REASON AND ACTION

BRUCE AUNE

University of Massachusetts at Amherst

REASON

AND ACTION

D. REIDEL PUBLISHING COMPANY

DORDRECHT-HOLLAND / BOSTON-U.S.A.

Library of Congress Cataloging in Publication Data

Aune, Bruce, 1933–
    Reason and action.

(Philosophical studies series in philosophy; v. 9)
Bibliography: p.
Includes index.
    1. Man. 2. Act (Philosophy) 3. Agent (Philosophy)
4. Reasoning. I. Title.
BD450.A86   128   77–8000
ISBN 90–277–0805–3

Published by D. Reidel Publishing Company,
P.O. Box 17, Dordrecht, Holland

Sold and distributed in the U.S.A., Canada, and Mexico
by D. Reidel Publishing Company, Inc.
Lincoln Building, 160 Old Derby Street, Hingham,
Mass. 02043, U.S.A.

Printed in The Netherlands

To Ilene

CONTENTS

PREFACE

Philosophers writing on the subject of human action have found it tempting to introduce their subject by raising Wittgenstein's question, 'What is left over if you subtract the fact that my arm goes up from the fact that I raise my arm?' The presumption is that something of particular interest is involved in an action of raising an arm that is not present in a mere bodily movement, and the philosopher's task is to specify just what this is. Unfortunately, such an approach does not take us very far, since a person could properly be said to raise his (or her) arm while asleep or hypnotized even though he (or she) would not be performing an action in the sense of 'action' with which philosophers are particularly concerned. To avoid this kind of difficulty I shall approach the subject of human action is a more academic way: I shall expound some important rival theories of human action, and introduce the relevant issues by commenting critically on those theories.

One of the issues I eventually introduce is a metaphysical one. A theory of action makes sense, I contend, only on the assumption that there are such 'things' as actions (or events). After considering some key arguments bearing on the issue I conclude that, as matters currently stand in philosophy, a metaphysically noncommittal attitude toward actions and events seems justified. In line with this conclusion I argue that a theory of agents can be developed as an alternative to a theory of action. To obtain such a theory we 'translate' the preferred theory of action into language that refers to agents and characterizes them by a special class of predicates. Thus, where a theory of action might assert that Tom's action of flipping a switch is identical with a certain physical movement, a theory of agents would assert that Tom flipped a switch if and only if he moved in a certain way. The assumption here is, of course, that predicates like 'flips a switch' and 'moves in a certain way' do not refer to actions or events: they characterize agents and do not *refer* to anything at all.

Having emphasized the possibility of transforming (or 'translating') a theory of action into a theory of agents, I put aside the metaphysical speculations of Chapter I and begin to speak freely about actions, events, states, and processes. My principal subject in Chapter II is the nature of the mental states or episodes involved in voluntary action. I examine the notions of volition, desire, intention, and purpose, and I consider such matters as the nature of intentional action and the logical structure of so-called purposive explanations. My underlying aim throughout the chapter is to identify the basic relation between thought (belief, intention, desire) and rational action. I eventually conclude that, to explain why an agent performs an intelligent, nonhabitual action, we must take account of the reasoning that prompts his action and guides it to completion. Toward the end of the chapter I explain how my account of the relation between thought and action could be expressed in terms appropriate to a theory of agents.

The reasoning that leads to intelligent behavior is called 'deliberation' or, more generally, 'practical reasoning'. My subject in Chapter III is the basic formal structure of such reasoning. To add perspective to my discussion, I begin with a critical account of Aristotle's view of deliberation, and I go on to expound and criticize related views that have been developed in recent years. I end the chapter with a sketch of my own views, arguing that deliberation does not always involve the derivation of a practical conclusion from antecedent premisses. When no such derivation occurs, the normative relation between the beginning and end of a deliberation can be clarified, I contend, by the principles of Bayesian decision theory. But when a derivation does occur, the logic of the deliberation seems to involve a special form of inference. My final chapter is largely devoted to a critical examination of three theories of practical inference. The conclusion I eventually reach is that, in spite of appearances, the formal logic of practical inference is really no different from the formal logic of ordinary, assertoric inference.

The unifying theme of the book is indicated by its title. Allowing for the possibility that statements about actions and mental states should be interpreted as mere *façons de parler* equivalent to statements about entities of a metaphysically less problematic sort, I might express my fundamental contention as follows: Intelligent, nonhabitual human action is invariably the product of reasoning, and to understand it adequately we must understand not only the general nature of action and how belief, desire, intention and so forth condition the reasoning leading to action (the topics of Chapters I and II) but also the logical structure of that reasoning (the topic of Chapters III and IV). A philosophical treatment of human action (or human agency) that does not come to terms with the logical structure of practical reasoning is, in my view, little more than a prolegomenon to the subject.

I began writing this book in the winter of 1973 when, thanks to a sabbatical leave from the University of Massachusetts, I enjoyed the hospitality of the Department of Philosophy, University of California at Irvine. I wish to thank the members of that department, particularly its chairman at the time, Nelson Pike, for the pleasure and stimulus of their company. I completed the book under ideal conditions at the Center for Advanced Study in the Behavioral Sciences, Stanford, California. I wish to thank the Center and its staff for their generous support during a truly extraordinary year.

Since the winter of 1973 I have given numerous seminars and public lectures on the subjects discussed in this book, and I have learned a great deal from the responses of my audiences. People who have been particularly helpful in commenting on the manuscript include Wilfrid Sellars, Hector-Neri Castañeda, Gareth Matthews, Stephen Schiffer, Michael Bratman, Patricia Barber and the members of my seminar in philosophy of mind during the fall semester of 1975. Permission to quote from my essay 'Sellars on Practical Reason' was granted by The Bobbs-Merrill Company, Inc., and permission to quote from H. N. Castañeda's *The Structure of Morality* was granted by Charles C. Thomas, Publisher.

Amherst, Massachusetts   BRUCE AUNE
November, 1976

Chapter I

THEORIES OF ACTION

The first part of this chapter is concerned with three rival theories of action. Each theory conceives of an action as an event or process in time, or as an aggregate of such events and processes; and each conceives of an action as adequately individuated by virtue of its causes and effects. I shall argue that, if a metaphysical commitment to events is accepted, no one of the theories is clearly preferable to the others. This is a surprising result, since the theories are espoused by philosophers as diverse in orientation as H. A. Prichard, Donald Davidson and R. G. Collingwood. In the last section of the chapter I argue that a metaphysical commitment to events is actually questionable and that, if it is rejected, a theory of agents must be accepted as clearly preferable to any theory that is explicitly concerned with actions and attempts to specify the conditions of their identity.

1. PRICHARD'S THEORY OF VOLUNTARY ACTIVITY

When Wittgenstein raised the question 'What is left over if you subtract the fact that my arm goes up from the fact that I raise my arm?' he was concerned with an example of what Hume called 'knowingly giving rise to a movement.'[1] For traditional philosophers, moving one's arm in this way is patently a conscious process. It is not just that, on 'giving rise' to the movement, one knows what the resulting movement will be; rather, it is that one brings about the movement *by* one's conscious, voluntary activity. This conscious activity was called 'willing'; and the traditional view is that, when we make a voluntary movement, we will that movement into being. The activity of willing is thus regarded as a kind of mental cause: it is a conscious process from which the physical movement of an arm or leg might naturally result.

Although philosophers espousing the view that we move our bodies by willing them to move have usually conceived of an action as, typically, the physical movements resulting from our willing, H. A. Prichard was an important exception. In a characteristically penetrating yet very puzzling article called 'Acting, Willing and Desiring' Prichard argued that an action must be understood as the process or activity of willing itself, and that this process, though having a physical movement as its typical result, cannot accurately be considered an activity of causing that result.[2] As he saw it, the willing is one thing, the result another. Both typically occur when an action is performed, but the action must be identified with the willing rather than with the result.

Prichard began his article by attacking the idea, defended even today,[3] that 'to do something is to originate or to bring into existence, i.e., really, to cause, some not yet existing state either of ourselves or of something else...' (p. 59). He acknowledged that this idea may be qualified in various ways — for example, by distinguishing the direct from the indirect production of a change — but he insisted that it is nevertheless untenable. An action, he said, is always an activity; and 'though we think that some man in moving his hand, or that the sun in attracting the earth, causes a certain movement, we do not think that the man's or the sun's activity *is* or *consists in* causing the movement' (p. 60). To this he added, 'if we ask ourselves: "Is there such an activity as originating or causing a change in something else?", we have to answer that there is not.'

The main thrust of Prichard's objection is clear: An action is an activity; there is no activity of causing or originating something; therefore, an action cannot be identified with the causing or originating of some change. What is not clear is what an activity is supposed to be, and why Prichard is so confident that there is no such thing as an activity of causing or originating something. He grants that we may speak of a subject causing a change, and he acknowledges that 'there is such a thing' as causing something. Yet he insists that, though an episode of causing may occur and may even require an activity, the causing itself is not an activity and therefore not an action. What is his basis for these claims?

I cannot say exactly what Prichard meant by the word 'activity', though he clearly restricted its application to events, occurrences, or processes that are properly regarded as causes. The principle behind his claim that causing is not an activity is easier to identify, however. Put in current terminology, his principle appears to be this: Statements of the form 'Thing or person S causes event E' are to be understood as elliptical for statements of the form '$(\exists A)$ (A is an activity by S and A causes E)'. Thus, we may speak of a thing or person causing a change, but if we have our philosophical wits about us we shall mean that the thing or person *does something* (that is, acts in a certain way) as the result of which the change occurs.

Prichard remarks that we often speak of a thing causing some result without knowing what change or activity of it is actually responsible for that result. When we say that a body caused a change 'by a force of attraction or repulsion, we are only expressing our knowledge that there is some activity at work, while being ignorant of what the kind of activity is' (p. 61). Statements of the form 'Thing S causes E' thus allude to activities only indirectly; they affirm that there is some activity or other of the subject that causes the relevant change to occur. To say, as Prichard does, that 'there is such a thing' (but not such an activity) as causing something is only to say, therefore, that there are, or can be, complex states of affairs that involve activities and what results from them.

After rejecting the claim that an action, being an activity, can be identified with the causing or originating of something, Prichard proceeds to develop his own view. As I have said, he contends that a human action is an activity of willing some change. His contention here should not be interpreted as involving a tacit denial that the statement 'John moves his hand' attributes to John a certain physical movement. His point is simply that John's *activity* in moving his hand — the action he thus performs — is accurately understood as an activity of willing his hand to move. There is no inconsistency in this position, for the statement 'John moves his hand' contains no singular term referring to an action. If the statement is true, there is no doubt some true counterpart statement that does contain such a singular term: it might be 'John's moving his hand occurs'. But although this statement may *imply* that John's hand actually moves, it does not tell us (Prichard would say) that John's *activity* in moving his hand is physical rather than mental.

To appreciate the rationale for Prichard's peculiar view, consider the action statement 'X moves Y's hand'. This statement affirms that the subject X brings about (that is, causes) a certain movement — namely, the movement of Y's hand. According to Prichard's thesis about causation, this claim about X is equivalent to '$(\exists A)$ (A is an activity by X and A causes the movement of Y's hand)'. Observe that, on this interpretation, the 'moves' in 'X moves Y's hand' does not itself connote a physical movement. Of course, if X moves Y's hand by pushing it with some part of his body, then X will have caused it to move by making a physical movement. But X need not, logically speaking, have proceeded this way; as Prichard points out, it is at least conceivable that X moves it by some kind of psychokinetic action. Although such a 'moving' may be no more than a bare logical possibility,[4] it allows us to see that the verb 'moves' has fundamentally different meanings in its intransitive and transitive uses. In 'Y's hand moves' it connotes a motion of Y's hand, but in 'X moves Y's hand' it alludes to an event or activity that causes Y's hand to move. Prichard's contention is that when 'moves' connotes an action, it is used in the latter sense: it means 'does something that causes a movement'.

Prichard's odd-sounding view of action follows naturally from these considerations. The statement 'John moves his hand' is equivalent to 'John moves John's hand'. Given Prichard's principles, we must analyze 'John moves John's hand' as '$(\exists A)$ (A is an activity by John and A causes the motion of John's hand)'. The relevant activity here may, of course, involve a movement, since John might move his hand by pushing it with his foot. But if his action is voluntary, he will probably (though not necessarily) move his foot without making some other movement that causes his foot to move.[5] In this case the moving of his foot (in the action sense) will not itself be a movement of his body. What activity, then, will cause his foot to move? Prichard says 'it almost goes without saying. . . [that it is] a *mental* activity of a certain kind, an activity of whose nature we are dimly aware in doing the action and of which we can become more clearly aware by reflecting on it. . . If we ask "What is the word for this special kind of [mental] activity?" the answer, it seems, has to be "willing" ' (p. 61).

Apart from any doubts one may have about the existence of a distinctive activity of willing, the obvious objection to Prichard's theory is that an action is surely something overt, something we can see. As P. J. Fitzgerald remarks in connection with a related theory:

'Caught in the act' conjures up a picture of the burglar creeping away with the swag over his shoulder: of the murderer standing over his victim, bloody knife in hand: not of a criminal contracting various muscles [or, we may add, of the criminal merely 'willing' to do something].[6]

But Prichard has a reply to this kind of objection. He would say that, when a voluntary act is successful, it has (at least typically) an observable result or upshot. But it is clearly a mistake, he would contend, to confuse the upshot with the act itself. A man who moves his arms while asleep performs no act — even though his arms move in the way they would move if they resulted from a voluntary act or activity.

It seems to me that Prichard has his finger on a shrewd point here, which is not adequately understood by some recent philosophers. J. L. Austin once called attention to an important feature of action language that Feinberg has called 'the accordian effect'.[7] Austin said that 'a single term descriptive of what [a man] did may be made to cover either a smaller or a larger stretch of events, those excluded by the narrower description being called "consequences" or "results" or "effects" or the like of this act'.[8] Feinberg expanded on Austin's remark, saying that, by an appropriate use of language, 'we can, if we wish, puff out an action to include an effect. . .; instead of saying "Smith opened the door causing Jones to be startled," [we can say] "Smith startled Jones".'

But Austin and Feinberg are mistaken in their description of the accordian effect. By tinkering with language, we cannot ourselves puff out, pull in, squeeze down, or stretch out an action; what we can puff out or pull in is the *description* of an action. Prichard would agree with this. Although we can include a reference to Caesar's death in describing Brutus's action, we cannot reasonably hold that Caesar's death was *part* of anything Brutus did. Brutus stabbed Caesar, and as a result Caesar died: the death was the causal consequence of the act, not part of it.[9] When we puff out the description of Brutus's action, we may include a tacit reference to the death − as in 'Brutus's killing of Caesar' − but this does not puff out Brutus's *act*. His act, however we describe it, was an activity of his (Prichard would say a mental activity); and the death of Caesar was the result or upshot of this activity − not part of it.

Although Prichard may thus elude the kind of objection Fitzgerald raises, other plausible objections quickly come to mind. Apart from questioning the notion of willing Prichard employs, some philosophers would want to reject his basic premiss about causation − namely, that statements affirming that a thing or person caused or brought about a result are reducible to statements of the form '$(\exists A)$ (A is an activity by S and A caused E)'. Thus, they would want to reject Prichard's view that so-called agent causation is reducible to what we might call 'event causation'.[10] They may well grant that, when the agent in question is an inanimate object, the agent causation is reducible to event causation; but they would insist that the same kind of reduction is not possible when the agent is a person.

It seems to me, however, that Prichard's view is clearly preferable on this matter. If we say that John moved his hand at time t, we may indeed add that

he caused his hand to move at that time. But to say this is not to say that he
was the irreducible cause of his hand's motion; if he were, then, since he
existed yesterday, his hand should have moved the same way yesterday too.
After all, if *A* is the irreducible cause of *B*, then whenever we have *A*, we
should have *B* as well. Clearly, if John did move his hand at a certain time,
then there must have been something about him at the time that accounts for
the occurrence, then, of his hand's movement. In this respect the case of John
does not differ from that in which we say that an empty car knocked over a
lamppost: the car, like the man, must 'do' something (in this case, strike the
post) that causes the result to occur.

When we think of a person's action, we do not, of course, think of a mere
response to some physiological change. We think of a person as a conscious
agent, and we regard the movements he voluntarily makes as somehow due to
his mental activity. Traditionally, the kind of mental activity considered the
cause of a person's voluntary movements is called 'willing'. This use of the
verb 'to will' is not just a philosopher's technicality, for it has been familiar in
English since before the time of Shakespeare.[11] Unless the traditional notion
of willing can be shown to be confused or objectionable in some fundamental
way, the idea that our voluntary movements are willed into being would *seem*
to be a natural presupposition of ordinary talk about action.

It is well known, of course, that many philosophers have challenged this
natural presupposition. Some have expressed an inability to understand what
willing could possibly be; others have simply denied that they are aware
of any distinctive mental process that could reasonably be called 'willing'.
Such philosophers do not always accept the thesis that agent-causation is
irreducible, however. Donald Davidson, for example, argues that causality is
properly a relation between events, and holds that the cause of a person's
voluntary movements may be the 'onset' of a belief or pro attitude – a view
that has important affinities with certain claims by Aristotle and Hume.[12]
Chisholm, a recent defender of the irreducibility thesis, has argued against
such views as Davidson's in a way that, oddly enough, seems to support
Prichard's position. He claims that the concept of action is 'essentially
teleological', involving the idea of endeavor or purpose, and that 'a man may
endeavor. . .to bring about what he does not desire and what he does not
even believe to be a means to anything he desires. . .'.[13] This claim is
surprising, coming from a defender of the irreducibility thesis, because it
suggests that agent causality is not irreducible after all. There is clearly some

close similarity between what goes on in the mind of a man who voluntarily raises his arm and what goes on in the mind of one who, knowing that he is paralyzed, 'endeavors' to raise his arm. Such endeavoring would seem to differ little from what Prichard called 'willing'.

To be consistent Chisholm must, of course, contend that, although endeavoring is a mental activity, it is not really the cause of the movements that the man, in the endeavor to do something, brings about. But this kind of claim is not easy to defend, for the notion of cause (in the 'event' sense) clearly seems applicable to the case in question. Obviously, the endeavoring Chisholm describes makes an important contribution to the resulting movement: if it had not occurred, those movements would doubtless not have occurred either. Since we normally regard the cause of a given event as that factor crucial for the control (production or inhibition) of events of that kind, it would seem perfectly appropriate to regard the endeavoring Chisholm describes as the cause of the relevant voluntary movements. If Chisholm is to reject this common way of speaking, he will have to offer some analysis of event causation that rules it out. But he has made no attempt to do this.

The philosophical controversy about the mental character of the state of an agent that results in his voluntary movements is very complicated, and I shall, therefore, defer further discussion of it to Chapter II. Here I shall merely say that the irreducibility thesis seems completely implausible, and that if (unlike Chisholm) we grant that a person's voluntary movements are the result of some characteristic mental activity on his part, then we may accept the general structure of Prichard's theory even though we reject Prichard's specific account of what this activity is. Since the term 'willing' is familiar in everyday discourse and since I shall eventually defend a qualified notion of willing against standard philosophical objections, I shall follow Prichard's lead in this chapter and refer to the relevant activity as that of willing. But my use of this term should not be taken as prejudging the interest of Prichard's view of action. One could hold that the activity of moving one's arm is a very complex one, involving beliefs and pro-attitudes, or that it is a special activity of 'endeavoring' or 'undertaking' to move it, which cannot plausibly be identified with willing. Both positions are consistent with the general structure of Prichard's theory.

Before ending this section I want to make a final remark about so-called event causation. Although it is natural to say, with Prichard, that the movement of an arm may be the result of an appropriate mental state, one might object to this way of speaking on the ground that such movements result from events closer to the agent's skin — that is, from events in his nerves or muscles. If an activity of willing has any physical result, it no doubt occurs somewhere in the agent's brain. I do not deny that willing may be thought to initiate a causal chain of great complexity, having the movement of an arm as a fairly remote member. But this does not commit one to denying that willing can be regarded as having an arm movement as its result, or that the willing can be regarded as *the* cause of the arm movement.

As I pointed out above, the familiar notion of causation is generally applied to those events or 'conditions' that we regard as instrumental in controlling (bringing about or preventing) a given phenomenon.[14] As Collingwood once put it, the cause is the event with the 'handle' on it.[15] Although many complicated changes undoubtedly intervene between the ingestion of poison and dying, we would still (in most cases) regard the ingestion of poison as the cause of the death — just as we are prepared to regard smoking as the cause of lung cancer even though we know that smoking could not possibly give rise to lung cancer without intervening changes of some complexity. The concept of a cause is thus a largely practical one applicable even in cases where the result is temporally remote from the occurrence we regard as crucial for its practical control. Since, from the ordinary point of view, a man's mental state is instrumental in the production of his voluntary movements, it is thus natural to regard his voluntary movements as the result of his mental state, even though we know full well that those movements would not occur unless appropriate changes took place in his muscles and nerves.

2. PRICHARD, DAVIDSON, AND THE NOTION OF AGENCY

As I have developed it thus far, Prichard's theory applies most directly to simple actions like moving one's hand. But not all actions are as simple as this, and some simple ones involve movements the agent did not will to occur. Thus, we may sink battleships as well as merely move our hands; and, as Prichard himself admits, we may will one movement but actually bring about another — in which case moving hand *B* cannot possibly be identified with the activity of willing that hand *B* move. In a recent article Donald Davidson has described results of both kinds — that is, the sinking of battleships and certain unintended bodily movements — by saying that the person bringing them about is 'the agent' of their occurrence.[16] Although Prichard has very little to say about such cases, his theory of action seems to commit him to the following definition:

(1) *S* brings about *E* in the sense of being the agent of *E*'s occurrence just in case *E*'s occurrence is the causal consequence of *S*'s willing something.

Consider the case of Jones who, as we should say, knocks over a teacup unintentionally. According to Prichard, Jones can be said to have acted only if he exercised his volition in some way. Assume that it was a movement of Jones's body that caused the teacup to be knocked over. If this movement was willed by him, we can say:

(2) $(\exists V)(\exists M)$ (*V* is an activity of willing by Jones & *M* is a movement of Jones's body & *V* caused *M* & *M* caused the teacup to be knocked over).

Assuming that the causing here is transitive, we may also affirm:

(3) $(\exists V)$ (*V* is an activity of willing by Jones & *V* caused the teacup to be knocked over).

But (3), according to Prichard's theory, is equivalent to

(4) Jones brought about the knocking over of the teacup.

By virtue of the accordian effect, we may interpret (4) as affirming that Jones knocked over the teacup, whether he did so intentionally or not.

We might observe in passing that a person can sometimes be the agent of a certain event when that event results from the movement of another person's body. Suppose I want to disrupt a dull conversation by knocking over the teacup I see perched precariously on Mary's knee. I note that nervous Harry is sitting next to Mary, and it occurs to me that if I startle him by abruptly moving my chair, he will jerk sideways, striking Mary's knee and dislodging the teacup. Consequently, I move my chair and the teacup falls. Given the peculiar sequence of events here, we should naturally say that *I* deliberately knock over the teacup: I do it *by* startling Harry. In one sense, of course, he knocks it over, but he does so only in the nonagency sense in which a stick thrown by a child could be said to knock something over. His contribution to the outcome is that of instrument rather than agent.

This last case should not make us suppose that, whenever a person's volition initiates a chain of events having a particular outcome, he must be considered the agent of that outcome. On the contrary, he is the agent only when his volition is sufficiently important or instrumental to the outcome to be considered its cause. Suppose, to vary the case just given, that Harry had guessed my intention and, being sympathetic with my aim, decided to bump against Mary's knee when I moved my chair. Even though my willed movement may have triggered off his interaction with Mary's knee and thus led to the teacup's falling over, he, not I, would be the agent of that event. The reason for this is that his decision, not mine, is the key causal factor in the bumping of Mary's knee and the consequent falling of the teacup. Had he not made his decision, the movement of my chair would presumably not have led him (given his knowledge of my intention) to strike Mary's knee.

As a general matter, an event early in a causal chain can be considered the cause (or even a key or perhaps 'major' cause) of an event later in the chain only under certain conditions. This means that, generally speaking, the relation of causing is not transitive. If e_1 causes e_2 and e_2 causes e_3, we cannot generally assume that e_1 causes e_3 or that e_3 is the result of e_1. Under certain conditions we can make this assumption; under many conditions we cannot. I shall not try to specify these conditions here: it is difficult to do so, and not really necessary for my task of describing a theory of action. *If an event is reasonably regarded as the result or causal consequence of an agent's volition, then and only then is he reasonably regarded as the agent of it.* This is Prichard's theory, as least as I am reconstructing it. The task of deciding whether this or that person is the agent of a given event is essentially a practical matter, which may be extremely difficult to resolve. (Maybe two people are jointly responsible for the event, and maybe neither could be considered the actual agent of it.) As Joel Feinberg has remarked, the question whether

a causally complex act is to be ascribed to a person whose relatively simple act [or volition, as Prichard would say] was a causal factor in the production of some upshot depends. . . on how important a causal contribution it made, as determined by our prior assumptions and practical principles.[17]

The view I have been attributing to Prichard is fundamentally similar to Davidson's. According Davidson, a person S is the agent of an event E just when there is a description D of E such that the complex predicate ⌐_____

brought about D intentionally⌝ is true of S.[18] To see the similarity of this view to the one I have attributed to Prichard, note that the following descriptions might, for Davidson, apply to the same event:

(5)   John's knocking over the teacup
(6)   John's lifting the platter of cookies
(7)   John's surprising his wife.

Davidson would regard the events described here as movements by John; and if just one movement were involved in all three cases, he would say that the three descriptions would have the same reference, respectively, as the following:

(8)   The movement by John that causes the knocking over of the teacup
(9)   The movement by John that causes the raising of the platter of cookies
(10) The movement by John that causes his wife to be surprised.

On the assumption that just one movement is involved in all three cases, we may infer that the events denoted by (5), (6), and (7) are identical – that is, one and the same event. Given that

(11) John's lifting the platter of cookies was intentional

is true, we may then infer, according to Davidson's theory, that the events denoted by 'John's knocking over the teacup' and 'John's surprising his wife' are actions John performed.[19]

The similarity between Davidson's and Prichard's views stands out even more sharply if we take account of Davidson's remarks on intentional action. According to the doctrine of his 'Actions, Reasons, and Causes', statements having the form (or surface structure) of 'S did A intentionally' appear to be equivalent to statements of the form 'S did A as the result of a primary reason R for doing A'. Given what he says about primary reasons, his view would appear to be something like this: S is the agent of an event E just when E is caused by the 'onset' of a complex state consisting of a pro attitude toward bringing about events with a certain property, and a belief that E, under a certain description, has that property.[20] The events immediately produced by such complex states of mind – that is, by what Davidson calls 'primary reasons' – are, for him, 'mere movements' of the agent's body.

These mere movements, Davidson says, 'are all the actions there are'. To this
he adds, 'We never do more than move our bodies: the rest is up to nature'. [21]
As we have seen, Prichard's view is more austere than this. For him we merely
will to move our bodies: even our physical movements are up to nature.

To avoid hasty objections to these theories we should emphasize that such
strong claims by Davidson and Prichard are hyperbolic. Obviously, both men
would agree that we can do a lot more than merely move our bodies or will
them to move: we can knock over teacups, start wars, and proceed to sink
battleships. Yet our actions in doing such ambitious things are analyzable,
they will insist, into more elementary activities that have the falling over of
teacups, the onset of wars, and the sinking of battleships as their more or
less distant consequences. The claim that actions described in causal terms
are analyzable into more elementary activities (or events) that have certain
consequences is not, in my opinion, bizarre; and neither theory is obviously
mistaken when its actual commitments are taken into account.

3. OBJECTIONS AND QUALIFICATIONS

Several lines of objection to Davidson's theory have been raised recently,
which are very instructive to consider. Cornman has argued that a man may
be considered the agent of a certain event even if there is no description of
that event under which the man intended to produce it. [22] Suppose, for
example, that a man unwittingly dropped a lighted cigarette in the woods
and that a forest fire resulted. Even though he had no intentions whatever
respecting the cigarette (he may have been paralyzed with fear at the sight
of a menacing bear) he would still have caused the fire by his 'action' and
thus be the agent of its occurrence.

This objection applies, of course, to Prichard's theory, since the fire did
not result from the man's volition to do something. I think both Prichard and
Davidson could respond to the objection as follows. The man did cause the
fire, but only in the sense in which a sleeping man might cause a lamp to fall
over by striking it with his arms while asleep. Clearly, there is no *conscious*
agency in such cases, and this is what Davidson's and Prichard's theories
are meant to apply to. It is true that the man just described may be held
responsible for the fire, but this does not imply that he must have been the
agent of the fire in the intended sense. A man can be held responsible for

omissions (things he failed to do) as well as for his acts; and although the man may not have intended to drop the lighted cigarette, he can be held responsible for lighting it in the first place (this might have been negligent on his part) or even for carrying matches and cigarettes into a dry forest area if he is the kind of man who is apt to light up a cigarette without realizing what he is 'doing'.

The second kind of objection has been developed in different ways by different writers; Alvin Goldman has developed it essentially as follows.[23] Jones kills Smith by shooting him. To shoot him Jones pulls the trigger of a gun. Since Jones makes just one movement that (a) causes the trigger to be pulled and (b) causes Smith to be killed, his action of pulling the trigger ought to be identical, in Davidson's theory, with his act of killing Smith. But although Jones's act of pulling the trigger causes the gun to go off, his act of killing Smith did not (it is claimed) cause this. Hence, it is a mistake for Davidson to identify these two acts of Jones.

The correct response to this objection is that Jones's particular act, which may be called a killing because of a relational property it possesses, may perfectly well be the cause of the gun's going off. It might sound odd to say such a thing, but this is because we tend to confuse a causal relation between events with an explanatory relation between statements or propositions. The fact that the gun went off is not causally explained, obviously, by the fact that Jones killed Smith. Yet the action Jones performed in bringing about Smith's death, which we might call 'his killing of Smith', may still have caused the gun to go off. To put this in the terminology used in explaining Prichard's theory, Jones's act of killing Smith is that activity of his that caused Smith to be killed; and this activity might well have been the one that caused the relevant trigger to be pulled.

A related objection is this. Jones shoots Smith, and Smith dies of the wound a day later. Thus, Jones kills Smith. According to Davidson's theory, Jones's killing of Smith is identical with his act of shooting Smith. But Jones shoots Smith before Smith dies. If the shooting were identical with the killing, Jones would have killed Smith before Smith died. But this is absurd. Consequently, Davidson's theory must be rejected.

Although it sounds odd to say that Jones could have killed Smith before Smith died, a defender of Davidson's thesis need only come to terms with the assertion that Jones's act of killing Smith occurred before the event of Smith's dying. But this assertion seems perfectly reasonable. If you want someone to die, you might attempt to kill him. The act of killing is the cause; the death, or the dying, the effect. But effects normally, if not always, succeed their causes: they occur after them. Consequently, if an act of killing is the cause of a certain death, it is bound to occur before the latter. This being so, Smith's death, or dying, *must* occur later than Jones's act of killing him. Of course, Jones's act is a killing only because it results in a death; and until we know that Jones's act has this result, we shall not know that it is an act of killing. But regardless of what we may know or come to know, if Jones does kill Smith, his act of killing him is bound to occur before Smith's death: in this kind of case, at least, causes unquestionably precede their effects.

Another objection may be expressed as follows. According to the Davidson-Prichard theory, an act of pumping water may be identical with an act of poisoning the inhabitants of a certain town. But although the pumping is done swiftly, the poisoning may be done slowly. Since no action can be both swift and slow, it follows that the theory is untenable.

This objection shows confusion about the logic of attributive adjectives. An act of poisoning is an act of bringing about a poisoning — that is, of bringing it about that someone or other is poisoned. If such an act is, intrinsically, a rapid pumping, then it is a rapid act (in relation to pumping) that brings about a poisoning. But this rapid act can also be considered slow in relation to the time taken in bringing about the result: a fast pumping may slowly bring about a poisoned community. 'Slow' and 'rapid' are relative terms, like 'large' and 'small'; and a particular action may well be slow in one respect while rapid in another — just as a baby elephant can be both large and small: large as a mammal and small as an elephant. If the pumping in question is done swiftly, then if the pumping is identical with the poisoning, the poisoning can be done slowly only in the sense that it slowly brings about the poisoned state of the relevant community. But this raises no problems for Davidson's or Prichard's analysis.

Goldman has posed an objection that is closely related to the ones just considered.[24] According to him, there can be no objection to saying that, by flipping a switch, Smith has turned on a light. But if Smith's act of flipping the switch were identified with his act of turning on the light, we should have to say that, by turning on the light, Smith turned on the light. And clearly this is false. The relation represented by the pronoun 'by' is both asymmetric and irreflexive: If S does A by doing B, then it is false both that S does B by doing A and that S does A by doing A. Yet if A and B are identical, 'there can be no asymmetric or irreflexive relation which one bears to the other'.

The first point to make about this objection is that it fails to establish its key premise — namely, that *acts* stand in a 'by' relation. If we use singular terms to denote the relevant acts, we could not meaningfully say:

S's turning on of the light by S's flipping of the switch.

The preposition 'by' is thus not a clear example of a relation word; in fact, it is used to connect sentences to verb phrases:

S turned on the lights by flipping the switch.

It seems to me, moreover, that a fair reading of this statement is:

S flipped the switch and thereby turned on the light.

For a Prichardian, this last statement can be analyzed as follows. On first approximation we have:

S caused the switch's being flipped and thereby (he) caused the light's being turned on.

Since agent causation is reducible to event causation, we then obtain:

($\exists A$) (A is an activity by S such that A caused the switch's being flipped and thereby caused the light's being turned on).

The word 'thereby' in these statements might connote a relation, as 'by' was claimed to do, but the relation would not hold between acts; at best, it would hold between the *results* of acts. Since the event of the switch's being flipped might naturally be said to cause the event of the light's being turned on, the act (or activity) of causing the first event might naturally be said, by the transitivity of causation, to be the cause of the second event. This approach to 'S turned on the light *by* flipping the switch' seems perfectly reasonable, and it is entirely compatible with the view that S's *act* of flipping the switch is identical with his *act* of turning on the light.

We should emphasize in this connection that when we make remarks of the form 'S did A by doing B', we do not always think that certain events connected with S's doing A and B are causally related. If S signals a turn by extending his arm in a certain way, we are not tempted to say that his arm movement causes a signaling to occur. What we want to say, at least if we are

attracted by the views of Prichard or Davidson, is that the act of extending
the arm *constitutes*, in the circumstances, an act of signaling. The remark 'He
extended his arm and *thereby* signaled a turn' should not, therefore, be taken
to imply that an act of signaling was brought about by a distinct act of
extending an arm; it should merely be taken to imply that certain acts of
extending an arm and making a signal are so related that by virtue of performing the first act one performs the second. An appropriate relation
insuring this consequence would be the identity of the 'two' acts: extending
the arm simply constitutes, in the circumstances, an act of signaling.

In his important book on action to which I have referred, Goldman
contends that when it is true that S does A by doing B, S's act of doing A
may be 'generated' from his act of doing B in four ways: it may be *causally*,
conventionally, *simply*, or *augmentally* generated by it.[25] As we have seen,
a follower of Prichard or Davidson would want to revise Goldman's contention that one act generates new acts in four ways. An alternative view would
be that if an agent does something B, he may be said thereby to do something
A for reasons of four distinct types. Each type of reason could be taken to
support the claim that the particular act of doing B is identical with the act
of doing A. We have already illustrated the first two types of reason. A
particular act of flipping a switch could be considered identical with an act of
turning on a light on the grounds that the act of flipping the switch is *the* act
that causes the relevant light to go on. Again, an act of extending an arm
might be regarded as identical with an act of signaling on the grounds that,
by virtue of certain *conventions*, the first act constitutes (in the existing
circumstances) an act of signaling. As an example of a reason corresponding
to Goldman's notion of simple act-generation, we could say that if George
jumps five feet and Bill jumps six feet, Bill's act of jumping six feet is
identifiable with his act of outjumping George because the former act is
simply what makes it true, in the circumstances, that Bill outjumps George.
No causal relation is essential here, and no special rules or conventions (as
in the signaling case) need be operative. Finally, for an example of a reason
corresponding to act augmentation, we could say that Bill's act of jumping
(on the occasion described) is identical with his act of jumping six feet; to
say this is just to augment the description of the act of jumping by adding
details.

A final objection to Davidson's theory, which applies also to Prichard's,
concerns the idea of explanation.[26] According to Davidson, a particular act

of playing the piano may be identical with a particular act of practicing for a concert. Yet (it might be contended) we explain the agent's act of playing the piano by saying that he is practicing for a concert where we cannot explain his practicing for a concert by saying he is practicing for a concert. If his playing were identical with his practicing, the latter explanation would have to be acceptable, for explaining the playing would then be the same as explaining the practicing. Consequently, we must grant that the playing is not really identical with the practicing.

This objection is fundamentally confused. In the first place, we do not really explain events; we explain *why* this or that event occurred or failed to occur.[27] And to explain why something happened or failed to happen is to answer the question why it happened or failed to happen. But to answer the question 'Why is S practicing?' is not to answer the different question 'Why is S playing?'. The expression 'S's practicing' may refer to the same event as 'S's playing' does, but the former gives the aim or purpose associated with the playing. If we know what this purpose is, we can give a reasonable answer to the question 'Why is S playing?'; we can say 'S is playing because he wants to practice'. But to answer the question 'Why is S practicing?' we must consider why S is playing with the aim of practicing. A satisfactory answer to this question might be 'S wants to give a good performance'. Thus, although a given act of playing may be identical with a given act of practicing (or playing with a certain aim), the question why the playing occurs is different from the question why the practicing occurs, and the answer to the first question (or the explanation why the playing occurs) is different from the answer to the second question (or the explanation why the practicing occurs).

We should now consider an important difficulty applicable specifically to Prichard's theory. As set forth by Prichard, the theory applies most directly to such actions as deliberately moving an arm or finger. As we saw, however, the theory can be extended to cover unintentional movements as well as actions of a very ambitious sort — for example, breaking a prize teacup or launching a submarine. The trick here was to regard these actions as mental activities having certain upshots or causal consequences. Our recent discussion has made it clear that further qualifications are required: corresponding to Goldman's principles of act generation, we must allow various principles of act constitution. As far as Prichard's theory is concerned, we must say that a particular action may be *causally*, *conventionally*, *simply*, or *augmentally* constituted by the willing (successful or perhaps not) of a particular result or upshot. Thus, if the appropriate criteria are fulfilled, we can say that the act of signaling is conventionally constituted by an appropriate mental activity that has a particular result or upshot.

Although the qualifications just mentioned go a long way toward rendering Prichard's theory plausible, reflection shows that they do not go all the way. One difficulty is that certain complex actions, such as building a doghouse or planting a garden, seem to resist being constituted according to the principles just discussed. There does not seem to be any form of mental activity by which these complex actions could be constituted — even when accompanied by certain physical upshots and occurring in particular circumstances. To accommodate such actions, we must supplement Prichard's theory along different lines. I suggest saying that complex acts are constituted by two or more simpler acts. When a cabinet-maker's assistant constructs a key-hole desk, he performs many sub-acts. He builds drawers, turns out legs on a lathe, planes boards, and assembles the finished units together according to a blueprint. He may have no intention of constructing a particular kind of desk (he is merely following instructions); and it would seem absurd for us to identify his act of making the desk with his mental activity during the whole period in question. It is entirely natural, on the other hand, to identify his act with his simpler acts that, taken together, bring the desk into being. Since the atoms for a complex act are ultimately the sort of thing Prichard's theory was explicitly designed to cover, this amendment to Prichard's theory preserves the spirit of the original. Strictly, the idea would be that a complex act is constituted by an aggregate (whole or sum) of acts of will — or that talk about a complex act is analyzable into talk about various acts of will. The claim, however, that a certain complex act actually occurred — for example, the claim that a man actually built a key-hole desk — would imply that the required physical movements (and their upshots) also occurred. In the following discussion this amendment to Prichard's theory will be assumed.

Although the theories of both Prichard and Davidson can elude the lines of criticism discussed in this section, it may seem obvious that Davidson's theory, being the more recent of the two, is far preferable. This point is by no means clear, however. Davidson identifies an action with a physical movement, but this maneuver is questionable, at least in connection with such simple acts as 'making' physical movements. As Prichard insisted, although we commonly bring about such movements when we perform such acts, the movements we bring about do not seem to be identical with our voluntary activity; they seem to be its visible results or upshots. This view is also supported by examples of actions where no physical movement is even intended. If a man deliberately blocks a doorway by not moving away from where he is standing, there need be no movement — not even an unintended one, such as the tensing of certain muscles — with which his action could plausibly be identified. His activity, his doing, *seems* to be purely mental.

These apparent advantages to Prichard's theory are not, of course, decisive; in fact, a lot more must be said about his theory before we can claim to understand it fully. The next section will be concerned with details of Prichard's theory that must be kept in mind when comparing it with alternative theories such as Davidson's.

4. SECONDARY USES OF ACTION LANGUAGE

Although the topic of willing is deferred to the next chapter, we may consider here an important problem that is generated by Prichard's view that an action is the willing of some result. This problem arises even on the assumption that the notion of willing can be explicated in some reasonable way.

If we will at all, it would seem that we will to act, to *do* something or other. But Prichard denies that we can will to act: 'what we will', he says, are physical movements, changes, or perhaps nonmovements if we can will to be motionless. He holds this view because the alternative involves, in his opinion, a vicious regress. His argument is essentially this: Since an action, properly speaking, is the willing of something, the willing of an action 'must in turn really be the willing of the willing of something else'. If we always willed to act, a vicious regress would result, because the 'something else' mentioned in the last sentence would be an action, which is the willing of something; and since this latter 'something' is, by hypothesis, an action, it too would be the willing of something, and so on without end.[28]

Prichard's argument here is not valid, however. In criticizing other writers on action Prichard makes it clear that he uses the expression 'what we will' to refer, not to the effect brought about by our willing, but to our end or aim in willing, to what we will to bring about. Given this, 'S wills x' is what logicians call an opaque context; and even if 'an action' is defined as 'the willing of something', we cannot infer 'S wills the willing of something' from

'*S* wills an action'. After all, if a man does not know that an action is the willing of something, he might will to act (that is, have the aim of bringing about an action) without having the aim of willing to will.

Although Prichard's argument is thus invalid, its spirit can be saved by an obvious amendment. If we accept Prichard's thesis about action, we shall use the expression 'I will an action' to mean 'I will the willing of something'. If, further, we accept the view that what we will is always an action, we shall have to acknowledge that the 'something' in 'I will the willing of something' refers, when *we* use it, to an action. Consequently, when we say 'I will the willing of something', we shall be committed to saying 'I will the willing of an action'. But this latter statement will mean, for us, 'I will the willing of the willing of something'. This last claim can in turn be expanded, and we shall be on our way to an infinite regress. Since the regress is generated by the thesis that we always will some action, it is thus reasonable to reject that thesis.

In spite of this argument it is difficult to deny that, if we will at all, we will to *do* this or that. Since the thesis that we will an action seems to be a technical way of saying that, when we will, we will to do something, it is natural to seek some means of avoiding Prichard's conclusion. A tempting strategy is to identify the action of doing *A* with the 'action' of bringing about some result (some movement or change) *M*. Given this identification, we could then argue that '*S* wills to do *A*' simply means '*S* wills to bring about *M*'. If we interpret Prichard's claim that what we will is a movement as meaning 'what we will to bring about is a movement', his thesis will be equivalent to the natural view that, when we will, we will to do something.

Tempting as this line of thought may initially be, it cannot be acceptable to Prichard. If *M* is a minimal movement — that is, one under our immediate voluntary control — then the activity by us that results in *M* is an activity of willing. For Prichard, there is, as we may recall, no activity of bringing something about: the locution '*S* brings about *M*' is simply short for '*S* does something that results in *M*'. Given this, the claim that *S* wills to bring about *M* can only mean that *S* wills to do something that results in *M*. But if *M* is minimal, the only activity that can have *M* as a result is a willing. Therefore, the claim that we might will to do something that has *M* as a result can only mean that we might will to perform or execute a willing that has *M* as a result. But Prichard declares that we cannot will to will.[29]

Since acting, for Prichard, is willing, there is no escaping the conclusion that he must disallow the possibility of our willing to act in the full sense of

the word 'act'. If we deliberately move our finger, we will our finger's movement, or we will that it move — but we do not will to *bring about* its
movement. We may say, it is true, that *we* bring about its movement, but
saying this is simply short for saying that we 'do something' (in this case, will
something) as the result of which our finger moves. To will to bring something about is to will to act, and Prichard cannot allow that this is possible.

Prichard's view that we cannot will to act, or to do something, depends, of
course, on the sense of 'act' or 'do something' specified by his theory. As we
have seen, however, causal verbs like 'moves' and 'does' are not always used
to ascribe actions to agents. When such verbs are so used, Prichard could not
object to our saying that we *can* will to move or to do something.

If a sleeping man's arm moves spontaneously, it is permissible to say
that he moves his arm — even though it is clear that the movement is not
voluntary. Similarly, when a man is the victim of a coughing spasm, it is
natural to say that he coughs or even that he does something (though not
voluntarily). In the case of such nonvoluntary 'doings', we are using typical
action language to connote movements, changes, or mere responses. The same
is true, Prichard would have to contend, of the word 'do' in the context '*S*
wills to do *A*': *S*'s aim here is that certain movements occur — those movements, namely, whose occurrence is implied by the statement that he has
done *A*. (Recall that '*S* moves his hand' implies '*S*'s hand moves'.)

Wilfrid Sellars, a philosopher who claims that we can and do will to act,
uses 'action' in something like the weak sense just mentioned. He says 'A
voluntary action in the primary sense is one that is caused by an act of
will'.[30] If we ask what is caused by *S*'s willing his arm to move, the answer
must be 'The movement of his arm' — and this would seem to be an action
in the relevant sense. Where Sellars and (we may recall) Davidson use 'action',
Collingwood and others use 'deed'. Collingwood used 'deed' because the word
'action' is, as he claimed, 'often by ancient and respectable usage employed
for the will as opposed to the deed'. As examples of this usage, he cited the
acts of parliament, the *acta* of any committee or deliberative body, the use
of 'act' in devotional literature, and the use of 'action' in well-known passages
from Shakespeare.[31]

Although the decision to speak of the upshots of volitions as actions,
deeds, or mere movements might seem to be a mere matter of nomenclature
having little if any philosophical interest, Prichard held strong views to
the contrary. In fact, he made a special point of criticizing a Professor

Macmurray, who claimed that the word 'action' is really ambiguous and may properly refer either to what is done, which he called 'the deed', or to the doing of it, which he called 'the action'. In opposition to this, Prichard flatly asserted, 'Obviously . . . there is no ambiguity whatever'. He continued:

When I move my hand, the movement of my hand, though an effect of my action, is not itself an action, and no one who considered the matter would say it was, any more than he would say that the death of Caesar, as distinct from his murder, was an action or even part of an action (p. 63).

For my part, the question whether to use the word 'action' for the willing or the result of the willing is not *crucially* important in the context of a philosophical theory. What is crucially important are the distinctions drawn and the illumination provided. Prichard's use of 'action', which is to a degree technical, is based on an analysis of cases in which a man's volitional causality (as it might be called) is exercised. Such causality is implied by certain uses of transitive verbs like 'moves', 'hits', or 'murders'. If a man moves his arm in the way that is distinctive of a rational agent, then he brings about a certain movement: the movement results from his volitional activity. For reasons we have discussed, Prichard contends that there is no activity of bringing something about: to say that S brings about E is only to say that E results from some activity of S's. This provides a reasonably clear, straightforward analysis of what most philosophers would regard as action-ascribing uses of 'S moves his arm', 'S kills Jones', and the like.

There are, of course, as most philosophers would acknowledge, nonaction uses of 'S moves his arm' — for example, 'S moves his arm while asleep'. How are we to understand such locutions? Clearly, no conscious agency is implied. We seem to be presented merely with the movement of a body — a bodily movement. In saying '*He* moves his arm' in such cases we are certainly not ascribing responsibility or whatnot to the agent, for there is no question of his being responsible (generally speaking) for the movements of his body while he is asleep. A Prichardian would no doubt contend that we are using action language here largely as a result of habit. We are presented with the kind of movement that occurs when a man voluntarily moves his arm; and although we believe that the man is not voluntarily making that movement, we describe him as if he were. The import of what we are saying, when we give such a description, is that the man's body moved in the way it would move if he voluntarily moved it. This nonaction use of locutions like '*He* moved his arm' is thus logically secondary; it makes sense only in relation to talk about actions proper.

Although it is possible to call the movements or changes resulting from our volitional activity 'actions', this practice, according to the Prichardian, is unnecessarily confusing. An action is normally understood as a doing, which is technically an activity. Yet the movement of an arm clearly seems to be the *result* of an activity, the activity of willing. Why call such results 'actions'? Why adopt a view having the consequence that the movement of Jones's arm might *be* Smith's action, as in a case of psycho-kinesis? Indeed, if Brutus could kill Caesar merely by willing him to die, which is certainly 'logically' possible, then Brutus's act of killing Caesar might be identical with Caesar's dying. But surely an act of killing could never be *identified* with an 'act' of dying. Prichard's way of speaking certainly seems preferable to this.

5. THREE THEORIES OF ACTION

In spite of the rhetoric a Prichardian may introduce in supporting his theory, an impartial observer might say that, at least as far as typical actions are concerned, Prichard's theory does not differ a great deal from the Davidson-Sellars alternative. Both affirm that a typical action involves both a mental, volitional component and a physical result. The key difference is simply that, for Prichard, the action is the mental state that has the physical result, while for Sellars and Davidson the action is the physical result (or upshot) of the mental state. Each seizes upon a different component of a complex situation that both sides acknowledge to exist and identifies that component with the action. Apart from this, they seem to be in general agreement about what is involved in a typical human action.

Actually, this observation is not quite correct. According to Prichard, even a simple action of moving one's arm is an activity with a physical result: one *brings about* the relevant movement, and this requires an activity, a 'doing', that is distinguishable from that movement. Sellars and Davidson must reject this idea; they must say that, although a distinction between doing and result may legitimately be drawn in some cases — for example, in the case of bringing about an explosion *by* pressing a button — there is no room for such a distinction in simple cases of voluntary movement. In these simple cases one's act is merely a physical movement that, by virtue of having an appropriate mental cause, is correctly called 'an action'.

A philosopher wishing to follow the general approach of Sellars and Davidson might be tempted to say that the schema 'X brings about M' is not properly applicable to simple cases of voluntary movement: to apply the schema is to open the door to Prichard's distinction between a purely volitional 'doing' and a physical result. Yet if, like Davidson, such a philosopher has no qualms about a commitment to events, he cannot deny that, if a person moves his hand, he *does* bring about a physical movement: he is the agent, as Davidson would say, of that event. If, holding to events, the philosopher is to avoid Prichard's position, he must say that the schema 'X brings about E' either has more than one interpretation or else is never properly interpreted as Prichard interprets it. If he accepts the first alternative, he might say that 'X brings about E' may mean either 'X does something that causes E' or 'X is the agent of E in Davidson's sense'. If he prefers the other alternative, he might say that 'X brings about E' always means 'X is the agent of E in Davidson's sense'.

It seems clear to me that 'X brings about E' (or words to that effect) commonly mean what Prichard says they mean — namely, that the agent X does something that brings about (or causes) E. Thus, to bring about an explosion is to do something — perhaps press a button — that causes the explosion to occur. This interpretation is not inconsistent with Davidson's view that, if one does something that causes an explosion, one's act can be described (in accordance with the accordian effect) as an act of exploding something. On the other hand, since this interpretation accords with customary usage, we must acknowledge that 'X brings about E' (or words to that effect) does *not* always mean 'X is the agent of E in Davidson's sense' or (roughly) 'E is caused by the joint occurrence in X of some belief and pro attitude that concern E'.

In spite of this, there is no evident absurdity in *explicating* some or even all uses of 'X brings about E' along the lines of 'X is the agent of E in Davidson's sense'. An explication, as Carnap defines it, is a technical equivalent of a vernacular locution; and such an equivalent need not be synonymous or even approximately synonymous with its vernacular counterpart.[32] Thus, if it is convenient or illuminating, in the context of a philosophical theory of action, to interpret some or all uses of 'X brings about E' in the suggested way, there would appear to be no serious objection to doing so. Prichard might well contend that his interpretation accords better with customary usage, but if (as seems obvious) his interpretation must also be viewed as an explication, neither can be said to be *correct*. The fundamental question to ask, for anyone concerned to choose between these explications, is 'Which of the alternative philosophical theories provides the best, most illuminating account of human behavior?'

As I have described them, the theories of Davidson and Prichard are extremes: one says that actions are (at least typically) mere movements; the other says they are mere mental causes of movements. Since either theory is awkward in places — Prichard's awkward in implying that we can strictly observe only the result or upshot of an action, not the action itself; Davidson's awkward in dealing with cases like that of the man whose action consists partly in *not* moving out of the way of his approaching friend — it might appear that a far better theory is a hybrid of the two. An action, one might think, is neither a mere mental state nor a mere physical movement but a whole or sum of both: at least in typical cases, it is a complex of mental state and physical movement.[33] As Collingwood once put it, speaking figuratively, a typical action has both an inside and an outside: it is a complex occurrence with more than one aspect.

Although this view might seem highly promising at first glance, it has awkward consequences for the ontological status of actions. Depending on how it is elaborated, it might imply either (a) that actions are abstract entities of some kind (sets, sums or perhaps states of affairs) rather than events in time or (b) that actions do not, strictly speaking, exist. The first alternative would result from acknowledging that actions are entities having components in some sense: they might be sets or mereological sums of mental and physical events, or they might be mental-events-causally-related-to-certain-physical-events, something that would not appear to be an event itself. The second alternative could be supported by the assertion that we do not have to acknowledge both mental causes, physical results, *and* composites (or whatnot) involving such. To say, according to this alternative, that a typical action occurs would be to say merely that mental events of a certain sort occur *and* are followed by certain physical effects. On this view, typical human actions would be 'logical constructions': talk about such things would be equivalent to talk about mental causes and physical effects. Though not patently untenable, neither alternative seems particularly attractive, or clearly preferable to the rival views of Prichard or Davidson.

A clearly developed theory of actions as involving both mental and physical events might, of course, avoid these alternatives or render one of them more attractive. But in the absence of such a theory we cannot confidently say that the hybrid approach is really preferable to either Prichard's or Davidson's; in fact, the cases that raise difficulties for these theories will also make trouble for the hybrid approach. In view of this we seem to be faced with a predicament: How can we possibly select a preferred theory from these well-supported alternatives? Instead of merely concluding that any choice is bound to be arbitrary, resting on nothing but whim or subjective preference, we might note that our predicament rests on an assumption that might reasonably be challenged.

When we are concerned with the question of what, exactly, an action is and of whether doing A is, or is not, identical with doing B, we are clearly assuming that there are such *things* as actions — things that may or may not be identical with one another. But from a metaphysical point of view this assumption is at least questionable.

6.   THE METAPHYSICS OR ONTOLOGY OF ACTION

A familiar contention in metaphysics is 'Only substances exist'. The claim is that, although we must acknowledge the existence of inanimate things (like rocks and molecules) and persons (like Prichard or Zeno), and although we must acknowledge that such 'substances' change or act in various ways, we do not also have to acknowledge the existence of things called 'changes' or 'actions'. We may, of course, speak of changes or actions both in our technical and in our everyday discourse, but our speech in this regard should be viewed as a mere manner of speaking. Singular terms purporting to refer to events and actions, like terms purporting to refer to propositions, properties, and states of affairs, can in principle be eliminated from our discourse: though perhaps highly convenient to use, they are not actually needed for describing what is or exists. Thus, while Nero fiddled on the occasion of Rome's burning, it is not necessary for us to describe the situation by using such terms as 'Nero's fiddling' or 'Rome's burning'. Instead, we can simply say such things as 'Nero fiddled *while* Rome burned'.

In recent years many philosophers have been indifferent to traditional issues in metaphysics, regarding them as meaningless, trivial, or at least irrelevant to their work in, say, action theory. But the metaphysical contention described above is clearly relevant to action theory, for the questions raised about action in the last section presuppose a particular metaphysical stand. Unless it can be shown that events and actions are not mere 'logical fictions', as Russell has called them − that terms apparently referring to them are not mere *façons de parler* − we are in an extremely poor position to admit, as philosophers, that questions about the identity of events really make sense at all. For this reason alone, no philosophical discussion about the nature of human action can be regarded as even remotely complete if it does not include a section on the ontological status of actions.

As far as I know, the only philosopher who has recently faced up to the basic metaphysical questions about action and offered clear reasons for adopting an ontology of events is Donald Davidson. His reasons are based on an analysis of the logical form of statements about events and actions − or, as he would also put it, on a semantical theory of such statements. An explicit statement by him on this matter is as follows:

... the assumption, ontological and metaphysical, that there are events [and thus actions] is one without which we cannot make sense of much of our common talk; or so, at any rate, I have been arguing. I do not know of any better, or further, way of showing what there is.[34]

Davidson's published reasons for adopting an ontology of events and actions (actions being, for him, 'concrete' events) are based specifically on an analysis of *adverbial modification* and of *singular causal statements*. I shall discuss these subjects in turn.

Adverbial Modification

In 'The Logical Form of Action Sentences' Davidson called attention to the following specimen sentence:[35]

> Jones buttered the toast in the bathroom with a knife at midnight.

Although most philosophers, at least before reading Davidson's article, would analyze the sentence as containing a five-place predicate 'x butters y in z with w at t', such an analysis has a crucial defect: it does not distinguish semantically important verbal elements that the sentence shares with 'Jones buttered the toast', 'Jones buttered the toast in the bathroom' and 'Jones buttered the toast in the bathroom with a knife'. These latter statements are logical consequences of the original statement; they follow by virtue of that statement's

logical form. If the original statement contained an unstructured five-place
predicate, its logical form would not justify these consequences: we could not
show that they follow as a matter of formal logic. Some other analysis of the
original statement must, therefore, be correct.

What is the correct analysis of that statement? Davidson says that we must
regard it as a statement about events: it tells us that an event occurred that
was an act of buttering the toast by Jones, that took place in the bathroom,
that was done with a knife, and that occurred at midnight. Put in symbols,
the general idea is that:

$$(\exists x)\,(Bxtj \cdot Ixb \cdot Dxk \cdot Oxm).$$

Since each adverbial phrase in the original is represented by a conjunct in the
symbolic counterpart, it is easy to see that the entailments in question are
demonstrable by standard quantification theory. Thus, 'Jones buttered the
toast' takes the form of '$(\exists x)\,(Bxtj)$', which follows immediately from the
formula above.

Davidson's canonical counterparts to ordinary action sentences are thus
existentially quantified, and the quantifiers range over a domain containing
events. Since the canonical counterparts disclose the logical form of the
ordinary statements, the latter commit us, Davidson believes, to an ontology
of events (at least among other things). One of his reasons for adopting such
an ontology, then, is that it seems forced upon us by the formal logic of
action statements.

Although Davidson is avowedly concerned, in his article, with the logic of
action statements, his subject is really much more general: it is the logic of
adverbial modification. To make his points about the semantical structure of
complex verbal structures, he did not have to choose a statement specifically
about actions; he could just as well have used the sentence 'The radiator
exploded in the bathroom at midnight on New Year's Eve'. What Davidson's
article really requires us to ask ourselves is whether the logic of adverbial
modification requires us to adopt an ontology containing events. Davidson's
approach in 'The Logical Form of Action Sentences' suggests an affirmative
answer to this, but other approaches are possible, which require no commitment to events. To gain perspective on the issue I shall point out certain
shortcomings to Davidson's treatment of adverbial modification, and then
indicate how a different treatment, not involving quantification over events,
avoids those shortcomings.

Consider the simple action-statement 'Jones traveled slowly'. As Davidson acknowledges, this statement cannot be interpreted as '($\exists x$) (x was a traveling by Jones and x was slow)'.[36] The difficulty here is that a modifier like 'slowly' cannot be detached from its verb and converted into a simple predicate true of events. If Jones's traveling were identical with his walking, then, if Jones walked extremely fast, the proposed analysis would require us to say that his action was, without qualification, both slow and fast. Since saying this would be absurd, some other analysis must be found. Davidson's approach provides no likely clues, however.

Another sort of case where Davidson's approach is unhelpful may be illustrated by 'Jones was rarely sober after dinner'. Although we seem to have a core sentence here, 'John was sober', modified by a number of adverbs, the sentence with the modifiers included does not entail the complete sentences embedded within it. Thus, 'Jones was rarely sober after dinner' does not entail 'Jones was rarely sober', let alone 'Jones was sober'. The specimen sentence discussed by Davidson differs significantly in this respect: it does entail the shorter sentences embedded within it. If we had a clear understanding of adverbial modification, we should be able to point to the structural features of the two types of sentence that account for this striking difference in their implications. Davidson's theory offers little help in this regard, for it throws no light whatever on the structure of sentences beginning 'Jones was rarely sober. . .'.

Apart from these limitations of scope, Davidson's theory encounters difficulties with sentences it was designed to handle. Consider this one:

John walked into the door.

According to Davidson, this sentence has the form of

$$(\exists x)\,(Wxj\,\&\,Ixd).$$

But suppose, consistently with Davidson's theory of action, that John's walking here is identical with his amusing Mary. Since his act of amusing Mary is *an* act of amusing her, and since it is also identical with the act that, according to the formula above, is *into* the door, we can then infer that

$$(\exists x)\,(Axjm\,\&\,Ixd).$$

But the vernacular equivalent to this statement is

John amused Mary into the door.

Clearly, this result is absurd, and it is not at all obvious that Davidson can avoid it. Davidson himself admits that if I fly my spaceship to the moon, my flying is *to* the moon — that is, stands in that relation. But if my act of flying is identical with my act of frightening my wife, then my frightening her would also stand in that relation, and the vernacular statement 'I frightened my wife to the moon' should be considered true.

A related example that generates a similar difficulty is this. Suppose Jones hits Smith with a small stick. Jones's movements in hitting Smith frighten Mary. Thus we may say that, according to Davidson's theory of action, Jones's hitting Smith is identical with his frightening Mary. By the kind of reasoning illustrated in the last paragraph we may conclude that Jones frightened Mary with a small stick. But the stick in question is, we may assume, very small — small enough so that Mary, from her perspective, did not actually see it. She saw Jones hit Smith, but she did not see that he hit him with a stick. It seems obvious that there is no way of interpreting the statement 'Jones frightened Mary with a small stick' so that it is even remotely true. Yet it must be considered true if Davidson is right both about action and about adverbial modification. In constructing this example I am treating the preposition 'with' just as Davidson treats it in his well-known example of buttering toast *with* a knife in the bathroom at midnight.

The last two examples recall Goldman's claim that acts may stand in a by-relation. In Section 3 of this chapter I argued that Goldman's claim is implausible and poses no genuine difficulty for the identity theory of actions, but anyone who accepts Davidson's approach to adverbial modification cannot brush it aside as easily as I have. According to Davidson's approach, the statement

John turned on the light by flipping the switch

presumably has the form of

$$(\exists x)\,(\exists y)\,(Txjl \;\&\; Fyjs \;\&\; Bxy),$$

and this formula does imply that actions stand in a by-relation. Since the by-relation, if there is such a thing, is asymmetrical, Davidson's approach to adverbial modification appears to be at odds with his theory of action.

Another drawback to Davidson's approach is that it cannot, at least in any evident way, account for certain entailments between adverbially modified statements. One such entailment involves the verb 'to exist'. Although this verb may be translated into a system of logic in more than one way, any acceptable translation of it should allow us to prove that 'John was drunk' formally entails 'John existed'. Similarly, any fully adequate theory of adverbial modification should allow us to prove that 'Jones was drunk on New Year's' formally entails 'Jones existed on New Year's'. Yet according to Davidson's approach these statements have the form of '$(\exists x)$ (x is a [state of] being drunk by Jones & x is on New Year's)' and '$(\exists x)$ (x is an existing by Jones & x was on New Year's)'. But inspection shows that there is no formal entailment between these formulas. They both contain *unstructured* predicates true of some event or condition involving Jones, and there is no logical basis for inferring that if the first predicate is true of some event or condition, the second must also be true of some event or condition. A fully satisfactory theory of adverbial modification should show us how to prove the relevant implication on purely formal grounds.

A difficulty of a more philosophical or metaphysical sort also arises from Davidson's approach. If we follow his strategy in exposing the structure of the predicate in 'Jones stood on his head in the living room at midnight', we shall no doubt follow the same strategy in exposing the structure of the predicates in the following sentences:[37]

> John had red hair on New Year's.
> John was excited about the game.
> John's passion for Mary ended on New Year's.
> John was absolutely motionless for three hours.
> John was physically mature at thirteen.

But if we follow his strategy in these cases we shall be committed to acknowledging some very peculiar entities: John's having red hair, John's being excited (or John's excitement), the ending of John's passion for Mary, John's absolute motionlessness, John's physical maturity, and so on. The entities here are, I suppose, examples of states or conditions. Some philosophers will not, of course, object to such entities, but it is hard to believe that we are actually committed to them merely because we use adverbial phrases to modify certain verbs.

In his book *Inquiry Into Meaning and Truth* Russell contended that, to avoid a commitment to an unknowable substratum, we should think of material things and persons as 'bundles' of qualities.[38] If we are committed to entities like John's excitement, John's tallness (got from 'John is tall now'), John's intelligence, and the redness of John's hair, we might be strongly tempted to follow Russell and simply *identify* John with a 'bundle' of these entities. If there is such a thing as John's intelligence, must it not partially constitute John? Surely, his intelligence, his tallness, his anger, and the like could not exist apart from him: if he were related to these items in any way other than whole to part, he would seem to be a kind of mysterious substratum. If this is right, it is actually misleading to say that *both* John and such things as his intelligence, his tallness, and his excitement exist; instead of existing apart from these more elementary things, he is *constituted* by them.

When a biologist tells us that we are really systems of scientific exotica (molecules, say) he can reasonably expect our assent. After all, he uses legitimate empirical methods of investigation, and he knows what he is talking about. But when a metaphysician tells us we are really systems of metaphysical exotica, he cannot expect us to assent just as readily — particularly if his claim is based merely on the logical analysis of a grammatical construction. Metaphysical objects like events, states, conditions, and states of affairs are not only obscure in themselves, but it is far from clear how they are supposed to be related to other things. If we can possibly avoid a commitment to them, we certainly ought to do so. As far as our philosophical theories are concerned, the exotic and obscure should not be multiplied beyond necessity.

Largely in response to Davidson's remarks on action sentences, theories of adverbial modification have recently been developed that do not involve quantification over events, states, conditions, and the like. Romane Clark's theory is a case in point.[39] His theory, unlike Davidson's, provides a thoroughly general account of predicate modifiers. His key idea is that predicate modifiers are not themselves predicates, or even predicates in disguise: they are operators, which make big predicates out of little ones. The adverb 'slowly' thus occurs as a modifier of 'travels', yielding the complex predicate 'travels slowly'. Since there are significantly different types of predicate modifier (apart from standard ones, Clark recognizes fictionalizers like 'mythical', enlargers like 'possible' in 'possible addict', negators like 'fake', and neutralizers like 'alleged') no single rule holds for all of them. According to the rule for a standard modifier like 'slowly', the sentence 'John traveled slowly' logically entails 'John traveled'; according to the rules for a nonstandard modifier like 'possible', there is no entailment relation between 'John was a possible addict' and 'John was an addict'. In Clark's system the statement Davidson discusses, 'Jones buttered the toast in the bathroom with a knife at midnight', is interpreted as having the form of a simple relational statement with a core predicate complicated by three modifiers. Each modifier introduces a singular term, and if, in line with the usual logical practice, we collect these terms at the end of the formula, we can represent Davidson's specimen sentence as follows:

> In [At [With [Buttered (Jones, the toast)] (a knife)] (midnight)] (the bathroom)].

Clark's basic idea, that predicate modifiers function as operators that generate complex predicates from simpler ones, is extremely plausible, but it appears to have the consequence that statements involving such modifiers are nonextensional. Although, as I shall argue in a later section (see pages 93 ff.), this consequence may actually be avoided, we can grant it for the time being. Many philosophers would be strongly tempted to reject Clark's theory on account of it, and it is worth pointing out that such a temptation is really hard to justify.

One mark of a fully extensional statement is that any statement occurring within it can be replaced by any other statement with the same truth-value without changing the truth-value of the whole. It seems obvious that the statement 'John shaved in the bathroom' does not possess this mark. Suppose that the statement is true and suppose also that Nero did, in fact, fiddle while Rome burned. The simple statement 'John shaved' thus has the same truth-value as 'Nero fiddled', but although 'John shaved in the bathroom' is true, the statement 'Nero fiddled in the bathroom' is no doubt false. Thus, modified statements like 'John shaved in the bathroom' seem to lack a distinctive mark of extensionality.

There is, however, another, perhaps more fundamental mark of extensionality that statements like 'John shaved in the bathroom' clearly seem to possess. If a statement is extensional, then any singular term (or name) occurring in it may be replaced by any other term with the same referent without changing the truth-value of the statement. This mark seems to be possessed by 'John shaved in the bathroom', because if, say, the title 'The President of the Board' refers to John, then it would appear that 'John shaved in the bathroom' is true if, and only if, The President of the Board shaved in the bathroom. This second mark of extensionality is related to a third mark, which also seems to be possessed by 'John shaved in the bathroom'. If a statement containing a singular term '*a*' is extensional, then it may be existentially generalized with respect to the position occupied by '*a*'. Since 'John shaved in the bathroom' seems obviously to imply '($\exists x$) (x shaved in the bathroom)', it would certainly appear that the statement about John possesses this third mark as well.

Some philosophers evidently believe that these three marks are coextensive – that if a sentence possesses one of them, it possesses them all; and that if it lacks one, it lacks the others as well. If this belief were correct, we should have to acknowledge that if 'John shaved in the bathroom' really does lack the first mark, it must, in spite of appearances, lack the others as well. This consequence would be very puzzling, however. If we could not validly infer '($\exists x$) (x shaved in the bathroom)' and 'The President of the Board shaved in the bathroom' from 'John shaved in the bathroom' and 'John = The President of the Board', then the statement 'John shaved in the bathroom' would not really be *about* the person John: the term 'John' would not possess its normal reference in that statement. As Quine has emphasized,[40] if a term '*t*' occurs purely referentially in a sentence *S*, the position it occupies must be subject to the substitutivity of identity and to existential generalization. Since it seems obvious that the term 'John' does refer to the person John in sentences like 'John shaved in the bathroom', the idea that such sentences are really nonextensional – that they really lack one of the distinguishing marks of extensionality – may thus appear highly questionable.

The reasoning here depends, of course, on the assumption that the three marks of extensionality are coextensive. Anyone accepting this assumption would thus prefer a theory of adverbial modification that, like Davidson's, interprets 'John shaved in the bathroom' as extensional. As we have seen, Davidson would interpret the sentence as having the form of '($\exists x$) (Sxj & Ixb)'. A sentence of this form does not contain a complete sentence within it; rather, it contains two formulas bound by a common quantifier. Although we cannot validly replace these formulas by statements, we can validly replace them by materially equivalent formulas. If, for example, the statement '(x) ($Sxj \equiv Axm$)' is true, then '($\exists x$) (Axm & Ixb)' is true as well. On Davidson's approach, the statement 'John shaved in the bathroom' is thus fully extensional. It may, on the basis of its surface structure, *appear* to lack a mark of extensionality, but when its logical form is identified, it can be seen to be extensional.

If the assumption on which all this reasoning is based were sound, Clark's theory of adverbial modification could reasonably be rejected on account of its evident nonextensionality. But there is no reason to believe that the assumption is sound. If sentences like 'John shaved in the bathroom' do, in fact, lack the first mark of extensionality, *this has nothing to do with their referential character: By the usual tests, they would appear to be referentially transparent.* As Quine insists, the referential features of a statement are owing to the singular terms (the names and bound variables) it contains; they are not owing to the predicates appended to such terms. Thus, when Quine explains why the positions occupied by referring terms are subject to the substitutivity of identity, he says 'the predication is true so long merely as the predicated general term is true of the object named by the singular term. . . ; hence the substitution of a new singular term that names the same object leaves the predication true'.[41] There is nothing in this remark to suggest that if a complex predicate, involving an adverbial modifier, is true of an object, then some other predicate (with or without that modifier) is also true of that object. Thus, even though John may have both shaved and showered on a certain day, the fact that the complex predicate 'shaved rapidly' is true of him while 'showered rapidly' is false of him should not suggest that the statement 'John shaved rapidly' is not *about* John.

If we take seriously the plausible idea that certain adverbial constructions actually function as adverbial modifiers, making bigger predicates out of littler ones, then we should not expect statements containing such modifiers to possess the first mark of extensionality. One reason for not expecting this is that a modifier making sense when conjoined to one predicate may yield nonsense when conjoined to another predicate true of the same person or thing. Thus, suppose that Mary, who abhors violence, ran to the store. If this supposition is true, the statements 'Mary ran' and 'Mary abhors violence' then have the same truth-value: they are materially equivalent. But while 'Mary ran to the store' is both meaningful and true, 'Mary abhors violence to the store' is neither: it does not make sense. This kind of absurdity is compounded if we suppose that 'Mary ran' can be replaced by *any* materially equivalent statement in the context of 'Mary ran to the store'. Take 'Plato was a philosopher' or even '2 + 2 = 4', for example. If 'Mary ran' is true, these statements are materially equivalent to it; yet the locutions 'Plato was a philosopher to the store' and '2 + 2 = 4 to the store' are nonsensical.

It is important to observe here that even *logically* equivalent formulas cannot be validly interchanged in statements involving the kind of adverbial modification we have been considering. To take a simple, nontechnical example: 'Mary smiled' is logically equivalent to 'If Mary did not smile, then the weather was good in all respects and bad in all respects'. Yet while 'Mary smiled happily' is (we may assume) true, 'If Mary did not smile, then the weather was good in all respects and bad in all respects happily' does not make clear sense. The general point here is that when we have a predicate modifier like 'happily', we cannot expect to interchange even logically equivalent statements in the position preceding it — that is, in the position indicated by the blank in '_____ happily'. This point does not hold for all adverbial modifiers, for some of them, like 'probably', are not even predicate modifiers: they modify complete statements. But when an adverb is used to modify a given predicate, it generates (if Clark is right) a complex predicate; and if (as I have been doing here) we view statements containing such a predicate as containing a core sentence, then we cannot allow that core sentences of this kind may be replaced by others that are even logically equivalent to them.

The fact that we cannot validly replace 'Mary smiled' by a logically equivalent statement in the context of a sentence like 'Mary smiled happily' is very important. By the strategy of an argument to be discussed later in this section it is possible to prove that if we *may* validly interchange logically equivalent formulas in a certain sentential context, then we may substitute singular terms referring to the same thing in that context just in case we may validly interchange materially equivalent formulas in it. This fact indicates that, for a large class of statements, the three marks of extensionality actually are coextensive. But this class of statements does not involve those containing 'standard' predicate modifiers — at least if statements containing such modifiers are viewed as containing simpler, core statements. (If statements containing predicate modifiers are not viewed this way, then, as I shall argue in the next chapter, they may be regarded as *fully* extensional.) Nonstandard modifiers like 'mythical', 'alleged' or 'deliberately' can be expected to yield strongly nonextensional contexts on any plausible theory, though this expectation might be defeated, at least in part, by a suitable analytical strategy.

If what I have been saying is correct, it would appear that statements like 'John shaved in the bathroom' should not (given the proviso I have mentioned) be considered totally nonextensional. In particular, it should not be supposed that they are somehow not 'about' the world, that the singular terms they contain do not possess their customary reference. The only thing logically special about them is that they involve a mode of predicate composition that renders inapplicable certain rules governing the valid interchange of equivalent formulas. But this does not seem objectionable. If the relevant rules of predicate composition can be clearly set forth (as they are in Clark's theory) we can claim to understand the logical structure of such sentences even though they lack some of the logical properties of statements that do not contain predicate modifiers.

Before introducing these remarks about Clark's theory of predicate modifiers, I pointed out certain drawbacks to Davidson's approach to adverbial modification. Although Clark's approach seems clearly preferable to Davidson's, I will concede that Davidson's totally extensional approach might possibly be modified and extended so as to avoid the drawbacks I have mentioned. I have no real interest in disputing this. What I do want to dispute is the idea that the formal logic of adverbial modification *requires* us to adopt an ontology containing events. It seems to me that this view has nothing to commend it. To prove that the view is correct, one would have to do far more than develop a complete theory of adverbial modification that carries such a commitment. At the least, one would have to show that no satisfactory alternative theory not carrying such a commitment is even possible. Davidson, of course, has never even attempted to prove something like this. Since at least one alternative to Davidson's theory has actually been worked out that (a) covers the whole field of predicate modification and (b) does not require a commitment to irreducible events, it seems safe to say that the formal logic of action sentences — or, more exactly, the adverbial modification they often involve — does not itself require us to adopt an ontology of events. And in not requiring such an ontology it does not *require* us to answer the questions about the identity of actions that we raised at the end of the last section.

Singular Causal Statements

As I pointed out, Davidson has offered other reasons for adopting an ontology of events. In an article called 'Causal Relations' he turns his attention to the logical form of singular causal statements like

(1)   The short circuit caused the fire.

According to the interpretation he develops, such statements are really about events.[42] As far as I can tell, he offers no direct argument for this interpretation; rather, he defends it indirectly by attacking a possible alternative. The alternative is that the specimen sentence (1) has the form of

> (2)   *The fact that* there was a short circuit *caused it to be the case that* there was a fire.

This alternative differs from Davidson's interpretation in construing the word 'caused' as elliptical for a statement connective — a complex connective constituted by the italicized words in (2).

Davidson's argument against the rival interpretation of (1) is unsatisfactory, however. He says:

It is obvious that the connective in (2) is not truth-functional, since (2) may change from true to false if the contained sentences are switched. Nevertheless, substitution of singular terms for others with the same extension in sentences like... (2) does not change their truth-value.... Surely also we cannot change the truth value of the likes of (2) by substituting logically equivalent sentences for sentences in it.... [But by a Fregean argument these assumptions lead] to the conclusion that the main connective of (2) is, contrary to what we supposed, truth-functional.[43]

Davidson regards the conclusion of his Fregean argument as posing a dilemma, which is best avoided by rejecting the interpretation in question and accepting his own approach.

It is hard to see why Davidson should think his argument presents us with a dilemma. What is directly shown by his argument is that, if (a) we may validly substitute logically equivalent formulas for one another in the context of sentences like (2), and if (b) we may also validly substitute coextensive singular terms for one another in such contexts, then (c) we may also substitute materially equivalent formulas for one another in such contexts. But since we know by an obvious counter-instance (which Davidson himself supplies in the passage above) that (c) is false, we *know* that (a) is false or (b) is false. In knowing this we know that one of the premises used in Davidson's argument is false, and that his argument does not, therefore, establish anything about the logical form of (1). The sentence (1) does not even enter into the argument set out above.

As I said, Davidson's Fregean argument proves that (c) follows from (a) and (b). Slightly reconstructed, the argument is as follows. The conclusion (c) — that we *may* validly substitute materially equivalent formulas for one another in the context of sentences like (2) — may be expressed somewhat more formally by saying that, for any statements P and Q, if P is materially equivalent to Q, then $S(P)$ is materially equivalent to $S(Q)$, where $S(P)$ is a sentence having the form of (2) and differing from $S(Q)$ only in containing P where $S(Q)$ contains Q. To prove that (c) follows from (a) and (b), assume (a), (b), and the antecedent of (c). It is sufficient to show, on these assumptions, that $S(P)$ implies $S(Q)$. Assume $S(P)$, then, and observe that P is logically equivalent to $\hat{x}(x=x \cdot P) = \hat{x}(x=x)$. Substitute this last formula for P in $S(P)$ and observe that, since P is materially equivalent to Q, the singular terms $\hat{x}(x=x \cdot P)$ and $\hat{x}(x=x \cdot Q)$ are coextensive. In accordance with premiss (b) substitute $\hat{x}(x=x \cdot Q)$ for $\hat{x}(x=x \cdot P)$ in the formula $S[\hat{x}(x=x \cdot P) = \hat{x}(x=x)]$ and get $S[\hat{x}(x=x \cdot Q = \hat{x}(x=x)]$. But the nested formula here, $\hat{x}(x=x \cdot Q) = \hat{x}(x=x)$, is logically equivalent to Q. Therefore, by premiss (a), we may conclude $S(Q)$.

This argument has been criticized by some writers on the grounds that the formula P is not really logically equivalent to $\hat{x}(x=x \cdot P) = \hat{x}(x=x)$.[44] Strictly speaking, the criticism is justified, for the two formulas are not equivalent in the narrow sense of the word 'logical'. They are, however, equivalent in a broad sense of the word: they may be proved equivalent in any set theory allowing a universal class, and corresponding formulas may be proved equivalent in other set theories.[45] Since set theoretical truths are often considered logical in a broad sense of 'logical', the Fregean part of Davidson's argument would seem to be acceptable. Davidson's apparent error in the passage quoted above is that of supposing that we might validly substitute logically (= set-theoretically) equivalent formulas *and* materially equivalent terms in a given context when we cannot validly substitute materially equivalent formulas in it. The Fregean argument shows that this supposition is false. Since Davidson's overall argument seems to be based on this false supposition, it does not, at least in any obvious way, pose a dilemma that should be resolved by rejecting the suggested interpretation of the specimen causal statement and by accepting Davidson's alternative. As I pointed out, the sentence whose interpretation is in question − namely (1) − does not even enter into Davidson's argument.

As far as I can tell, the most that can be inferred from Davidson's argument is that sentences with the form of (2) have a puzzling or problematic logical structure. Since we know, by virtue of obvious counterinstances, that we cannot validly interchange materially equivalent formulas in the context of such sentences, we must acknowledge that at least one of the other principles of substitution fails for such contexts. But which principle is this? Or do both principles fail? The answer is not entirely clear. On the face of it, the principle allowing the interchange of set-theoretically equivalent formulas seems to fail. One would not normally suppose that a fact about the identity of two sets — two abstract objects — would *cause* it to be the case that there was a fire. On the other hand, it is far from obvious that the truth of causal statements can always be preserved by interchanging co-referring singular terms in them having the complex structure of $\hat{x}(x=x \cdot P)$. Until we are clear about the bearing of these principles on statements like (2), we shall have to regard these statements as logically problematic.

In view of these last considerations it might seem that, although Davidson's specific argument does not really support his interpretation of causal statements, his interpretation is clearly preferable to the alternative involving statements like (2). But, again, the matter is far from clear. Davidson himself points out cases of singular causal statements that his interpretation apparently cannot handle, and he suggests another interpretation for these special cases.[46] Some of these cases are as follows: 'The failure of the sprinkling system caused the fire'; 'The slowness with which the controls were applied caused the rapidity with which the inflation developed'; 'The collapse was caused, not by the fact that the bolt gave way, but by the fact that it gave way so suddenly and unexpectedly'; 'The fact that the dam did not hold caused the flood'. In connection with these examples Davidson says: 'I suggest. . . that the "caused" of the sample sentences [just given] . . . is best expressed by the words "causally explains" '.

It is obvious that the interpretation suggested for the special cases works perfectly well for the ordinary cases. Thus, instead of saying that the short circuit caused the fire, we could say that the fire is causally explained by the fact that there was a short circuit; and instead of saying that something caused the fire, we could say that there is a causal explanation for the fire. The possibility of saying such things shows that Davidson has actually supplied an alternative interpretation of singular causal statements that does not require a commitment to an ontology of events. Since it is simpler, philosophically, to interpret all singular causal statements according to a single pattern than to interpret some according to one pattern and others according to a different pattern, Davidson has unwittingly given us reason to interpret *all* singular causal statements on the pattern of 'S causally explains S^*'.

If we think about this alternative interpretation for just a minute we can see that, oddly enough, it does not differ appreciably from the interpretation Davidson attacks with his Fregean argument. The most felicitous way of replacing the variables in 'S causally explains S*' will result in assertions of the form 'The fact that P causally explains the fact that Q', and such assertions seem mere variants of 'The fact that P caused it to be the case that Q'. If Davidson's argument against interpreting singular causal statements as having the form of the latter were valid, it would hold equally against one affirming that they have the form of the former. It is very surprising, therefore, that he should have made this particular suggestion about how to interpret the special cases.

One difficulty with the alternative suggestion is that it seems to commit us to an ontology of facts. Actually, such a commitment would have to be demonstrated. The mere fact that we use certain singular terms does not show, or even provide a strong presumption for thinking, that those terms are used to stand for something. Quine's, and I suppose Davidson's, criterion for a commitment to entities of a certain kind requires that they be 'quantified over';[47] yet the alternative in question involves no quantification over facts. As we shall see in Chapter II, assertions of the form 'The fact that P causally explains the fact that Q' can actually be understood as fully extensional and as referring to statements or inscriptions (see pages 104 - ff below).

The idea that we might be able to deal with causation without postulating events may seem bizarre. One might expostulate, 'Surely there are causal relations, and surely causal relations hold between events!' But it is not madness to deny that there are causal relations. In fact, only a Platonist would want to maintain that there are (really) *relations* of any kind at all. If we do not acknowledge events, we can, of course, speak *as if* there were such things; we can use the language of causes and effects as a convenient *façon de parler*. As a convinced opponent of events might argue: 'In more careful moments we can speak of causal laws rather than causally related events; and we can say that causal explanations are distinguished by the laws or principles they involve or allude to. Although familiar causal principles contain causal language (compare "If a dry, well-made match is scratched in the presence of oxygen, it will light") they do not require any quantification over events. More sophisticated causal laws are not given the epithet "causal" because they are about events, or types of events, that may be parsed into causes and effects; they are given this epithet because they remind us of the familiar causal principles that involve the primitive causal language of, say, "...a match is *scratched*". Ideally, causal laws no matter how sophisticated concern the behavior of individuals: they tell us what *individuals* of such and such a kind will do (how they will behave) if, say, they collide with individuals of a certain other kind. It is simply a mistake to think that causal laws – particularly in the advanced sciences – have to be concerned with causes and effects. They can tell us how things behave without objectifying the "ways".' So speaks the opponent of events.[48]

To return, however, to Davidson. Although his Fregean argument for adopting an ontology of events is not successful, he makes some additional remarks in 'Causal Relations' that seem to support such an ontology. He contends that

(3)   Jack fell down *before* Jack broke his crown

seems to have a logical structure parallel to that of

(4)   Jack fell down, which caused it to be the case that Jack broke his crown.

He then argues that (3) has the form of

(5) $(\exists x)(\exists y)(\exists z)(\exists w) [Fxj \cdot t(x) = z \cdot Byj \cdot t(y) = w \cdot z < w]$,

where the variables z and w take 'pure numbers' as their values and the functor '$t(x)$' is read 'the time of x'. Since on this interpretation (3) tells us that one event *precedes* another, the parallelism in question leads Davidson to say that (4) should be understood as saying one event *causes* another.[49]

This line of thought does not really give us good reason to interpret (4) as tacitly about events. In the first place, Davidson bases his contention about the logical form of (3) on his Fregean argument, which applies, he says, 'just as well against taking the "before" in [3] as the sentential connective it appears to be'.[50] But, as we saw, the Fregean argument is based on inconsistent premises, and thus does not prove anything of interest about the logical form of particular sentences. Secondly, Davidson's contention that (3) has the form of (5) is based on his belief that 'events are on hand' – that is, on his belief that we already have an event ontology.[51] If this belief is put in question, his claim about the logical form of (3) – and thus his conclusion about the logical form of (4) – remains unsupported.

Even though Davidson has not given us good reason to interpret (4) as a statement about events, an interpretation of this kind is bound to be tempting to any philosopher at home with modern logic. Nevertheless, a mere temptation, no matter how strong, is clearly insufficient to establish an ontology of events. We might, after all, adopt a strategy of rendering vernacular statements in a certain formalism merely as a matter of convenience.[52] There is generally more than one way of construing a statement; and though it is convenient to treat the 'before' in the context 'P before Q' as Davidson does (and as Frege did), there does not appear to be anything *wrong* with treating this 'before' as the sentential connective it appears to be.[53] As we have seen, Davidson's argument fails to cast any doubt on this idea. Of course, if we interpret 'before' as a temporal connective, we must indicate its logical powers by certain axioms — for example, by '$(P$ before $Q) \supset \sim (Q$ before $P)$'. But there does not appear to be any particular difficulty in working these axioms out.

We might note in this connection that philosophers interested in the philosophy of time have generally argued that we must acknowledge some basic (or 'primitive') temporal predicate. A familiar candidate is 'wholly-precedes'.[54] Most philosophers concerned with temporal discourse would argue that we cannot order events temporally merely by associating numbers with them; we must relate our scale of numbers to a corresponding order of moments. As is well known, Russell argued that moments could be 'constructed' from overlapping events and that all events could be ordered, temporally, by a single basic relation.[55] A philosopher wanting to avoid a basic commitment to events would resist Russell's strategy in constructing moments, but he would naturally contend that, to talk adequately about temporal matters, we need a basic temporal expression. Instead, however, of using Russell's 'wholly-preceeds' as the basic temporal expression, he might adopt the temporal *connective* 'before' and say 'Mary scowled before Bill left' where Russell would say 'A scowling by Mary wholly preceded a leaving by Bill'. But just as Russell needed special axioms for his primitive predicate, we shall need special axioms for our primitive connective. The latter axioms will, of course, have a striking structural similarity to the former ones.

I have not been concerned to prove, in this section, that an ontology of events is, in fact, dispensable; I have merely tried to show that, as matters currently stand in philosophy, there is no good reason to suppose that we *must* accept such an ontology. I incline to the view that events are really best understood as what Russell called 'logical fictions' — that is, as entities belonging to the same ontological basket as propositions, facts, properties, and states of affairs — but I am not sure that this view is wholly defensible: to be sure, we should need a fully worked out system of metaphysics. Until we know that the view is indefensible, however, we do not really have to adopt a theory of what events are and be seriously concerned with answering the question posed at the end of the last section — namely, 'Are actions mental causes, physical effects, or a combination of both?' This question can arise only on the assumption that there really are such things as events. As far as I know, this is an assumption we have no *good* reason to accept.

7. CONCLUDING REMARKS

Suppose that we do not wish to adopt an ontology of events. What kind of action theory is possible for us? The answer is that, strictly speaking, no *action* theory is possible for us, but we may have a theory that corresponds to an action theory. This corresponding theory might be called a 'theory of agents', for its fundamental subject matter will be rational agents rather than the supposed acts that agents perform. A distinctive feature of such a theory is that it will employ predicates where an action theory employs referring singular terms. Thus, instead of saying that John's act of hitting Tom caused Mary's anger, a philosopher espousing a theory of agents might say (at least as a first approximation) that Mary was angry *because* John hit Tom. The agent theorist's preferred locution clearly includes what might loosely be called 'action predicates', but since such predicates are not referring terms, they do not commit him to actions or events.

As this last example might suggest, a theory of agents may be viewed as a kind of translation of a theory of action. I say 'kind of translation' because an acceptable theory of agents need not have a counterpart to every assertion in a plausible theory of action. On the other hand, counterparts of this sort can generally be expected. When I defended Prichard against various objections, I pointed out that his theory must be augmented by principles of act constitution that correspond to Goldman's principles of act generation (see page 16 above). For example, where Goldman claimed that an act of signaling may be generated from a distinct act of moving one's arm, Prichard should say that an act of signaling may be constituted by an act of moving one's arm. Now, a philosopher espousing a theory of agents would want to adopt principles corresponding to those of Goldman and the augmented Prichardian. But instead of applying to acts, his principles would apply directly to agents. According to one of them, if an agent S extends his arm in a certain way while in a particular region of the intersection, then S signals a turn. According to another, if a person launches a torpedo and the Bismark sinks because he launches the torpedo, then he sinks the Bismark. This last principle is clearly an application of a general principle that corresponds to Goldman's principle of causal act-generation. My conjecture is that, if a philosophical opponent of actions and events can work out a satisfactory interpretation of causal statements (perhaps along the lines suggested earlier), he should encounter no fundamental difficulty in working out a satisfactory theory of agents.

The position I am taking in this book is not, again, the strong one that a commitment to events, actions, states, conditions and so forth is positively unnecessary; it is the more modest position that it is really an open question whether we need to acknowledge such entities. As I said, I happen to believe that an ontology rich in exotica is ultimately avoidable; but I do not think I can prove it, at least in this book, and it would be absurd to recommend my belief as something to be accepted on faith.[56] My official position here concerning events, states, and the like should, therefore, be viewed as one of metaphysical neutrality: all things considered, a commitment to such entities may or may not be required.

In view of my official position on events, actions, and states, I cannot brush aside theories of action as unworthy of detailed investigation; in fact, I consider it vitally important to come to terms with the supposed mentalistic aspects of actions, something I neglected in discussing the views of Prichard and Davidson. In accordance with this conviction, I shall devote the following chapter to the so-called springs of action. In discussing this subject I shall use terms like 'Mary's belief that snow is white' and 'Tom's intention to enter college' as if they referred to something real. I shall even go so far as to say that beliefs are mental propensities and that intentions are similar to beliefs. My view is that, if a commitment to states and conditions proves to be unavoidable, we are fully justified in referring to beliefs and intentions, and we may conceive of them in the ways I suggest. On the other hand, if it is possible (as I actually believe it is) to avoid a commitment to such entities, then the claims I make about various mental states can be translated into the metaphysically preferable language of a theory of agents. My claim, for

example, that a belief *is* a certain kind of mental propensity can be trans-
formed into the claim that a person believes such and such *just when* he
has a certain propensity — that is, just when (to put it roughly) certain
hypotheticals are true of him. I shall not attempt to work out a detailed
theory of agents, for this would require (among other things) a thorough
analysis of causal statements, which is beyond the scope of this book. Nevertheless, I shall explain how someone holding a theory of agents can deal with
some of the most difficult problems uncovered by a plausible theory of
action.

I have said that I believe, but shall not here assume or attempt to argue,
that an ontology of states and events is ultimately avoidable. Suppose I am
mistaken in this belief. The chapter to follow will show how we might then
conceive of various mental states. But what about actions? It seems to me
that if we must ultimately accept a theory postulating actions, any of the
three theories discussed at the end of the last section could be rendered
acceptable by suitable qualifications. As I pointed out, all three theories are
in general agreement about what is involved in a typical action; they disagree
mainly in carving the joints in different places. I noted that the hybrid or
'composite' view of Collingwood and Thalberg has certain awkward consequences, but since every metaphysical theory must inevitably come to terms
with composite entities of one kind or another, those awkward consequences
cannot be decisive. (In fact, it would appear that both Prichard and Davidson
would have to acknowledge that certain actions are complex entities — for
example, those of building a house or writing a book.) My general view, then,
is that if we find it necessary to conceive of the world as containing things
called 'actions', we have three alternative ways of picking them out. We may
take our choice.

NOTES

[1] See Ludwig Wittgenstein, *Philosophical Investigations*, tr. Anscombe (Oxford, 1953),
I, sec. 621; and David Hume, *A Treatise of Human Nature*, Bk. II, sect. III.
[2] H. A. Prichard, 'Acting, Willing, and Desiring', in Prichard, *Moral Obligation* (Oxford,
1945), pp. 89–98. Reprinted in A. R. White, *The Philosophy of Action* (Oxford, 1968),
pp. 59–69. My references in the text are to the reprint in White.
[3] White, p. 2.
[4] According to a popular article, 'Parapsychology in the U.S.S.R.', *Saturday Review*
(March 18, 1972), feats of psychokinesis have been carried out experimentally at the

Institute for Technical Parapsychology in Moscow. The article includes a photograph of 'the noted Russian "sensitive" Nina Kulagina. . .[causing] a plastic sphere seemingly to float in the air. . .'. We are told that 'Mrs. Kulagina's other psychokinetic accomplishments supposedly include separating the yolk from the white of an egg, moving a pitcher filled with water across a table, and stopping the heartbeat of a frog' (p. 36).

5 Here I am ignoring the various physiological 'movements' that must occur if the man's foot is to move.

6 P. J. Fitzgerald, 'Voluntary and Involuntary Acts', in A. G. Guest (ed.), *Oxford Essays in Jurisprudence* (Oxford, 1961), pp. 1–28. Reprinted in White, pp. 120–143. The quote passage occurs on p. 126 of White.

7 See Joel Feinberg, 'Action and Responsibility', in Max Black (ed.), *Philosophy in America* (London, 1965), p. 146; see also the reprint in White, p. 106.

8 J. L. Austin, 'A Plea for Excuses', in *Philosophical Papers* (Oxford, 1961), p. 149.

9 See Prichard, p. 63.

10 See R. M. Chisholm, 'Freedom and Action', in Keith Lehrer (ed.), *Freedom and Determinism* (New York, 1966), pp. 28–44.

11 Recall the passage in Marlowe:
> Nature that fram'd us of foure Elements. . .
> Wils us to weare our selves and never rest,
> Until we reach the ripest fruit of all. . .,
> *Tamburlaine the Great*, II, vi, 869–878 (1590).

12 Donald Davidson, 'Actions, Reasons, and Causes', *Journal of Philosophy* 69 (1963), 685-700. Reprinted in White, pp. 79–94.

13 Chisholm, p. 29.

14 See H. L. A. Hart and A. M. Honoré, *Causation and the Law* (Oxford, 1959), Ch. 1.

15 R. G. Collingwood, *An Essay on Metaphysics* (Oxford, 1940), p. 296.

16 Davidson, 'Agency', in Robert Binkley *et al.*, *Agent, Action, and Reason* (Toronto, 1971), pp. 3–25.

17 See Feinberg, p. 159.

18 Davidson, 'Agency', p. 7. This formulation of Davidson's view is mine; it differs from his more informal statement in what I hope is an unimportant respect.

19 *Ibid.*, pp. 21–25.

20 See Davidson, 'Actions, Reasons, and Causes', pp. 82–89.

21 See 'Agency', p. 23.

22 James Cornman, 'Comments', in Binkley *et al.*, p. 32.

23 See Alvin Goldman, *A Theory of Human Action* (Englewood Cliffs, N.J., 1970), p. 2.

24 *Ibid.*, p. 5.

25 *Ibid.*, pp. 20–30.

26 A related objection is discussed in Goldman; see *ibid.*, p. 5.

27 See Israel Scheffler, *The Anatomy of Inquiry* (New York, 1963), pp. 55–76.

28 Prichard, p. 64.

29 *Ibid.*

30 Wilfrid Sellars, 'Fatalism and Determinism', in Keith Lehrer (ed.), *Freedom and Determinism* (New York, 1966), p. 159.

31 See R. G. Collingwood, *The New Leviathan* (Oxford, 1942), pp. 97f.

32 See Rudolf Carnap, 'Two Concepts of Probability', in H. Feigl and W. Sellars (eds.), *Readings in Philosophical Analysis* (New York, 1949), p. 330.

[33] This view seems to have been held by Collingwood in *The Idea of History* (Oxford, 1946), p. 213. More recently it has been defended by Irving Thalberg in 'Constituents and Causes of Emotion and Action', *Philosophical Quarterly* 23 (1973), 2–14.

[34] Donald Davidson, 'Causal Relations', *Journal of Philosophy* 64 (1967), p. 703.

[35] Davidson, 'The Logical Form of Action Sentences', in Nicholas Rescher (ed.), *The Logic of Decision and Action* (Pittsburgh, 1967), p. 83.

[36] *Ibid.*, p. 82.

[37] Romane Clark has called attention to similar sentences in 'Concerning the Logic of Predicate Modifiers', *Noûs* 4 (1970), p. 317.

[38] Bertrand Russell, *An Inquiry Into Meaning and Truth* (London, 1948), p. 97.

[39] See fn. 37 above. For further discussion of adverbial modification, see J. A. Fodor, 'Troubles About Actions', in D. Davidson and G. Harmon (eds.), *Semantics of Natural Language* (Dordrecht, Holland, 1972), pp. 48–69; Terence Parsons, 'Some Problems Concerning the Logic of Grammatical Modifiers', *Synthese* 21 (1970), 320–333; Richard Montague, 'English as a Formal Language', in Richmond Thomason (ed.), *Formal Philosophy: Selected Papers of Richard Montague* (New Haven, Conn., 1974), pp. 188–221; and M. J. Cresswell, *Logics and Languages* (London, 1974), Ch. 9.

[40] See W. V. O. Quine, *Word and Object* (Cambridge, Mass., 1960), pp. 141–151.

[41] *Ibid.*, pp. 142f.

[42] Davidson, 'Causal Relations', pp. 691–703.

[43] *Ibid.*, p. 684f.

[44] See J. L. Mackie, *The Cement of the Universe* (Oxford, 1974), pp. 248–255.

[45] In a set theory without a universal class the term '$\hat{x}(x=x)$' may be replaced by one like '$\hat{x}(x$ is a man & $x=x)$'. See, e.g., Patrick Suppes, *Axiomatic Set Theory* (Princeton, N.J., 1960), pp. 69f.

[46] See 'Causal Relations', pp. 702f.

[47] See W. V. O. Quine, 'On What There Is', in *From a Logical Point of View* (Cambridge, Mass., 1953), p. 12.

[48] Wilfrid Sellars has argued in a number of essays that ordinary discourse does not commit us to an ontology containing events; he holds that terms like 'John's hitting Bill' are eliminable in favor of 'that'-clauses. See especially his 'Actions and Events', *Noûs* 7 (1973), 179–202, and 'Time and the World Order', in H. Feigl and G. Maxwell (eds.), *Minnesota Studies in the Philosophy of Science*, vol. 3 (Minneapolis, 1963), pp. 527–616. Although Sellars rejects the view that everyday discourse commits us to events, he acknowledges that scientific theory may require such a commitment. For details, see his 'Time and the World Order'. In my book *Knowledge, Mind, and Nature* (New York, 1967), pp. 256–261, I also acknowledge that scientific theory may require such a commitment, but I would deny that this possibility has any implications for the analysis of everyday discourse or for a philosophical theory of actions or agents. In a splendid essay Paul Ziff argues forcefully against the need for postulating events on grammatical grounds; see his 'The Logical Structure of English Sentences', in Ziff, *Understanding Understanding* (Ithaca, N.Y., 1972), pp. 39–56.

[49] 'Causal Relations', p. 696.

[50] *Ibid.*, p. 695.

[51] *Ibid.*, p. 698.

[52] See Quine's defense of this idea in 'Methodological Reflections on Current Linguistic Theory', in Gilbert Harmon (ed.), *On Noam Chomsky: Critical Essays* (Garden City, N.Y., 1974), pp. 104–117.

[53] See Sellars, 'Time and the World Order', pp. 550ff, and P. T. Geach, 'Some Problems About Time', in P. F. Strawson (ed.), *Studies in the Philosophy of Thought and Action* (Oxford, 1968), pp. 175–191.

[54] See Bertrand Russell, *Human Knowledge: Its Scope and Limits* (London, 1946), p. 288.

[55] See *ibid.*, pp. 284–294. Russell also argued the point in his *Analysis of Matter* (London, 1927), pp. 209–312.

[56] Some relevant considerations can be extracted from my article, 'On Postulating Universals', *Canadian Journal of Philosophy* 3 (1973), 285–294.

Chapter II

THE SPRINGS OF ACTION

An assumption common to the theories of action discussed in the last chapter is that voluntary action has a distinctive mental aspect. Although I raised a general metaphysical doubt about the basis for those theories, I shall now put that doubt aside, at least initially, and attempt to work out a plausible view of how the mental aspects of action are best understood. Toward the end of the chapter I shall show how a philosophical opponent of actions and states can come to terms with the view I develop.

1. PRELIMINARY REMARKS ON VOLITION

As we saw in Chapter I, traditional philosophers such as Hume and Prichard regard volition or will as the ultimate source of voluntary behavior. According to Prichard, willing is 'a *mental* activity of whose nature we. . .[are] dimly aware in doing [an] action and of which we can become more clearly aware by reflecting on it'.[1] This is a natural approach to willing, but Prichard was not able, apparently, to elaborate upon it, for he added that the 'nature [of willing] is *sui generis* and so incapable of being defined, i.e., of having its nature expressed in terms of the nature of other things'. Hume's famous conception of the will is similar: 'by the will', he says, 'I mean nothing but *the internal impression we feel and are conscious of when we knowingly give rise to any new motion of our body, or new perception of our mind*. This impression. . . is impossible to define. . .'.[2]

The view of willing naturally suggested by these remarks has been vigorously attacked by philosophers ever since Ryle made fun of 'the myth of volitions' in *The Concept of Mind*.[3] The main difficulty, which seems particularly evident in connection with Hume's definition, is that most of us are simply not aware of any distinctive impressions whenever we consciously do something, or make some movement voluntarily. On introspective grounds such impressions seem to be fictions. Another difficulty concerns the causal role of volitions, which philosophers like Prichard insist upon. As Hume describes it, willing seems to be a causally unnecessary adjunct to voluntary movement: even if we are conscious of a special impression when we knowingly give rise to a new motion of our body, this impression does not seem to qualify as the mental process that generates or brings about that motion. A final difficulty concerns the moral significance that willing is supposed to have. One who wills to break a valuable dish or harm an innocent neighbor is supposed to be more deserving of blame or censure than one who does such a thing without willing to do so. Yet the moral significance of a Humean impression seems completely illusory. If one 'knowingly gave rise' to the smashing of a dish or the maiming of a neighbor, one would appear to be just as deserving of blame or censure whether a Humean impression occurred or not. Thus, the impression Hume speaks of seems positively irrelevant to the morally significant distinction between voluntary and nonvoluntary movements.

These objections to willing as Hume conceives of it seem entirely conclusive: if his impressions are not utter fictions, they patently lack the causal and moral significance willing is supposed to possess. But weighty as these objections are in relation to Hume's official definition, they do not prove that there is no such thing as willing. What they do prove — and prove without question — is that if there is such a thing as willing, it cannot be characterized by Hume's definition. The possibility that Hume has simply misdescribed the sort of phenomenon willing is supposed to be should not be neglected, for it is consistent with important critical remarks of those who attack the doctrine of volitions most vigorously. One of Ryle's key arguments against the myth of volitions is that it is subject to a vicious regress; yet no regress is even faintly suggested by Hume's definition. The impression he describes is something that just occurs when one 'knowingly gives rise' to a movement. As such, a Humean volition is not an act of bringing something about that might, in turn, be brought about by another such act. It is simply an 'original existent' that is supposedly experienced *when* we do something voluntarily.

Although Hume's official definition is thus inapplicable to the sort of thing defenders of volitions presumably have in mind, another conception of willing can be extracted from his remarks if we consider, not the impression he speaks of, but the very process of 'knowingly giving rise to a motion of our body'. It is not unnatural to suppose, with Prichard, that this is a *mental* process. As we have seen, Prichard said that the process, or 'activity', of willing cannot be defined in the sense of 'having its nature expressed in terms of the nature of other things', but he did go on to make an incidental remark about it, which is very important. In objecting to the theories of James and Stout that what we will is what we perhaps directly bring about by willing, Prichard insisted that what we will and the effect of our willing 'are totally different'.[4] We can, he said, will one thing but bring about something else.

This last claim of Prichard's adds to the idea of willing as a mental process, for it suggests that willing is an activity that involves the idea of some end: in contemporary jargon, it has an 'intentional object'. This suggestion also seems to be implicit in Hume's talk about 'knowingly giving rise' to a motion of our bodies: it is not just that we know what motion we are giving rise to, but that we know (as Chisholm would say) what motion we are 'endeavoring' to give rise to. Kant defined the will as 'the faculty of bringing about objects corresponding to conceptions, or of determining oneself to do so whether the physical power be present or not'.[5] Though obscure in typical Kantian fashion, this definition is well in line with the suggestions of Prichard and Hume, for it implies that willing is a mental process that involves the idea or conception of a result to be brought into existence and has that result as an expected consequence.

It should be observed at this point that even writers like Davidson, who emphatically reject the doctrine of volitions, would agree that the process or state that gives rise to a voluntary movement has the two features suggested by Kant's definition. As we have seen, Davidson holds that such a movement is caused by a primary reason, which is a complex of belief and pro attitude. Such a complex consists, he says, of a pro attitude toward actions with a certain property, and a belief that the movement the agent will make (or the action he will perform) has that property.[6] Clearly, this latter belief 'involves the idea' of a result to be brought into existence and has that result as an expected consequence. Consequently, to single out a mental state by reference to the two features mentioned in Kant's definition is not to imply that the state is thereby an act of will. An act of will, if there is such a thing, presumably has the two features, but not every state having those features would reasonably count as an act of will. In fact, virtually any philosopher can be expected to grant that a voluntary movement results from a process having the two features, though most philosophers nowadays are extremely suspicious of alleged acts of will.

If one is convinced that there is such a thing as willing, one might be inclined to improve upon Kant's conception by saying that willing to do

something involves intending to do it. This approach is not without prece-
dent, for some twentieth century philosophers have contended that willing is
simply a special form of intending. R. G. Collingwood held this view,[7] and
Wilfrid Sellars has defended it in recent years.[8] To decide whether such a
view is really acceptable or whether an alternative like Davidson's is preferable, we must obviously consider the role of intention in voluntary behavior.
This is particularly important because Davidson has recently claimed that,
strictly speaking, there are no such things (no such mental states or dispositions) as intentions. If Davidson is right, the views of Collingwood and
Sellars on willing are misguided from the very beginning. To come to terms
with the exact character of the process of 'knowingly giving rise to a new
movement of one's body' I shall, therefore, begin with Davidson's views on
intention.

2. INTENTIONS AND OTHER PRO ATTITUDES

According to Davidson, 'the expression "the intention with which Jones went
to church" has the outward form of a description, but in fact it is syncategorematic and cannot be taken to refer to an entity, state, disposition, or
event'. Its function, he says, is 'to generate new descriptions of actions in
terms of their reasons'.[9] Clearly, if Davidson is right about this, we must
agree that there are no states, events, or whatnot of intending. If 'Jones'
intention in going to church' does not refer to an intention, it is hard to see
how any term could refer to one.

As we saw in Chapter I, Davidson seems to hold that statements with the
surface form of 'S did A intentionally' are equivalent to corresponding
statements affirming that the action in question was caused by a certain sort
of primary reason.[10] Although Davidson did not spell out his interpretation
fully, his basic idea, which he would want to qualify somewhat, seems to be
this: To say that a person did something intentionally is to say that the
person's act was caused by the 'onset' of a complex state consisting of (a) a
pro attitude toward actions with a certain property and (b) a belief that
the action in question 'under a certain description' has that property. As
examples of pro attitudes, Davidson includes 'desires, urges, promptings and
a great variety of moral views, aesthetic principles, economic prejudices,
social conventions, and public and private goals and values in so far as these

can be interpreted as attitudes of an agent directed toward actions of a certain kind'.[11] Since pro attitudes are, for Davidson, genuine mental states, episodes, or dispositions, he is clearly claiming that a statement like 'Jones went to church intentionally' is true just in case the relevant behavior is caused by a suitable complex of belief and pro attitude, where the pro attitude is something other than a state, event, episode, or whatnot of intending.

The first thing I want to say about Davidson's syncategorematic approach to intention is that it does not seem very plausible. For one thing, Davidson is not arguing in favor of the metaphysical view that mentalistic terms never really refer to events, states, or dispositions. As we saw in the last chapter, he has no general objection to such entities. If, then, we assume with Davidson that terms like 'John's desire for wealth' and 'Mary's belief that Jones is mortal' do refer to states or dispositions, we should find it very natural to assume that 'Jones's intention in going to church' also refers to a state or disposition. On the face of it, at least, there appears to be no more reason to deny that intentions are genuine mental states than there is to deny that beliefs or desires are genuine mental states. Davidson, as far as I know, has offered no explicit defense for his reading of 'S's intention in doing such and such', and in the absence of such a defense his reading should be regarded as *prima facie* implausible.

The implausibility of Davidson's view gains support from a number of considerations. As we normally speak, a person can be said to have an intention he has never acted upon; thus the singular terms apparently denoting the good intentions that pave our way to Hell cannot be analyzed in the way Davidson suggests. Apart from this, the word 'intending' is (as Austin observed[12]) very closely related to 'choosing' and 'deciding', both of which seem to apply to mental activities characteristically involved in deliberation. In the process of deciding what to do, one is frequently faced with alternatives between which one must choose. If, on reflection, one chooses to do A rather than B, one has made a decision. But to decide to do A is, among other things, to *form the intention* of doing A. If one does 'form' an intention in such a case, it would seem obvious that one thereby intends to do something — just as one comes to believe something when one has formed a belief. Consequently, if believing something is a genuine state of mind, intending to do something would also appear to be such a state.

A more direct difficulty with Davidson's evident account of doing something intentionally is that the responses elicited by the pro attitudes he discusses cannot generally be expected to be intentional, no matter how they are described or conceived. Intuitively, to do something intentionally is to *mean* to do it — to carry out, as it were, a plan, idea, objective or even resolution.[13] But a desire, passion, or other pro attitude may conceivably be so strong that a man loses control of himself (as people used to say) and 'does' things that he does not mean to do. Again, one could conceivably give in to a passing desire, whim, craving or yen — also without really meaning to do so. In such cases one need not have lost control; one may simply not have exercised it. If desires and Davidson's other pro attitudes are not restricted to intentions, then the fact that they, together with a belief or group of beliefs, may prompt a person to respond in a certain way will not be sufficient to insure that his response has the possibly deliberate but certainly *meant* character of an intentional response — that his response is something he really intended to produce.

It is important to realize that Davidson's approach may also be rejected by a philosopher who wishes to avoid a commitment to events, states, or conditions. Although such a philosopher may well agree with Davidson that terms like 'the intention with which Jones went to church' are syncategorematic and do not refer to any state, event, or disposition, he can consistently deny that intention-predicates such as 'intends to please his mother' are eliminable in favor of predicates involving 'believes', 'desires' and the like. As far as the key point made above is concerned, he can insist that 'Jones did *A* intentionally' implies 'Jones meant to do *A*', and that no conjunction of statements of the form 'Jones believed *P*' and 'Jones desired *X*' have the same implication. At the end of this chapter I shall explain how such a philosopher might come to terms with the notion of doing something intentionally (see pages 103 ff); for my purposes here, it is sufficient to say that Davidson's view of intention is not rendered acceptable merely by a general metaphysical objection to states and events.

What I have been principally concerned to show here is that a primary reason (as Davidson seems to conceive of it) is not *sufficient* for doing something intentionally. Such a reason may, however, be necessary for intentional behavior. This possibility is worth discussing, because a long line of philosophers, beginning with Aristotle, have held that 'reason itself cannot move a man to act'.[14] According to Hume, for example, we can be prompted to act only by some 'passion', such as desire. Reason can move us to act only indirectly, either by exciting a passion that directly prompts an action or by showing us what action on our part will satisfy a passion that we already have. If two or more passions conflict, the stronger will determine our action; in no case does reason itself (or any purely intellectual faculty) have a 'motive power'.[15] Although few philosophers today are likely to accept this view of Hume's without serious qualification, there is undoubtedly some truth to it, and examining it briefly will no doubt improve our understanding of action on desire and perhaps make us clearer about what intentional, deliberate, or willed action might actually involve.

According to Hume, 'when we have the prospect of pain or pleasure from any object, we feel a consequent emotion of aversion or propensity, and are carried to avoid or embrace what will give us this uneasiness or satisfaction'.[16] An important question to ask is how we are to conceive of the emotion of aversion or propensity, which intervenes between the idea that something is pleasant or painful and the disposition to avoid or embrace it. Hume regards it as an impression, an 'original existence' that must be experienced to be properly conceived of.[17] It is this impression, and not the thought of the pleasant or painful object, that disposes us to pursue or avoid the object; it possesses the 'motive force' that disposes us to act.

Since, for Hume, desire is a direct passion, immediately evoked by the prospect of pleasure, we may interpret him as holding that the prospect of gaining pleasure from some object excites a feeling of desire and that this feeling evokes, in turn, a disposition to pursue the desire object. There can be no doubt that Hume's view is partly correct: the thought that something is pleasant may well excite a desire for it, and the desire excited certainly prompts one, in some degree, to pursue the desire object. But it does not seem correct to characterize a desire as a mere feeling. A desire may no doubt be accompanied by certain feelings, but no special feeling seems to be present whenever a desire is felt. Also, many desires seem to be far more intellectual than a mere feeling, involving the *idea* of a friend's happiness or the end of a brutal war. If one were to express such desires in words, one might say 'Would that Mary were happy' or 'I want the war to end'. Finally, one may desire certain things for a lengthy period of time without experiencing constant feelings of propensity of continually thinking of the things desired.

These drawbacks to Hume's account should not, of course, blind us to its merits. An impulsive, unreflective person who feels (as we should naturally say) a momentary desire to whistle or slap his hands may proceed to do so (or attempt to do so) without hesitation. Here an inclination seems to be felt or experienced, and a propensity to act seems to result. But even a simple desire to do something uncomplicated does not generally operate this way in more reflective people. In such people the consequences of acting on a given desire immediately come to mind, and their view of these consequences will largely determine how they will proceed to act. Sometimes an impulse to act will be inhibited by a single consideration; sometimes a great deal of thinking may be required. I desire another drink, and have the bottle in my hands. But I have had a lot to drink already. Should I have another drink or not? What will my companions think? Will I end up by making a fool of myself? Will I be in a good condition to drive safely home? Clearly, my decision-making in this case could be fairly complicated; I might decide not to give in to my desire for remarkably sophisticated reasons.

The limitations of Hume's account assume greater significance when we consider more complicated examples. Suppose I desire that a certain war shall end. What will I do? The answer depends largely on my various beliefs, my other desires, my shrewdness or stupidity, and so forth. If I believe that certain things I can do will contribute to ending that war, I may or may not be disposed to do them. Some of these acts may have what I take to be totally unacceptable consequences; others may require sacrifices that I am not prepared to make. Of the class of actions that do not strike me as having unacceptable consequences or as requiring excessive sacrifice, I will presumably be disposed, if I am rational, to perform the one that, all things considered, I regard as the most satisfactory. In performing this action I will, moreover, be acting with intent; I shall be doing it *because* I view it as a satisfactory means of satisfying (or helping to satisfy) my desire. On the other hand, if I am not aware of any reasonable steps I can take to satisfy my desire, I need not remain inactive. I might naturally *seek* some means of realizing my desire: I might begin to read certain books, make certain inquires, and the like.

Since desires are generally not momentary impulses, as Hume's account suggests, but often fairly long-lasting attitudes, it seems best to regard most of them as propensities or dispositions rather than as occurrent conscious states. Such propensities are normally very complicated, as the example about the war indicates, but it seems plausible to regard those distinctive of most desires as essentially propensities to seek acceptable means of bringing about some states of affairs and, if such means are found, to act on them *because* they are thus viewed as satisfactory. This conception seems applicable to cases where the agent does have beliefs about how he can satisfy his desire, for even minimally rational agents will be moved to adopt only those means that they take to be satisfactory. In the case of highly rational people, a satisfactory means to a desired end will have to meet any number of conditions: it will have to be consistent, for example, with the satisfaction of numerous other desires and of various policies, moral commitments and the like. Less rational people are apt to be more impulsive and to place fewer restrictions on a satisfactory means to a desired end, but even the most irrational person will place some restrictions on such means: he will not be moved to do just anything he thinks will satisfy his desire. More often than not a desire can be satisfied by more means than one, and the agent will have to make a choice between alternatives.

If we take this dispositional conception seriously, we must acknowledge that desires are not just 'passions' that trigger off actions; they are usually propensities that affect our behavior only by affecting the thinking that leads us to act. This kind of thinking is called 'practical thinking', and its rational upshot is typically a decision. We desire to bring about some state of affairs and, if we are at all rational, we seek some satisfactory way of doing so. Various possibilities come to mind, and we consider which, if any, is really satisfactory. If one stands out as particularly promising, we may decide to adopt it. Such a decision may be more or less explicit (but more about this later); the important point is that, when we act rationally on most desires, our behavior is ultimately motivated by a decision, which reflects our assessment of a practical situation. Consequently, if, as philosophers, we are seeking an ultimate trigger that propels our actions, desire is a poor candidate. Typically, desire moves us to act only indirectly; it does this by conditioning the thought that directly moves us to act.

Although Hume's view of a person as being pushed and pulled by various 'passions' no doubt has some element of truth, his idea that reason is entirely inert would seem to be false. Hume claimed that our reason or understanding merely 'asserts itself after two different ways, as it judges from demonstration or probability'.[18] Yet even judgments of reason are not merely inert states of mind that do or do not correspond with reality; they are propounded, held, or accepted with various degrees of confidence or conviction. As Peirce contended,[19] the mark of a confidently held belief is that, given appropriate circumstances, its holder is prepared to act on it. The traditional division of the mind into active and inert faculties — with reason wholly on one side and passion wholly on the other — cannot, therefore, be correct: we are moved to act by reason (by beliefs, thoughts, and decisions) as well as by our 'passions'.

In discussing the nature of desire I may have thrown some useful light on the genesis of intelligent behavior, but I have not come to terms with the question whether desire is necessary for intentional behavior. To one not entrenched in the Aristotle-Hume tradition, a negative answer to this question seems obvious: Haven't we all done countless things — and done them deliberately — when we haven't wanted to do them? Philosophers in the Platonic tradition would certainly say 'Yes'. For them, reason is far from inert: it is not only at constant war with passion, but it frequently wins. For my part, the Platonic tradition seems right in this matter. Although we commonly do what we desire to do, we often do things we don't want to do — not always because we are forced to do them, but because, sometimes, our sense of what is right, proper, fitting, or obligatory leads us to decide upon them — to form the conscious intention of doing them.

In spite of its obvious plausibility, the contention just made always strikes some philosophers as fundamentally mistaken. Another comment on it may, therefore, be useful. Suppose that I do not *want* to keep my appointment with the dentist. My friend argues with me, emphasizing that if I do not visit the dentist at this time, I shall lose my delightful smile. I struggle with my feelings and eventually decide to keep my appointment. Some relevant facts are these: I do want to keep my delightful smile; I do not *want* to visit my dentist; I believe that if I do not visit my dentist, I shall lose my delightful smile. Let us grant that my desire to keep my smile is actually stronger, in some sense, than my desire to avoid the dentist. If we accept the identity theory of action, we may also grant that my act of going to the dentist is identical with an act of preserving my smile. But even granting these points, we may allow that I do not *want* to visit my dentist. There is no inconsistency in this contention, for the context 'I want . . .' is referentially opaque: If 'I want A' and '$A=B$' are both true, it may yet be false that I want B. Thus, although I visit my dentist — and visit him because I want to preserve my smile — I still do something I do *not* want to do, and I do it intentionally.

It is true in this case that, although I deliberately go to the dentist without wanting to, I also do something that I positively want to do — namely, to perform an act necessary for preserving my smile. Since this necessary act is (we are assuming) identical with the act of visiting my dentist, my two wants clearly conflict: they cannot both be satisfied. Given that one of them is stronger, more pressing or insistent, than the other, I might have satisfied it by an impulsive act — something that, as we have seen, need not be intentional. Yet if I did stop to think with a view toward selecting the most reasonable course of action, I *could* have decided to act on the weaker desire. Had I done so, I would no doubt have been moved by some other consideration — perhaps by an intention to avoid paying fees to people with unacceptable political views. An intention of this sort qualifies as a pro attitude, but it should not be interpreted as just another desire. As we have seen, one may desire to do something without intending to do it, and one may intend to do something without desiring to do it. Intending to do *A* and not wanting to do it is not, by the way, a simple matter of ambivalence, of wanting and not wanting the same thing. In the case just considered I did not want to visit the dentist *at all*: I shuddered at the thought of doing so. Nevertheless, under the impact of my friend's urging, I fully intended to make the visit.

When I criticized Hume's conception of desire, I argued that, as far as rational beings are concerned, most desires are essentially propensities to seek some acceptable means of bringing about a certain state of affairs and, when such a means is discovered, to act on it because it is viewed as thus satisfactory. My discussion made it clear that, at least in cases where a high degree of rationality is involved, a decision is reached to adopt the means that seem preferable. Now, a decision is just an intention formed as the result of deliberation. Consequently, when one acts rationally on all but the simplest desires, one forms the intention of doing something that satisfies them. This suggests that, at least in rational cases, intention forms the key link between desire and action.

I began this section with a discussion of Davidson's approach to intentional action; I shall end it with a final remark about his approach. As I pointed out, Davidson views the cause of an intentional action as the 'onset' of a complex state consisting of a belief and some pro attitude, such as desire. Yet the onset of such a state is not simply an event that causes intentional behavior. A particular desire typically leads to rational action only by means of a line of reasoning or deliberation whose outcome is partly determined by a variety of beliefs and other pro attitudes. When such a line of reasoning is fully explicit, its final step or conclusion expresses a decision, which is simply an intention formed in a special way. Consequently, although an intentional action may ultimately be traced back to a desire or, more realistically, to a complex of desires, beliefs and other pro attitudes, it is eventually brought into being, at least typically, by a decision or intention. If this is right, Davidson's account of the genesis of intentional behavior is seriously over-simplified and his syncategorematic interpretation of intentions cannot be correct.

3. INTENTION, BELIEF, AND ACTION

What is the relation, exactly, between intention and intentional action? One general formula that relates intending to doing is this:

If an agent intends to do A in circumstances C, believes he is in C and has no conflicting intentions, then if he is able to do A in C, is not prevented from doing A, and really is in C, he will probably do A, and do it intentionally.[20]

This general formula illustrates, though it does not imply, three points of considerable importance — namely, (1) that an intention by itself has, in general, no particular effect on a person's overt behavior, (2) that a belief by itself has no particular effect on a person's behavior, and (3) that individual intentions and beliefs 'combine' in favorable circumstances to produce intentional behavior. When this special combination of intention and belief occurs, we may proceed to act intentionally whether we actually *desire* to act this way or not.

What are beliefs and intentions, and how can they 'combine' to produce intentional behavior? To clarify the relation between intention and action, these questions will have to be answered, if only in a general way.

The most influential account of belief in recent times is due to Gilbert Ryle. According to him, 'believing that such-and-such' is a complex state 'involving abilities, tendencies or pronenesses to do, not things of one unique kind, but things of lots of different kinds'. For example,

believing that a certain patch of ice is thin is a matter of being unhesitant in telling oneself and others that it is thin, in acquiescing in other persons' statements to that effect, in objecting to statements to the contrary, and so forth. . . . It is also to be prone to skate warily, to shudder, to dwell on possible disasters and to warn other skaters. It is a propensity not only to make certain theoretical moves but also to make certain executive moves, as well as to have certain feelings.[21]

I cannot deny that a person having the belief in question might well have the propensities Ryle describes. But these propensities are not really distinctive of *the belief* that a certain expanse of ice is thin; they are distinctive of a certain person who has that belief. A different person, having the same belief, may have radically different propensities to behave. If he is malevolent, suicidal, a great taker of risks, he may encourage others to take to the ice: he may gleefully bound out upon it himself, relishing the thought of falling through. Again, if he believes that falling through thin ice is good for the health or encouraged by his favourite god, he may also skate upon it and urge others to do so as well. There is, in fact, no limit to the possible ways a person having the belief may be inclined to behave or even feel, for the thoughts and attitudes consequent upon a given person's belief will depend on countless other beliefs, attitudes, and the like.

In speaking of behavior here I have in mind overt behavior, since I think that there is subjective *mental* behavior that is distinctive of belief. This mental behavior consists in using the 'proposition' believed as a premiss in one's reasoning and in mentally assenting to its truth should an appropriate occasion arise. Philosophers commonly say that a person believing that P must at least be disposed to say that P, but saying is an overt act having consequences all its own. I might believe that my friend is a terrible philosopher, but it is not easy to imagine conditions under which I should want to express this belief to anyone. Of course, if the disposition to speak in question is that of saying that P *if* you believe that P and intend to express this belief, then no doubt everyone having the belief would have the speech disposition — but so, then, would everyone else. Dispositions specified in this way are clearly useless in explaining what a given belief is or consists in.

Since using a proposition as a certain kind of premiss — that is, one not simply assumed, say, for purposes of a conditional proof — may be regarded as a way of assenting to it, we may conceive of believing that P as a disposition or propensity to affirm that P in one's thinking.[22] It is natural to regard a belief as a disposition or propensity, because one can believe something when one is not thinking about anything at all — when, say, one is asleep. As far as the behavioral manifestations of a given belief are concerned, they will always depend on the individual person and what his attitudes, intentions, desires and other beliefs happen to be. Thus, if a man believes that his wife is frivolous, then if he is asked a suitable question about his wife and decides to give a truthful answer, he might well say 'She is frivolous'. But this response will be distinctive of *the man* in a certain practical situation; it will not be distinctive of the belief itself. Since beliefs are always held more or less firmly, we must, of course, think of the relevant propensity to affirm or assent to the appropriate proposition (or thought) as involving a certain *degree* of assent or *strength* of affirmation. But I shall ignore this qualification in what follows.

I turn now to the concept of an intention. As I see it, an intention is very similar to a belief.[23] It too is a mental disposition or propensity, for we can have the intention of doing something even when we are not thinking about doing it. But although an intention is in many respects similar to a belief, it is not a disposition to assent to the truth of some proposition; it is, at least primarily, a disposition to have practical thoughts of the form 'I *will* do such and such' or to reason in accordance with such thoughts. (I shall explain what I mean by 'reasoning in accordance with a thought' later on.) The practical thoughts involved in intentions may have a very complicated logical structure: one may intend to do A if P, to do everything one deems necessary for realizing some end E, and so on. In addition to such complicated intentions, however, one may have simple categorical intentions to do things here and now. These latter intentions have a particularly close connection with intentional behavior; in fact, the thoughts characteristic of them provide the ultimate connection between reason and action.

If the idea of doing A is that of a simple or, as I shall say, 'minimal' action, then the thought 'I will do A here and now' will not require an additional belief to prompt the intended behavior. This is because such thoughts themselves involve an awareness that the conditions are appropriate for realizing them. In this respect simple categorical intentions differ from those expressed by statements of the form 'I will do B in circumstances C', for the latter will generally lead one to act only when one has the information that one is in C. This latter information 'combines' with the intention in the sense that the information 'I am in C' and the thought 'I will do B in C' serve as premises from which a here-and-now practical thought is inferred. And it is this latter thought that, at least in ideal cases, brings about the appropriate behavior.

Two key points are fundamental to an understanding of the relation of belief and intention to intentional behavior. The first is that the thoughts distinctive of beliefs and intentions have a logical structure, which permits conclusions to be derived from them. The second is that certain practical conclusions may be categorical and involve an awareness that the conditions are appropriate for realizing them. Thus, a belief B and an intention I may give rise to the intentional behavior E by virtue of the fact that a practical thought of the form 'I will (here and now) do E' is derivable from the thoughts distinctive of B and I. The question of how such thoughts may jointly imply a practical conclusion will be dealt with in later chapters, when the logic of practical reasoning is discussed. But the question of how practical thoughts of the form 'I will do A here and now' can be expected to issue to appropriate behavior may be dealt with here.

The key point is this:[24] We have to learn to think in conceptual terms, and in learning this we develop propensities to behave (verbally and otherwise) in ways appropriate for various thoughts. Part of what is involved in learning to think in a volitional way is that we develop a propensity to make appropriate movements in response to thoughts like 'I will now do such and such'. Thus, the words 'I will now raise my hand' may run through our minds, but if they do not trigger off a propensity to move our hand in the required way, they will not express, for us, the relevant *volitional* thought.

Now if, given appropriate learning, we make certain movements as a consequence of thinking 'I *will* now do such and such', the relation between the thought and the movement may be regarded as *causal*. But what about the relation between more complex intentions, general or particular beliefs, and appropriate movements? Can this be considered causal as well? The answer is 'In a sense, yes'. There is an indirect causal relation between such states of mind and the appropriate movements. In learning to think conceptually we also learn to reason according to certain patterns. As I have said, beliefs and intentions are best understood as propensities to think certain things (or to use certain premisses), and a simple pattern of reasoning involving thoughts appropriate to both beliefs and intentions is this: If we have the premisses 'I will do A in C' and 'I am now in C', we will tend to conclude 'I will now do A'. By virtue of our propensity to reason in this way, the transition from such complex thoughts to the appropriate movements may be viewed causally: the premisses prompt the volitional conclusion, and the volitional conclusion triggers off the movements. There is thus a causal chain from thought to action.

In later sections of this chapter I shall qualify this simple picture of the relation between intention, belief and physical movement, for the connection between thought and action turns out to be far more complicated than this simple picture suggests. The basic idea illustrated by the picture is

nevertheless sound and worth presenting in the simplest possible terms —
namely, that the ultimate connection between intention, belief and action lies
in our propensity to reason according to certain formal patterns. In ideal
cases, where everything commonly tacit or implicit in an agent's practical
reasoning is explicit, his intelligent, nonhabitual actions will ultimately result
from a volitional thought that is based on premisses appropriate to certain of
his beliefs and intentions. This assertion may be viewed as a thesis that I shall
attempt to make credible as the chapter proceeds.

4.   A CONCEPTION OF VOLITION

The remarks I have just made are easily related to the subject of volition,
which I introduced at the beginning of this chapter. If intelligent, nonhabitual
actions are ultimately generated by volitional thoughts, an appropriate
name for such thoughts might be 'acts of will'. I noted earlier that R. G.
Collingwood and Wilfrid Sellars conceive of willing as a special form of
intending (Sellars would call it 'an act of intending'[25]); and a volitional
thought, as I have described it, is a manifestation or expression of intention.
The following quotation from Collingwood shows how close his conception
of willing comes to what I have said about volitional thoughts:

A will, as distinct from the corresponding deed, is an example of *practical thinking*. So
far as it is thinking, it expresses itself (like all thinking) in words; thus the intention to
shut the door is expressed as thought by saying 'I will shut the door'.
   But in addition to being a thought, it is also practical; and as practical it expresses
itself by the initial stage of the action of shutting the door; for example lifting my hand
in the appropriate way.[26]

If we add that the practical thought Collingwood calls 'a will' has a certain
logical form, so that it can be regarded as something inferable from practical
premisses, then his conception comes very close to my conception of a here-
and-now practical thought.

   Philosophers accustomed to disparaging so-called acts of will may prefer
not to use the expression 'act of will' at all. But thoughts are generally
described by philosophers as 'mental acts', and a volitional thought would
seem to be the sort of thing that defenders of acts of will, at least in their
more fortunate moments, are groping for. As we have seen, the incidental
remarks of Hume and Prichard suggest that they tacitly viewed willing as a

fairly simple mental process that (1) involves the idea or conception of a result to be brought into existence and (2) has that result as an expected consequence. Clearly, volitional thoughts, as I have described them, conform to this conception — as they also conform to Kant's definition of the will. Since this is so — since the conception of an act of will as a volitional thought makes good sense of the more fortunate remarks of Hume and Prichard and also fits in nicely with the key contentions of Kant and Collingwood — it would seem fair to regard it as a clarified version of a traditional idea.[27]

There are, of course, other conceptions of willing that are equally consistent with Kant's definition and the happier remarks by Hume and Prichard. A related one, which has some plausibility, is that an act of will is a thought having the logical form of a self-directed command.[28] According to this conception, when I explicitly will to do something *A*, I think to myself 'Aune, do *A*!' This approach not only provides a natural semantic interpretation for volition, but it seems to have considerable intuitive support. As Anscombe remarked, 'the only sense I can give to "willing" is that in which I might stare at something and will it to move'[29]. Since a person who tries to will an object to move is apt to think 'Move (you)!', the interpretation of willing naturally suggested by a remark like Anscombe's is that willing is a form of commanding or ordering — self-directed or other-directed, as the case may be.

There is, however, a serious theoretical difficulty with this approach. When (or if) I will an object to move, I endeavor to impose my will on it. A natural way of doing such a thing, at least when the 'object' is another human being, is to tell it — or, if one has the authority, to command it — to do what one wants. But I do not (at least normally) have to impose my will on myself; I do not have to treat myself as another agent who must be told what to do. On the other hand, when I am told to do something by some other agent, I may or may not assent to the order. If I do assent (or decide to obey), my thinking, made fully explicit, would involve the step 'So I'll do it'. An analogous step should be possible, or make sense, even with a self-directed order or command. If I were to say to myself 'Aune, do *A*!', it should be possible for me, as agent, to respond with 'All right, I'll do it' or 'No, I won't'. My final thought here, if affirmative, would thus seem conceptually closer to action — and thus a better model for volition — than the command to which it is a response.

To avoid misunderstanding I should emphasize that I have not based my conception of volition on the facts (1) that we unquestionably do will to act and (2) that volitional thoughts provide the best interpretation of willing. On the contrary, I have based my conception on the facts (1') that, when our practical thinking is fully explicit, we do have volitional thoughts and (2') that the concept of volitional thought provides a reasonable explication of what philosophers who speak affirmatively of acts of will seem to be trying, however inadequately, to describe. When I say that a certain volitional thought 'provides a better model for volition' than some command to which it is a response, I am merely alluding to the fact that, if we are inclined to use the language of 'will' or 'volition' at all, we should want to apply it to those mental states or episodes that we regard as the proximate causes of voluntary behavior.

In describing the two rival interpretations of volition, I have spoken of the logical form of a thought. This idea may be somewhat puzzling, at least initially, but it is far from novel: it has been familiar in the philosophy of mind at least since Descartes, though Kant was no doubt the first to place major emphasis upon it. As far as I am concerned, the logical form of a thought is determined solely by its semantic features. It is a commonplace of analytical philosophy that the physical structure of a statement is a very poor indicator of its logical form; thus, the idea is actually widespread that logical form is determined by something other than perceptible structure. The structure relevant to logical form is conceptual (or semantic) structure; and this may be possessed by a thought as well as by a statement.

Wilfrid Sellars and Peter Geach have propounded and defended analogical theories of thinking, and I have expounded a similar theory in my book *Knowledge, Mind, and Nature.*[30] According to these theories, we conceive of a thought on the analogy of a candid utterance or saying. To follow such a theory in making sense of the logical form of a thought, it is not necessary to press the analogy between thinking and saying very far. We do not have to assume, for example, that thinking is a kind of inner speech, involving the sort of verbal imagery one is apt to experience when reciting a poem silently to oneself. All we have to assume is that thought is like speech in having a certain semantic character — specifically, that the semantic features of a thought are analogous to the semantic features of a corresponding statement. Thus, if a thought has the logical form of a material conditional, then it has semantic features that parallel those common to materially conditional statements: its truth-value will be a particular function of the truth-values of two of its main constituents. Again, if a thought has the logical form of the statement '$(x)Fx$', then it is true just when every member of some universe of discourse has some appropriate property.

Analogous thoughts and statements may be called 'semantical counterparts' of one another. Thus, Jones's thought that snow is white is a semantical counterpart of any statement (by Jones or anyone else) that snow is white; it is, for example, a counterpart of Jacques's statement that snow is white. [31] To make his statement Jacques says 'La neige est blanche'. We, whose language is English, regard Jacques's statement as *a statement that snow is white* because we tacitly view it as a semantic counterpart to our statement 'Snow is white'. To be such a counterpart, Jacques's statement does not have to bear any physical resemblance to 'Snow is white'; it does not have to sound like it, for example. It is a semantic counterpart to our statement because we regard it as having the same semantic features — because, in a word, we regard the two statements as good translations of one another.

Quine is noted for contending that all translation is relative or, as he sometimes says, 'indeterminate'. [32] When we offer translations for what we regard as the words of some language, we are tacitly accepting a system of analytical hypotheses, which not only 'segment' the language (the relevant verbal behavior) into short recurrent parts (that is, words) but correlate these segments with what we regard as the words of our own language. In his view no one system of analytical hypotheses can be considered 'absolutely' correct. Countless systems of such hypotheses are always available, at least in principle; and though we may have adopted one system as the result of a long scholarly tradition, it is not any truer than its alternatives. Of course, once we have adopted a system of analytical hypotheses, we can consider it objectively correct to translate Jacques's 'Il pleut' by our 'It is raining' — but the correctness of this translation is fundamentally relative: it is correct, not 'absolutely', but relatively — relatively to one particular way of correlating distinguished segments of the two languages. The chosen way may be a highly convenient as well as thoroughly habitual way of correlating the languages (or behaviors), but there are always others, at least in principle.

Quine's view of translational indeterminacy is, of course, controversial, and I shall neither defend it nor attack it here. [33] I can say, however, that his theory is at least consistent with what I have said of thoughts as semantic counterparts of statements. To endorse my theory a defender of translational indeterminacy (and its consequence, referential indeterminacy) must simply add that a certain 'mental' state or process can be considered a thought *that it is raining* only in relation to a particular system of analytical hypotheses. These hypotheses could not, of course, be founded on an observation of the agent's mental behavior, for that behavior is not open to view. Nevertheless, when we attribute silent thought to a person, we are postulating a covert counterpart to his overt verbal behavior — and this postulation will require a system of analytical hypotheses. A defender of Quine's thesis will have to contend that many systems of such hypotheses will yield a workable theory of thinking, and that the system we happen to adopt is no more correct, 'absolutely speaking', than numerous others. The fact that we must postulate something we cannot hear or see may prompt familiar epistemological questions, but it does not affect the metaphysical point at issue here — namely, that when we regard certain 'inner states' as thoughts *that* such and such, we are giving them a semantic interpretation that, if Quine is right, must be considered relative rather than 'absolute'.

It is time, now, to return to the topic of volition. According to the view I have been expounding, to say that willing to do *A* is an act of thought having the form 'I will (here and now) do *A*' is merely to say that it is a mental semantic counterpart to some expression of intention (some verbal expression) having that form. I shall not attempt to explain what is meant by 'the logical form of a verbal expression', for the locution is thoroughly familiar in current philosophical writing.[34] If Quine is right, however, a verbal expression, or statement, can be said to have a certain logical form only in a relative sense. To determine the logical form of an expression or statement, we must assume a system of analytical hypotheses by which to identify the expression's logical words and to correlate it with a formula in our background language or 'canonical notation'.

Given the assumptions we commonly make about silent mental behavior, we can improve our account of why, if we are prepared to use the traditional language of 'will' and 'volition', we should naturally apply it to thoughts having the specific form of 'I will (here and now) do such and such'. I have already explained why it is natural to call certain thoughts 'acts of will', and why such thoughts should not be confused with covert self-directed commands. I can now explain why a specific logical form seems appropriate to volitions. To begin with, in any reasonable conception of volition a person who wills to do something *A* here and now must have some idea of what he aims to do — the idea, specifically, of doing *A* here and now. This idea has, for him, the same reference as the words 'my doing A here and now'. By virtue of this common semantic relation to an action, his volition is naturally viewed as the semantic counterpart of some statement involving the words 'my doing A here and now'. But a person who wills to do something must have a certain volitional attitude, presumably the sort of attitude expressed by the 'shall' in the slightly stilted prefix 'It shall be the case that. . .'. If we put these points together, it seems reasonable to conclude that a so-called act or volitional state of willing to do A here and now is a semantic counterpart of the statement (or expression of intention) 'My doing A here and now shall be the case'. But this statement seems to be semantically equivalent to the less stilted locution 'I *will* do A here and now', where the word 'will' is understood as expressing a volitional attitude. This last locution, or statement, would thus seem to be a semantic counterpart of the volition in question, and the two could be said, therefore, to have the same logical form.

If we consider what is implied when a chess player is said to think 'If he attacks with his queen, I will castle', we find that his thought is merely affirmed to have a certain formal character — specifically, to be the expression of a conditional intention that pertains to what he is committed to doing if his presumed opponent does a certain thing with his queen. To have this thought it is not necessary to have any mental imagery at all — verbal or otherwise. One does not even have to be able to visualize the opponent's queen or have the word 'queen' in one's active vocabulary. All that is necessary, if one has the thought in question, is that something going on in one's head should be describable as having a certain semantic character — a certain reference, a conditional form, and so on. As far as the nonsemantic or empirical features of the thought are concerned, it is entirely possible that they are describable in the language of neurophysiology. The same holds true for those categorical practical thoughts that I am calling 'volitions' (or 'acts of will').

If, as I am contending, an act of will is reasonably conceived of in semantic terms and need not be accompanied by imagery of any kind, it is easy to understand why philosophers have failed to discern any characteristic mental objects when they do something voluntarily: they are looking for items with tell-tale phenomenal marks, and willing does not invariably or even (so far as I can tell) typically possess any phenomenal marks at all. On the other hand, philosophers without a behavioristic axe to grind have no doubt that they are mentally active when they 'knowingly give rise to a movement' (as Hume put it). They know that their mental activity involves the *idea* of what they are endeavoring to accomplish, but like Prichard they cannot adequately describe what this mental activity is like. They cannot do this, if I am right, because they too are unwittingly supposing that their states of mind must, like their feelings, have a distinctive phenomenal character. But though we can all avow our thoughts, or say what we are thinking, we can really describe only their semantic features: what they are about, what must be true if they are true, and so on.

Thus far I have emphasized that willing, like thinking generally, need not involve imagery, even verbal imagery. It is clear, however, that it sometimes does involve imagery, though the imagery tends to be somewhat scrappy. A man playing tennis may be aware of saying to himself, on hitting the ball, 'There!' In saying this his attention is often focused on the place he wants the ball to go. If he is not responding automatically (as one commonly does in playing a familiar game) he may actually will to hit the ball into the place in question. But he does not mumble to himself 'I will now hit the ball *there*'. The word he does mumble may nevertheless be regarded as a partial expression of a more complete thought. When a person says to another, 'Go away', the subject 'you', is grammatically understood. Similarly, when the tennis player mumbles '*There*', the elements of a more complete thought might be understood: he may actually be thinking of *doing* a particular thing there and then, but only the word 'there' turns up in his covert monologue.

J. L. Austin once remarked that a philosophical discussion is apt to have two parts: there is the part where you say it, and there is the part where you take it back.[35] I have had my say about the positive nature of volition in the preceding pages; I shall now make some remarks and qualifications that will bring my views on volition more into line with the familiar contention, which I actually accept, that many things we do voluntarily or even deliberately are not things we explicitly will to do.

In the first place, the behavior we will to perform is sometimes very complicated, and we are not always conscious of the particular motions we make in bringing it about. When a child is first learning to play the piano, and wants to play a particular note, he may actually have to think of pressing a certain key with his right thumb. Yet when he becomes highly skilled, he can play a cadenza without even thinking of the individual notes. His complex hand movements are voluntarily brought about, but it is absurd to suppose that he willed each individual finger movement. As a general matter, when we have mastered a certain routine or procedure, we may will the whole into being while hardly conscious of its parts. The parts are brought about voluntarily or even deliberately — but only in the sense that they make up a whole that is voluntarily or deliberately brought about.

But there is an even more interesting sense in which we can voluntarily do something without explicitly willing to do it. This can be described by reference to what Quine has called 'the transitivity of conditioning'.[36] As I explained in the last section, someone having the premisses 'I will do A in circumstances C' and 'I am now in C' firmly in mind will tend to conclude 'So I will do A now' — and this conclusion will naturally result in appropriate behavior. But, as often happens, a person trained to reason in accordance with a certain pattern will gradually tend to skip elements in the pattern. This is a key reason why so much of our reasoning in everyday life is enthymematic. Our tendency to move from available premisses to a practical conclusion thus becomes altered; and instead of actually drawing the conclusion, we may make the physical movements that would otherwise be elicited by it. In such a transition from premisses to movements the practical conclusion may be called 'tacit' or 'implicit', for the consequent movements are made in accordance with it and are explainable, ultimately, only by reference to it.

These sketchy remarks on how we may reason or act merely 'in accordance with' various premisses do not, of course, exhaust the subject. If we have the intention of doing A if P, we may, for example, have very little tendency actually to think 'I will do A if P'; rather, we may be disposed to reason in accordance with this premiss, directly concluding 'I will do A' when we become aware that P. If the conclusion in question concerns an action (or movement) immediately within our power, the thought that P may, in fact, elicit our action directly — by the 'transitivity of conditioning'. Though I use a technical locution to describe this latter phenomenon, it is not really necessary for me, as philosopher, to endorse a particular theory of how it is best explained scientifically. For philosophical purposes, it is enough to insist that the phenomenon is thoroughly familiar; its importance, philosophically, is that it helps us to understand how reference to an agent's reasons can provide a satisfactory explanation of what he does — particularly in those cases where the agent himself is unaware of an explicit reasoning in which his reasons occur as premisses.

The considerations that will explain how reasoning becomes enthymematic will no doubt also explain how individual thoughts and statements become elliptical. In everyday discourse our remarks are rarely fully explicit: our sentences contain gaps, and they are often begun or ended with smiles, nods, or shrugs. Although a complete thought, like a complete statement, is ideally expressed by a complete sentence, most of our thoughts are no doubt highly abbreviated, significantly incomplete, and best expressed by grammatical fragments. A shrewd critic has emphasized that the prose we learn to speak or write is not the language of everyday conversation;[37] he could equally have said that the thoughts we express in even reasonably well-mannered prose are not the thoughts of most waking hours.

A few paragraphs back I described a case where a supposedly complete volitional thought was accompanied by a mere fragment of verbal imagery; a less contrived case would be one where the volitional thought is itself a fragment. Although many familiar scraps of thought are no doubt too disconnected to carry significant implications, and thus to serve as premises in reasoning, others are justly regarded as elliptical for conceptually more complete thoughts. The mark of an elliptical thought is, I suppose, an elliptical verbal expression, but our means of identifying it are not important in the present context. What is important, at least here, is that our thoughts are commonly elliptical and that something as complicated, conceptually, as "I will now hit it there" can evidently be contracted into a mere 'There'. As the result of our natural tendency to ellipsis and contraction, our reasoning thus tends to be doubly gappy: key inferences are enthymematic and explicit premises or conclusions appear as fragments. I cannot hope to explain why such scrappy, gappy reasoning seems to be the rule rather than the exception. We shall understand this phenomenon only when we have learned more than is known at present about the way our brains work and how linguistic behavior is related to neural functioning.[38]

The qualifications I have been making to my account of willed behavior — particularly my claim that willing may be merely implicit or tacit — bring it fairly close, at least on the surface, to the position made popular by Gilbert Ryle. According to him, to do something voluntarily or on purpose is to make appropriate movements while in a particular 'frame of mind', this being a state of readiness to respond with appropriate remarks, explanations, queries, avowals and so forth, depending on an enormously wide variety of contingencies.[39] Such a description of what actually goes on when a person does something is frequently correct: nothing else actually, or explicitly, occurs. But this is only because a rational pattern of thinking has been abbreviated. Ideally, in cases where everything implicit in voluntary action is made explicit, we actually will the behavior (or large-scale segments thereof) that we voluntarily produce. If, like Ryle and many others, we ignore these tacit or implicit elements in our philosophical account of voluntary actions, we cannot adequately explain the relation of thought (of belief and intention) to action or even give a satisfactory account of human agency.

The qualifications I have been making do not, by the way, rule out a qualified endorsement of Prichard's theory of action. If we can accept events as genuine entities, we could still adopt the augmented Prichardian view. To do this we would have to say that mere movements are often described by action language. When it is said that a man moves his arms while asleep, the movements of his arms are described *as if* they were brought about voluntarily by that man. Similarly, when it is said that a man voluntarily moves his arms without willing them to move, the man would be described (according to a Prichardian) *as if* he actually did what he did only implicitly or tacitly — namely, willing them to move. The man's movements would be made 'in accordance with a volition' in the way that the conclusion of an enthymematic argument is drawn 'in accordance with' its missing premisses.

In the chapters to follow I shall show, in much greater detail, how crucially important the notion of reasoning one's way to a practical conclusion is for the philosophy of mind. I cannot pretend that the picture of rational or purposive action I offer does not portray human beings in a very Aristotelian role as rational animals. Yet it seems to me that the model or ideal of human behavior enshrined in our traditional language for human action is clearly Aristotelian in this way. I agree that our actual behavior commonly lacks elements writ large in the model and that the model is, to a degree, unrealistic. But it is the only coherent, workable model we actually have, at least as yet; and it is only by reference to it that we can make clear sense of the descriptions and explanations of nonhabitual, intelligent human behavior given in our everyday language.[40]

5. REASONS AND PURPOSIVE EXPLANATIONS

My claims in this chapter about the relation between belief, intention and voluntary action allow a straightforward treatment of two matters about which there has been considerable confusion in the recent philosophical literature — namely, the notion of an agent's *reasons* for doing something, and the nature of a purposive explanation. I shall begin with the notion of a purposive explanation.

As is well known, the explanations we offer in common life do not appear to conform to any simple pattern.[41] This is largely owing, I believe, to the context-dependent character of what counts as a satisfactory explanation. When we offer an explanation of why a person did something, or why such and such events occurred, we generally provide only a minimum of information: typically, we call attention to important facts or considerations that we believe are unknown to our listeners and that, taken together with what we presume our listeners do know or might reasonably expect, provide a relatively full explanation of the action or event. This relatively full or complete explanation, which is rarely formulated explicitly, shows that the action or event conforms to some 'intelligible pattern'. A fundamental problem about explanation is to say just what the relevant pattern amounts to either in general or in various representative cases.

As Hempel has argued, 'all scientific explanation involves, explicitly or by implication, a subsumption of its subject matter under general regularities'.[42] A fully explicit explanation of why an event E occurred under the conditions C would thus identify some law or causal principles that, taken together with a statement affirming the conditions C to have obtained, warrants the conclusion that E occurred. Although every fully explicit explanation should possess this feature, it must possess other features as well. Unfortunately, not all the necessary features of a good explanation seem to have been identified by writers on explanation, and a satisfactory general definition, applicable to all forms of explanation, does not appear to be available.[43] For this reason, we must acknowledge that the general nature of scientific explanation remains somewhat obscure.

My concern in this section is with the specific form of explanation appropriate to purposive behavior. I shall not attempt to provide a strict definition of this form of explanation; in fact, I am not sure that this can even be done in a suitably general way. My aim is merely to identify some of the key features of an acceptable purposive explanation and to show, in useful detail, how the identification of an agent's reasons for doing something helps us to understand why he behaves as he does.

When we explain why a person performs a certain action by giving his reasons for performing it, we are at least tacitly alluding to an important regularity in his mental behavior. This regularity concerns his propensity to reason according to a certain formal pattern. My thesis is that a person's operative reasons for doing something A are the premisses from which, or in accordance with which, his intention of doing A was derived or formed. I say 'operative reasons' here, because a person may have premisses (beliefs or intentions) that would have been a good basis for his intention to act but that did not even tacitly enter the reasoning leading him to that intention. When a person offers what is, strictly speaking, a rationalization for doing something A, he generally provides good reasons for his action, but these good reasons were not the actual or operative reasons that prompted him to perform that action. This is why a rationalization is not a genuine explanation of behavior: it provides a rationale for the behavior, but it does not provide the correct rationale.

An extremely simple though not fully explicit explanation of why Jones did A might have the form:

> Jones did A because (1) he intended to bring about a state of affairs E and (2) he believed that he could bring about E only by doing A.

An explanation of this form is satisfactory only to the extent that the assertions (1) and (2) allow us to identify *the* reasons that were operative in leading Jones to do A. For these reasons to be operative, Jones must have used them as at least tacit premisses in a line of reasoning leading to a decision (tacit or explicit) to do A. The obvious line of reasoning, fully spelled out, would be this:

> 1′.   I will bring about E.
> 2′.   I can bring about E only by doing A.
> 3′.   So, I will do A.

The fact that Jones's reasoning conforms to this pattern will be sufficient to explain his behavior only if Jones, like most sophisticated agents, has a propensity to draw practical conclusions like (3′) from premisses like (1′) and (2′). If he has such a propensity, the transition in his thinking from (1′) and (2′) to (3′), and the transition from (3′) to the movements appropriate to doing A, may be regarded as causal. The ultimate pattern of events exemplified in Jones's mental and physical behavior if he does A because of the belief and intention in question is thus that of a causal regularity. This was the concluding theme of the last section.

As I have described it, the case of Jones is no doubt idealized; in an actual case the agent's thinking is not apt to conform explicitly to the pattern I have mentioned. Nevertheless, if the belief and intention in question do account for a person's behavior, the corresponding premises must enter his thinking in at least a tacit or implicit way. A person may, that is, think merely 'in accordance with' one of these premises; but if neither occurs explicitly in his thinking, his behavior could not really be *explained* by the stated belief and intention. If the explanation offered above for Jones's behavior were made fully explicit, it might take the following form:

> Jones did A because (1) he intended to bring about E; (2) he believed he could bring about E only by doing A; (3) his intention and belief provided him with practical premises of the form 'I will bring about E' and 'I can bring about E only by doing A' (4) Jones has the propensity to employ premises of these forms in a valid line of reasoning having 'I will do A' as, at least, a tacit conclusion; (5) Jones has a propensity to act in accordance with his tacit or explicit thoughts of the form 'I will do X'; and (6) the propensities mentioned in (4) and (5) were manifested in Jones' mental and physical behavior at the time in question.

The reasons following the 'because' here can be seen to entail that Jones did A. Ideally, at least, fully explicit explanations should have this feature: their explanans entails their explanandum.

In elaborating upon the explanation of why Jones did A, I have indicated that Jones has the propensity to reason according to a valid practical pattern. Although an assumption of this kind is only tacit in most purposive explanations, it is actually very important, because some people have a propensity to reason in accordance with various invalid patterns. Thus, a student, Smith, may have a stubborn tendency to commit the fallacy of Affirming the Consequent, and this tendency may be crucial for understanding why he says and does certain things. The fact that Smith's premises are sometimes logically unrelated to the conclusion he acts upon does not, therefore, disqualify them from being *the* reasons behind his behavior. We normally assume, of course, that mature people are capable of valid inference, and we do not normally call explicit attention to the logical structure of their supposed reasoning. But this does not show that the logical structure of their reasoning (whether valid or not) is unimportant for understanding why they behave as they do.

Some philosophers, no doubt impressed by the fragmentary character of their thinking when engaged in certain tasks, have contended that, when we offer a purposive explanation, we are merely placing an 'interpretation' on an action: we are, in effect, saying 'See it in this light'.[44] In saying this we are not implying that the agent actually reasoned, or deliberated, in a certain way; we are merely implying that one who had the beliefs and intentions in question might naturally have reasoned this way. In showing how the agent might have reasoned, we place his action (his movements and so forth) in the context of a familiar pattern: we 'structure' his action in a familiar way, placing an intelligible pattern on it. When we have succeeded in doing this sort of thing, we have given a rational explanation of the action. Such an explanation is all we expect in everyday life, and it requires no conjectures about the actual character of an agent's thinking.

The fundamental difficulty with this approach is that it does not really allow us to say 'He did such and such *because* he viewed his action in the indicated way'. In not allowing us to say this, it does not really provide an explanation of his movements; it does not show us why *he* made them.[45] It may have been perfectly natural for a person to have reasoned in the way indicated, but if the agent in question did not reason this way, the supposed explanation throws no explanatory light on his actual deed. Thus, while placing a certain 'interpretation' on a given action might be fun or interesting, if it is not the right interpretation − if it does not get us to see the action in the way the agent did − it gives us no understanding of *why* it actually occurred. Some agents, after all, are absurdly unreasonable, at least on occasion, and they often have strange or even silly beliefs. To try to explain their actions by telling the story a reasonable man might give is simply to confuse fact with fiction.

I remarked that philosophers who adopt the 'interpretation' view of purposive explanations are no doubt impressed by the fragmentary character of their thinking when engaged in various tasks. Another reason for doubting that purposive explanations conform to the general model set forth by philosophers of science is this: Purposive behavior is apt to be remarkably novel; a given instance of it may never have been observed before and may never be observed again. This fact makes it clear, one might think, that purposive explanations cannot be causal explanations. If an item of behavior is truly novel, we shall not know of any causal principle, or regularity, that could serve to explain it. It has, of course, been argued — notably by Davidson — that when we give causal explanations we often do not know the law that relates cause to effect: we may know full well that the thrown rock caused the window to break, but we may be unable to specify any *law* that relates flying rocks to breaking windows.[46] This kind of response does not meet the difficulty in question, however. The breaking of windows is a familiar phenomenon, and we have ample experience of how such effects are brought about. But we have no similar fund of experience by which to identify the cause of a novel form of behavior. If the behavior is really novel, as much purposive behavior clearly is, we simply have no experience of its being produced at all.

To resolve the difficulty here we need only consider *why* purposive behavior is apt to be novel. The answer, obviously, is that human beings have the capacity to think up means of achieving their ends that have not been employed (or even thought of) before. If we are to explain a novel form of purposive behavior, we must, therefore, take into account the *reasoning* that led the agent to adopt that form of behavior. My account of purposive explanations is based on this idea. A propensity to reason according to certain patterns provides a regularity, in the mental behavior of an agent, by which we may identify the mental causes (or 'reasons') for even highly unusual forms of behavior. Thus, although we may have no experience of a constant conjunction (as Hume would put it) between beliefs and intentions of a certain kind and a novel form of behavior, we may be perfectly familiar with the manner in which a given agent is likely to reason; and this manner (or pattern) of reasoning can provide the regularity by which we may predict the behavioral consequences of even anomalous beliefs and intentions. If, for example, Jones believes there is a werewolf loose in his neighborhood and intends to hunt it down, then if he believes werewolves are vulnerable to brass bullets and attracted, like Humbert Humbert, by blonde nymphets, it will not be difficult to predict, at least in a general way, the steps he will take in hunting it down.

Although I am officially concerned with purposive explanations in this section, I have not yet said anything specifically about purposes. Generally speaking, a purpose is a goal or leading intention, something one hopes to realize *as the result* of taking certain steps, or *by* adopting certain means. If I do *A* with a view to bringing about a result *R*, then my purpose (or at least one of my purposes) in doing *A* is to bring about *R*. In doing *A* with this purpose I clearly intend to bring about R: my purpose here does not differ from my intention and may be identified with it. On the other hand, though in doing A intentionally I intend to do A, my intention here would not normally be considered one of my purposes in doing it. When I do something with a certain purpose, I adopt means to an envisaged end, and my end is conceived of as distinct from the means I adopt to realize it.

As I have intimated, we may have many purposes in performing a given action. Sometimes the relevant purposes are all on the same level, as it were. I may do A not just to bring about an end E, but to bring it about with style, verve and imagination; I may also intend to do something that will impress my friend Mary, and doing A may realize this purpose. In this case my intentions to bring about E, to do something with style, verve and imagination, and to impress Mary could all be considered my purposes in doing A. The purposes that lie behind an action need not be on the same level, however; sometimes they form a hierarchy. A relatively immediate purpose in doing something B may be formed as part of a plan to realize a higher-order purpose; and this higher-order purpose may have been adopted (along with others) to implement a still higher-order purpose, and so on. Aristotle evidently thought that all rational beings have a single supreme purpose, under which all other purposes can be arranged, but this idea seems extremely doubtful. Recent work by psychologists on the structure of plans discloses a very different picture.[47] Our various plans may conflict, fit into rival strategies, and even belong (as it were) to different branches of different deliberative trees. The totality of a person's plans (and thus purposes) is, in fact, about as well organized as he is said to be. A highly organized person is apt to have well-organized plans that fit together in a well-organized way; the plans of a disorganized person are apt to be confused and disorganized — just as he is.

Not all the purposes bearing, directly or indirectly, on a given action are appropriately singled out in explaining that action. This is owing, mainly, to the context-dependent character of an acceptable explanation. Sometimes certain purposes are taken for granted when an explanation is given, and we call attention only to those purposes of which our listeners are presumably unaware. Sometimes the terms in which an action is described make it inappropriate to mention certain purposes. Suppose Jones punches Smith to hurt him and thereby to avenge an insult for the sake of upholding the reputation of his family. If we accept an ontology of actions and identify them as Davidson or Prichard would, we might contend that Jones's punching Smith = Jones's hurting Smith = Jones's avenging a certain insult = Jones's upholding the reputation of his family. Although Jones's immediate purpose in punching Smith was to hurt him (and not, for example, to kill him) we would not allude to this purpose in explaining Jones's action if his action were described in the terms 'Jones's hurting Smith'. In describing his action in this way we are already tacitly crediting him with a purpose, and if we are concerned to explain why he did what we say he did, we must allude to a further purpose. If our interest in Jones is very great — or if, for some reason, we want a particularly thorough explanation of Jones's action — we might mention his purpose in upholding the family reputation. It might, however, be sufficient, in the circumstances, to say that his purpose was to avenge an insult.

I began this section by emphasizing that the explanations of supposedly rational behavior we actually give are commonly abbreviated and context-dependent. This point is illustrated to some extent by the case just described, but further illustrations may be helpful. Although purposive explanations, when elaborated upon, will identify at least some of the agent's purposes, they may in practice not explicitly mention any purpose at all. Thus, we might explain Jones's act of hammering on a vending machine by saying that he thinks his coin is stuck in the mechanism; we should probably regard it as otiose to add that his purpose in hammering on the machine was to retrieve his coin. On the other hand, we might find it unnecessary to mention any operative beliefs in explaining an action, saying merely 'She took the train because she wanted (intended) to save money'. Sometimes, in fact, we may allude to an important reason only very indirectly, as when we say 'He bought that car because he is stupid'. In saying this we may (in the context) be understood as meaning that the man bought the car because of certain naive or obviously erroneous beliefs about it — perhaps that it would require few repairs and be comfortable to ride in. When we offer such an explanation, we might not even know what the person's beliefs were: we might, that is, have only a very rough idea of why he decided to buy the car.

It is important to realize that the explanations we give are often responses to specific questions, and the terms of a question make a particular kind of answer appropriate. Thus, if we are asked 'What made Jones do that?' the presumption may be that Jones did not really want to do what he did, that his action was owing to some kind of duress. Our answer may thus locate the kind of duress involved. In providing such an answer we may indirectly convey an idea of the man's aim or purpose in so acting. His actual thinking may remain obscure, but we shall have some understanding of the considerations that prompted his action. This understanding is not ideal, though it is frequently the best we can hope for in practical affairs. The explanations we give in such cases are thus highly incomplete; they barely count as what Hempel calls 'explanation sketches'.[48]

In these remarks on purposive explanations I have drawn no distinction between reasons and motives. I do not deny that such a distinction can be drawn, but it is apt to be misleading when discussing rational action. The term 'motive' is used very loosely in ordinary English; it seems applicable to anything that may 'move a man to act'.[49] Philosophers in the Aristotle-Hume tradition, who hold that 'reason cannot itself move a man to act', generally insist on the importance of the distinction, regarding mere beliefs as reasons and intentions (and other pro-attitudes) as motives. In rejecting the Aristotle-Hume view on this matter, I feel no need to distinguish reasons from motives — particularly if they are both understood as at least tacitly functioning as premises in a man's reasoning. Of course, some things commonly called motives do not affect behavior in this way. If a man is moved to do something out of jealousy or vanity, we may say that his action was motivated by jealousy or vanity, or that jealousy or vanity was his motive for doing what he did. But we do not assume that the thought 'I am jealous' or 'I am vain' entered his thinking as a premiss. Consequently, jealousy or vanity are not, in the strict sense, reasons for action.

A jealous or vain person does, of course, have characteristic reasons for his jealous or vain actions. A jealous husband is apt to feel jealous when his wife pays attention to another man, and he may proceed to insult the man because he resents the attention she has paid him. If his behavior is not just an irrational outburst but a deliberate act, his purpose in uttering the insult may be to discourage the man from talking to his wife or to make clear his anger or contempt. Though we speak of such a person as 'feeling jealous', we do not mean that the person has a characteristic feeling or sensation: we mean that he has a certain attitude. An attitude, viewed generally, is a disposition or propensity; and a jealous man has a propensity to resent and fear various forms of behavior in others. (The specific kinds of behavior he will resent or fear will depend not only on his beliefs and other attitudes but on the target of his jealousy — on what he is jealous of.) Ryle was calling attention to this dispositional character of an attitude when he said:

The statement 'He boasted from vanity' ... is to be construed as saying 'He boasted on meeting the stranger and his doing so satisfied the law-like proposition that whenever he finds a chance of securing the admiration and envy of others, he does whatever he thinks will produce this admiration and envy.[50]

Ryle's claim has been justly criticized, for it is not accurate in detail. A man may boast from vanity without being a vain man — without having a permanent or long-term tendency to seek the admiration and envy of others. And even a vain man may fall short of satisfying the law-like proposition Ryle describes. What we can say, however, is that a man who boasted from vanity boasted because of the kind of propensity a vain man characteristically has. This propensity is more polymorphous than Ryle implies, but it is a propensity (or group of propensities) nevertheless.

I spoke a paragraph back of 'the strict sense' of reasons for action; I must, therefore, think that there are reasons for action in a less strict sense of the word. This is true. We use the word 'reason' very loosely, I believe, to apply to a wide variety of explanatory factors that have a key importance in bringing about some result. Sometimes, in fact, we use 'reason' almost synonymously with 'cause'. Thus, we may say 'The reason for the explosion was a ruptured gas pipe'. I am inclined to think that this use of 'reason' is always derivative. If 'A happened because C happened' is true, then 'C happened' tells us why A happened and thus 'gives a reason' why A happened, whether A's happening had anything to do with an intelligent agent or not. Once we have agreed that 'C happened' gives us a reason why A happened, it is natural to speak of C's happening as a reason for A's happening. Such a reason has only a remote connection with human reasoning, and it is sometimes (but only sometimes) best understood as a mere cause.

This last claim deserves elaboration. Suppose it is agreed that Bill shot Tom because Tom shot Bill's father. One might then say that the reason Bill shot Tom was that Tom shot Bill's father. Should one agree that Tom's shooting Bill's father was the *cause* of Bill's shooting Tom? It depends, I should think, on the character of the chain of events leading from the first shooting to the second. If this chain is sufficiently short or compact (an extremely vague supposition) then it might be reasonable to think of the first shooting as the cause of the second one. But in general it seems questionable to describe the matter this way — especially if the second shooting was done intentionally. *That* Tom shot Bill's father is the reason why Bill shot Tom because the state-

ment 'Tom shot Bill's father' is the accepted answer (we are supposing) to the
question 'Why did Bill shoot Tom?' As the accepted answer to this question, the
statement provides a reason in relatively 'causal' terms why it is true that Bill
shot Tom. This last fact discloses the connection that a reason for an occurrence has with human reasoning. If 'A occurred because C occurred' is acceptable, then 'C occurred; so A occurred' is also (generally speaking) acceptable;
and this last sentence represents an acceptable move in one's reasoning.

If we agree that 'Bill shot Tom because Tom shot Bill's father' is true, have
we thereby located *Bill's reason* for shooting Tom? I think we should normally agree that we have located his reason. But just what is this reason? Is
it, as Schwayder has claimed, the *fact* that Tom shot Bill's father?[51] If my
claims in this section are correct, the answer is 'No'. Bill's reason is his
thought or belief that Tom shot his father. Even if Tom had not, in fact,
shot Bill's father, Bill could have the very same reason for shooting Tom —
namely, that (as he believes) Tom shot his father. If Tom did shoot Bill's
father, then what Bill believes about Tom is, as we say, a fact; but this only
means that Bill's belief is true. When we say 'Bill shot Tom because Tom shot
Bill's father', the content of our claim is partly determined by the context. If
we intend to give Bill's reason for shooting Tom, then our claim would be
more perspicuously expressed by saying 'Bill shot Tom because he was aware
that Tom shot his father'. The phrase 'because he was aware that' seems
preferable to 'because he believed' because our unqualified claim implied that
Tom did shoot Bill's father.

My chief aim in this section has been to show that purposive explanations,
at least when made reasonably explicit, involve a crucial reference to the
agent's practical reasoning. Although in the examples I have considered this
reasoning has a very simple logical structure, it may sometimes be highly
complicated. The chapters to follow will be specifically devoted to complex
forms of practical reasoning and to the logical principles underlying them.
But before pursuing these subjects I must deal with some of the loose ends
left hanging in earlier sections of this chapter.

6. VOLUNTARY AND INTENTIONAL ACTION

Thus far I have spoken of voluntary actions (or voluntary 'doings') in a very
rough and ready way. Having clarified the notion of volition, I can now be

more precise about the nature of voluntary action. Since, as I shall argue, a voluntary action is very closely related to an intentional one, my discussion of the voluntary will lead me back to a discussion of the intentional, which will turn out to be the major subject of this section. My basic approach to intentional action has been foreshadowed in my recent discussion and in my criticism of Davidson, but it has not been developed in detail. It is now time to do this.

Voluntary Action

The notion of a voluntary *action* (or doing) might seem comparable to the notion of a human man. How could an action or doing be anything other than voluntary? As we saw in discussing Prichard's theory, however, we can justifiably refer to various episodes as 'doings' without thereby implying that they are voluntary. For example, we can say that, while asleep, Jones knocked over a lamp, even though we would not acknowledge that he *did* so voluntarily. Since such doings may be considered nonvoluntary, or even sometimes involuntary, there can be no objection to saying that certain actions may be nonvoluntary or involuntary. In saying such a thing we shall, of course, be using the word 'action' in a minimal or perhaps secondary sense.

If we accept a theory of volition, we might naturally contend that a doing is voluntary just when it is willed by the agent. This approach does not seem satisfactory, however. Suppose I decide to exterminate the mouse that has made a nest in my garage. I consider various means of carrying out my decision, and choose to employ my neighbor's cat. Having brought the cat to my garage, I will to release it and, since the cat does kill the mouse, I realize my intention of exterminating the mouse. But although it seems reasonable to say that I voluntarily exterminated the mouse, I did not, strictly speaking, *will* to exterminate the mouse. I intended to exterminate him, but I actually willed to do something that brought about his extermination. The act that I strictly willed to perform may, of course, be identified with my act of exterminating him; but since the context '*S* willed to do *A*' is referentially opaque, we cannot infer that I therefore willed to exterminate the mouse.

In view of this kind of case we might want to say that a doing is voluntary just when it is directly or indirectly brought about by an act of will. This view would seem plausible because a doing brought about in this way could be

regarded as an action in the strict, agency sense of the word – and we have
noted that, when the word 'action' is used in this way, it seems to connote
something voluntary. Unfortunately, such a view has objectionable consequences. If, like Prichard, we are prepared to speak of acts of will, we may
acknowledge that anything I do in the sense of being the agent of is a consequence of my willing something. Yet many things I thus do are done
unwittingly, accidentally, or by mistake; and it seems clearly wrong to say
that such things are done voluntarily. I intend (or will) to pass the sugar,
and do so absentmindedly with the result that I knock over the teacup and
spoil my hostess's new dress. Clearly, *I* spoil her dress, but I do not do so
voluntarily.

A very simple conception of voluntary action that avoids the difficulties
of the conceptions already considered is this: A doing is voluntary just when
it is intentional. It seems to me that this conception has considerable merit,
though it cannot stand without qualification. Consider the matter of necessity. Can we say that a doing is voluntary *only if* it is intentional? There is no
doubt that many of the things we do voluntarily are also done intentionally,
but it would appear that some things done voluntarily are not intentional in
any strict sense of the word. Suppose that I play a complicated melody on
the piano. In doing so I press a certain key with my right thumb. I am not,
however, conscious of using my thumb in this way, though I have played the
melody countless times and intend to play it in the usual way. It is doubtful
that I actually intend to make the thumb movement in question; what I did
intend to do was to make a series of movements that, on examination, I see
to have included the thumb movement. I did not, on the other hand, make
that particular movement inadvertently, accidentally or by mistake, for it
was an essential component of what I did intend to do. Although that movement was not, I should say, strictly intended, I did make it voluntarily.

Other examples of nonintentional but perhaps voluntary actions are
suggested by the principle of double effect, which is often invoked in moral
disputes.[52] Suppose, to take a morally neutral example, that I deliberately
take a long automobile trip, knowing that I am thereby wearing down the
tires on my car. Although I do not actually intend to wear down my tires, it
would seem that, given my knowledge, I do voluntarily wear them down.
This case might be assimilated to the one just described on the ground that, if
I deliberately do what I know will wear down my tires, I must at least intend
to bring about a total state of affairs having the wearing down of my tires as

an unwanted but nevertheless foreseen 'part'. Although considerations pertaining to the logic of deliberation seem to make this assimilation reasonable (see below, pages 135 f) there is no need to insist upon it. We can acknowledge that we have another exception to the thesis that an action (or doing) is voluntary *only if* it is intentional.

In spite of these exceptions it seems that the thesis is at least on the right track. In fact, we can easily amend it by saying that an action or doing is voluntary only if it is either intentional, an essential part of something intentional, or a foreseen consequence of an intentional act. The notion of an essential part is, of course, vague, but the notion of a voluntary action (or doing) would seem to share this vagueness.

On the assumption that we have identified a plausible necessary condition for doing something voluntarily, we may now consider the matter of sufficiency. Is it reasonable to adopt the converse of the thesis just formulated — to say, that is, that a doing is voluntary *if* it is either intentional, an essential part of something intentional, or a foreseen consequence of an intentional action? From a metaphysical point of view, the idea does seem reasonable, but there are complications to consider. Suppose that a man is threatened by a gunman who utters the words 'Your money or your life!' If he complies with the threat, his action would seem to be intentional (at least 'under an appropriate description'), but it may be doubted whether it is voluntary, or fully voluntary. According to P. J. Fitzgerald, there is, at least in the law,

a very important distinction between what a man does voluntarily and what he does under compulsion, duress, necessity, etc. Before admitting a confession in evidence, for example, the Judge may have to determine whether it was voluntary, or whether it was obtained by some threat or inducement.[53]

Although it seems doubtful that the existence of a mere inducement would be sufficient to render an action legally nonvoluntary, the suggestion seems clear that, at least in the law, actions done as the result of duress are not considered voluntary, whether they are intentional or not.

Some philosophers would contend that, even in everyday contexts, the word is so used that actions resulting from duress do not count as voluntary.[54] There is no doubt that the word is sometimes used in this way. If we say that a person voluntarily contributed ten dollars to a charity, we should normally want to deny that he was required to make the contribution as a condition, say, of keeping his job. But as any dictionary makes clear, we do not always use the word in this way. Sometimes we use it to imply that an action or doing was consciously brought about by the agent — that he 'knowingly gave rise to it', as Hume would say. When we use the word this way, we can say that even the robbery victim acts voluntarily. His options are limited, to be sure, but he voluntarily adopts one of them in preference to the others. He may willingly hand over his money, or he may act on the maxim that even death is preferable to dishonor.

An implication of most senses of 'voluntary' given in dictionaries is that a person does something voluntarily when he does it of his own free will. The notion of 'free will' is, of course, one of the darkest, or at least most problematic, notions in all of philosophy, and it would be absurd to try to clarify the term 'voluntary' by reference to it. A less problematic way of viewing the matter is this: Voluntary doings are generally described as proceeding from the agent's will, choice or intention; the stricter senses of 'voluntary' result from limitations on the conditions under which the doings are thus produced. In the weakest sense, a doing is voluntary when it is willed or intentional; in the stronger sense, a doing is voluntary only if the volition, intention, or choice leading to it is not formed as the result of compulsion, duress, necessity, and the like. In view of these different senses of the word — none of which is very precise — an explication in Carnap's sense seems called for here.[55] The most satisfactory explication, in my opinion, results from combining the necessary and sufficient conditions that we have considered. According to this explication, a doing is voluntary just when it is either intentional, an essential part of an intentional doing, or a foreseen consequence of such a doing.

Thus far I have been concerned with actual rather than possible, or perhaps potential, voluntary actions. Such potential actions should at least be mentioned here, because the term 'voluntary' seems to have a special meaning when applied to them. If we think of the things a person *can* voluntarily do, we shall be thinking (it would appear) of things he can do 'at will': these are things he could be expected to do, in general or in specific circumstances, if he willed to do them. The close connection between this sense of 'voluntary' and the notion of willed action not only recalls the etymology of 'voluntary', but it may help explain our tendency to say that the unintended thumb movement I make in deliberately playing a complicated melody on the piano is at least voluntarily produced. It is certainly something that I can produce at will. In this respect it differs significantly from an involuntary movement.

A word on the distinction between involuntary and nonvoluntary doings may be helpful at this point. A doing is nonvoluntary just when it is not voluntary; it is involuntary just when it occurs independently of the agent's volition. Classic examples of involuntary doings are the kicking movements a person makes when his patellar tendon is struck or the sneeze he may emit on smelling freshly ground pepper. Such doings are also, of course, nonvoluntary, but many nonvoluntary doings are not involuntary. An example was given earlier. If, in passing the sugar, I accidentally knock over a cup of tea and spoil my hostess's dress, I do not voluntarily spoil her dress (I do so nonvoluntarily) but my action is not thereby involuntary. Had I not willed to pass the sugar, I would not have spoiled her dress: I did the latter because I willed to pass the sugar and did not pay sufficient attention to the foreseeable consequences of my act.

Intentional Action

Since my explication of 'voluntarily doing something' was based on the notion of an intentional action, I must now attempt to clarify this difficult notion. In Section 2 of this chapter I criticized Davidson's account of doing something intentionally and I developed a conception of intention in Section 4. But I have not yet offered a positive account of intentional action, at least in a usefully detailed way.

The first thing to say about intentional action is that the subject is a highly peculiar one. As Davidson has remarked, 'It is a mistake to suppose there is a class of intentional actions: if we took this tack, we should be compelled to say that one and the same action was both intentional and not intentional'.[56] Suppose that Jones intentionally hits Smith and that, in hitting him, he angers Mary. Given Davidson's approach to action, we might then say that Jones's action in hitting Smith was identical with his action of angering Mary. If we allow that there are intentional actions, Jones's act of hitting Smith would be one; and since this act was identical with Jones's action of angering Mary, we should have to say that his action of angering Mary was intentional. Yet Jones may have had no intention whatever of angering her; he may, in fact, have been totally unaware of her existence.

To avoid problems like this philosophers sometimes speak of actions as intentional only 'under certain descriptions'. But what could we mean in saying that Jones's action of angering Mary was intentional under the description 'Jones's hitting Smith'? The only sense I can attach to this is that Jones hit Smith intentionally and that his action of hitting Smith was identical with his action of angering Mary. Yet this last claim is none too clear. If it does not allow us to infer that Jones angered Mary intentionally, exactly what information does it convey? To answer this question we must, at the very least, have a clear understanding of the sentence 'Jones hit Smith intentionally'. This sentence has peculiar logical properties that deserve careful attention.

Quasi-intensionality. When Davidson discussed rationalizations for actions, he called attention to the quasi-intensional character of certain action statements.[57] A statement like 'Jones hit Smith intentionally' may be called quasi-intensional (at least on a straightforward reading that does not amount to 'Smith is such that Jones hit him intentionally') because it has some of the logical properties of a typical extensional statement and some of the properties of a nonextensional, or 'intensional', statement.[58] Thus, the position occupied by the name 'Jones' is open to existential generalization and the substitutivity of identity, which are marks of extensionality; but the position occupied by 'Smith', though perhaps open to existential generalization,[59] is not open to the substitutivity of identity. If Smith, unknown to Jones, bears the title 'The Poor Man's Friend', then 'Jones hit Smith intentionally' may be true while 'Jones hit The Poor Man's Friend intentionally' may be false. Another nonextensional feature of sentences like 'Jones hit Smith intentionally' is that we cannot validly replace the simpler sentences occurring within them (in this case 'Jones hit Smith') by materially equivalent sentences. Even if 'Jones hit Smith' and '2 + 2 = 4' have the same truth value, we cannot infer '2 + 2 = 4 intentionally' from 'Jones hit Smith intentionally'.

Some of the logical features of 'Jones hit Smith intentionally' may, of course, be accounted for by the mere fact that the statement contains an adverbial modifier. As we saw in Chapter I, adverbial modifiers generate a context that, at least on the face of it, is not open to the interchange of materially equivalent formulas. Also, on any plausible theory of adverbial modification, the position occupied by 'Jones' in 'Jones hit Smith intentionally' is referentially transparent. Nevertheless, 'Jones hit Smith intentionally' has logical features that are not owing to the mere possession of an adverbial modifier. Consider, for example, 'Jones hit Smith viciously'. No matter what theory of adverbial modification we adopt, we shall have to admit that the position of 'Smith' is referentially transparent in this sentence. But we have seen that the position of 'Smith' is not referentially transparent in 'Jones hit Smith intentionally' (at least on a straightforward reading of the sentence).

If we are to understand the peculiar logical features of sentences like 'Jones hit Smith intentionally', we cannot, therefore, merely assimilate them to sentences like 'Jones hit Smith viciously'. A more promising strategy is to compare them with other sentences that seem quasi-intensional. Consider the following, which Quine has made famous:[60]

(1)   Giorgioni was so called because of his size.

Although this sentence is extensional in implying that Giorgioni existed and was called something or other because of his size, it is not fully extensional because, from the identity statement 'Giorgioni = Barbarelli', we cannot infer that Barbarelli was so called because of his size. The peculiar logic of this statement is easily understood and accounted for, however, as soon as we observe that it is elliptical for

(2)   Giorgioni was called 'Giorgioni' because of his size.

In this statement the positions of all terms are open to the substitutivity of identity. If Giorgioni = Barbarelli, we may infer that Barbarelli was called 'Giorgioni' because of his size. But since the identity of Giorgioni and Barbarelli does not imply the identity of the names 'Giorgioni' and 'Barbarelli', we have no basis for inferring that Giorgioni was called 'Barbarelli' because of his size, or that Barbarelli was called 'Barbarelli' because of his size.

In analogy with (1) I want to contend that 'Jones hit Smith intentionally' is also elliptical for a longer statement — namely,

(3)   Jones hit Smith with the intention of hitting Smith.[61]

This view seems plausible, because if we ask ourselves just why we cannot expect to substitute 'The Poor Man's Friend' for 'Smith' in 'Jones hit Smith intentionally', the answer would be: 'Maybe Jones did not intend to hit The Poor Man's Friend; maybe one of his reasons for hitting Smith was to hit the avowed enemy of The Poor Man's Friend'.

If we regard (3) as an expanded version of 'Jones hit Smith intentionally', we can easily see, even without a thorough understanding of its logical structure, that (3) has the key logical properties we intuitively attribute to the simpler sentence. Thus, the position occupied by 'Jones' is referentially transparent, 'Jones hit Smith' follows, and the position occupied by 'Smith' is referentially opaque in the sense that, if Smith is The Poor Man's Friend, we may not infer that Jones hit The Poor Man's Friend intentionally. This latter inference is ruled out because even if Smith is The Poor Man's Friend, the intention of hitting Smith would seem to differ from the intention of hitting The Poor Man's Friend.

Another point to observe is this. If we view sentences like 'Jones hit Smith intentionally' in the way I am suggesting, we can support Davidson's claim that, strictly speaking, there are no such things as intentional actions — that is, no such things as actions with the property of being intentional. What we can say is that the predicate 'is intentional' does not connote a property at all: it is syncategorematic, eliminable in favor of an expression containing words of the form '(done) with intention i'.

Although this maneuver makes good sense of Davidson's claim, it unfortunately generates a problem of its own, which can be resolved only by further discussion. The problem is: Are there such things as actions *done with an intention*? To put it in another way: Does the expression '(done) with an intention' connote a property that actions might possess? To see the point of the problem, note that if we interpret '(done) with an intention' as connoting a property of an action, we should have to agree that, if Jones's act of hitting Smith is identical with his act of angering Mary, then if Jones hit Smith with the intention, say, of avenging an insult, he angered Mary with that intention. But this is a very dubious consequence. If Jones were totally unaware of Mary's existence, it would seem wrong to say that he angered her with any intention at all.

Adverbial Modification.   Since the meaning of sentences like (3) is not entirely obvious, we should attempt to clarify it. A natural first step in doing so is to consider the logical role of the modifiers such sentences contain. As we saw in Chapter I, two approaches to adverbial modification are currently available. According to Davidson, a sentence like (3) should be viewed as involving a tacit quantification over events. If, for convenience, we abbreviate 'the intention of hitting Smith' by the letter 'i', we can say that, according to Davidson's *general* approach to adverbial modifiers,[62] (3) has the form of

(4) $(\exists x)\,(Hxjs\ \&\ Wxi)$.

As we saw in Chapter I, however, this approach generates serious problems, particularly with modifiers like 'with'. Thus, if Jones hit Smith with a stick, then if Jones's act of hitting Smith is identical with his act of angering Mary, we should have to conclude that Jones angered Mary with a stick. This would not be satisfactory, because although Mary may have seen Jones hit Smith (and thus become angry) she may not have seen the small stick with which Jones hit him. Obviously, a related difficulty arises if we interpret (3) according to Davidson's approach: we shall then have to allow the objectionable conclusion that Jones angered Mary with the intention of hitting Smith. For these reasons alone, it would appear that (3) is best interpreted according to some alternative theory. The alternative we discussed was worked out by Romane Clark.

According to Clark, the modifier 'with. . .' functions as an operator that generates a complex two-place predicate '. . .does A with. . .' when applied to the one-place predicate '. . .does A'. If we adopt this view of the modifier 'with. . .' we can say that (3) has the form of

(5) $WHjsi$,

where the predicate '. . .hits. . .with. . .' is abbreviated as 'WH'. Although, as we pointed out, statements with the form of (5) seem to be referentially transparent, they also *seem* to lack an important mark of extensionality: evidently, materially equivalent formulas cannot be validly interchanged within them. Thus, if Jones hit Smith and thereby angered Mary, we cannot infer that if Jones hit Smith with a stick, he thereby angered Mary with a stick.

I said that sentences with the form of (5) *seem* to lack an important mark of extensionality, not that they actually do lack such a mark. I put the point in this guarded way, because if we accept Clark's approach to predicate modification, we can say that sentences like (5) only *appear* to contain sentences within them. The idea is that when we uncover their logical form, we can see that they contain a single complex predicate generated by an operation of adverbial modification. Of course, the *symbols* 'Hjs' occur in the formula '$WHjsi$', but the letter 'H' does not function as a predicate there and 'Hjs' does not function as a core sentence there. Thus, although the formula '$WHjsi$' may appear to consist of a core sentence 'Hjs' modified by an adverbial phrase 'Wi', it actually consists of a single, syntactically complex predicate 'WH' flanked by three singular terms, 'j', 's' and 'i'. Since '$WHjsi$' contains no core sentence and no predicate other than 'WH', the rule permitting the interchange of equivalent formulas is simply inapplicable to it (except in the trivial sense that the whole formula '$WHjsi$' can be interchanged for itself) as is the rule permitting the substitution of predicates coextensive with 'Hxy'. Since these rules are inapplicable to '$WHjsi$', they cannot be violated or falsified by that formula. Consequently, the formula can be regarded as extensional.

This approach to sentences like (5) is comparable to the approach other philosophers have taken to various sentences that appear, on the surface, to be nonextensional. Take 'Jones said that snow is white', for example. This sentence appears to contain a subsentence, 'snow is white'. If we accept this appearance at face value, we shall have to acknowledge that the sentence is nonextensional: 'Grass is green' has the same truth-value as 'snow is white', but 'Jones said that grass is green' may well be false when 'Jones said that snow is white' is true. But some philosophers do not interpret the sentence in this nonextensional way: they will admit that the words 'snow is white' occur in the sentence, but they deny that those words function as a sub-formula on which logical operations may be performed. Sellars and Davidson are notable examples of such philosophers.

According to Sellars, the 'that' clause in 'Jones said that snow is white' functions as a complex adverb modifying 'said'.[63] In his view the words 'snow is white' are merely *exhibited* in the adverb: they are on display. The function of such an adverb is to generate a predicate true of a person just when he used words that correspond in a certain way to those on exhibit in the predicate. The exhibited words do not, however, function as a formula on which logical operations may be performed. Davidson's theory is similar to Sellars's. According to him, 'Jones said that snow is white' has the form of '$(\exists x)$ (Uxj & Ax & Px & Rx, that). snow is white'. The words 'snow is white' are merely on display here; they function simply as verbal tokens to which the term 'that' refers. The quantified formula has the sense of 'For some x, x is an utterance by Jones that is a saying or asserting, that occurred in the past, and that is (roughly) a translation of *that*. snow is white'. (It is here assumed that a verbal token can count as a translation of itself.) The words 'snow is white' do not, again, function as an assertion in *this* context; they are merely on exhibit, an informative element of orthographic decoration in a fully extensional sentence about a human utterance.[64]

Extensional analyses of apparently nonextensional sentences are thus entirely familiar in recent philosophy. The claim that, in spite of appearances, sentences involving modifiers like 'with x' may be viewed as fully extensional should not, therefore, be viewed as patently absurd. The reasons for viewing such sentences this way are, of course, different from those Sellars or David-son would give for viewing sentences like 'Jones said that snow is white' as extensional. No words are merely on exhibit in a sentence like 'Jones hit Smith with a stick'. The extensional interpretation in this case is based on the idea that a complex predicate may be generated by applying a modifier to a simpler predicate: in the context of the complex predicate the symbol that otherwise functions as a simpler predicate no longer has *that* function. As a result, logical operations that otherwise may be applied to the simpler predi-cate are no longer applicable and extensionality is preserved.

If we take the suggested approach to statements like 'Jones hit Smith with a stick with the intention of hitting Smith with a stick', we can easily account for their distinctive logical consequences. By virtue of Clark's rules for standard modifiers, we can conclude from this illustrative statement that Jones hit Smith with a stick, that he hit Smith with something, and that, more simply, he hit Smith. We may also infer that if Jones bears the title 'The Avenger' and Smith bears the title 'The Enemy of the People', then The Avenger hit The Enemy of the People with a stick with the intention of hitting Smith with a stick. On the other hand, if The Avenger did hit The Enemy of the People with this intention, we may *not* infer that he hit The Enemy of the People intentionally. To draw this conclusion we need the premiss that Jones hit Smith (or The Enemy of the People) with the intention of hitting the Enemy of the People.

Another advantage to taking this approach is that we can easily explain why it is a mistake to suppose that *(done) with a certain intention* is a pro-perty of an action. As we pointed out earlier, if we allow that actions may have such a property, then if Jones's act of hitting Smith were identical with his act of angering Mary, we should have to agree that if Jones hit Smith with, say, the intention of avenging an insult, he angered Mary *with this intention* whether he was aware of her existence or not. But this difficulty cannot arise in the approach I am suggesting. In the context of 'Jones hit Smith with the intention i' the expression 'hit. . .with. . .' functions as a single complex predicate generated by an operation of predicate modification. If, for the sake of argument, we allow that predicates do connote properties, the pro-perty (or relation) connoted by 'hit. . .with. . .' is exemplified by pairs con-sisting of persons and intentions, not actions and intentions. If we adopted

Davidson's approach to adverbial modification, we should naturally interpret 'with' as connoting a relation between actions and intentions, so that the expression 'with intention i' could be said to connote a relational property possessed by actions alone. But in the approach we are taking 'with' functions merely as a part of a complex predicate that is true, not of actions, but of persons and intentions.

Concerning 'the Intention of Doing A'. It is important to observe that, according to Clark's interpretation of standard predicate modifiers, the position of *every* singular term in 'Jones hit Smith with Mary's book' is referentially transparent. As a consequence of this, we may infer that if Jones did hit Smith with Mary's book, then if Mary's book is identical with Tom's gift, then Jones hit Smith with Tom's gift. We may also infer that if Jones hit Smith with this book, then Jones hit somebody with something. Although corresponding inferences should be warranted by the statement 'Jones hit Smith with the intention of hitting Smith', it is difficult to feel equally confident about them.

The main source of perplexity lies in the remarkable polysemy of the word 'with'. My desk dictionary lists *eighteen* different senses for this little word.[65] Philosophical ingenuity might, of course, effect a significant reduction in the number of these distinct senses, but it seems undeniable that the word has very different implications in the context of 'S did A with a stick' and 'S did A with a certain intention': the sense in which you can hit a man with a stick is very different from that in which you can hit a man with an intention. Thus, until we have some understanding of what 'with' means in a context like 'Jones did A with the intention of doing B', we cannot be fully confident that the terminal position in such a context is really referentially transparent.

Let us assume, however, that the position occupied by 'the intention of doing A' in 'S did A with the intention of doing A' is referentially transparent, and let us make the natural assumption that the expression 'the intention of doing A' functions as a singular term referring to a certain mental state. Are there any obvious difficulties with these assumptions? None immediately comes to mind. The state of intending, as I have described it, is a propensity to think in a certain way (to have certain practical thoughts); and if Jones does something *with* a certain intention, it would seem reasonable to conclude that he does it *with* a certain propensity. Since we are interpreting expressions like 'the intention of doing A' as singular terms referring to mental states, we must, of course, acknowledge that 'Jones does A with the intention of doing A' entails '$(\exists x)$ (Jones does A with x)'. Obviously, this last formula must be distinguished from the corresponding formula entailed by 'Jones does A with Mary's book'. One way of drawing this distinction is to attach subscripts to the relevant uses of 'with'.

Even though we are assuming that the position occupied by 'the intention of doing A' in 'Jones did A with the intention of doing A' is referentially transparent, we must admit that the term 'the intention of doing A' has, at least on the face of it, an opaque structure. Suppose that Jones stabs Smith with the intention of killing Smith. As it happens, Smith bears the title 'The Enemy of the People'. We may infer from this that Jones stabbed The Enemy of the People with the intention of killing Smith, but we may *not* infer that Jones stabbed him with the intention of killing The Enemy of the People. For all we know, Jones may have intended to kill Smith as a means of protecting The Enemy of the People: he may have believed that Smith, the real Enemy of the People, was The Enemy of The Enemy of the People. Thus, if there is one intention Jones did *not* have in stabbing Smith, it is no doubt that of killing The Enemy of the People. In view of this case and countless others that could be produced, it *seems* reasonable to say that terms like 'the intention of killing Smith' are referentially opaque: they are not open to the kind of substitution we have been considering.

I have said that it *seems* reasonable to regard terms like 'the intention of killing Smith' as referentially opaque, not that it actually is reasonable. My reason for caution here is that, if we adopt Frege's theory of meaning, we shall want to insist that the referential positions inside such terms must be understood as transparent.[66] Insisting on this point will not require us to allow the kind of substitution just considered. Frege held that every term has a meaning or 'sense' as well as a reference, and that a term's sense and reference may vary with the context in which it occurs. In a statement like 'doing A = doing B', the terms 'doing A' and 'doing B' have their customary reference: they refer to the actions of doing A and doing B. But in an expression like 'the intention of doing A' the term 'doing A' does not have its customary reference; it now refers, Frege would say, to its customary sense or meaning. Since, according to his view, a term a may be substituted for a term b in a context C just when a and b have the same reference *in that context*, we can consistently deny (if we accept his view) that 'doing B' is validly substituted for 'doing A' in 'S did A with the intention of doing A' when 'doing *A*' and 'doing *B*' have the same *customary reference*. To make this substitution we need the information that 'doing *A*' and 'doing *B*' have the same *customary meaning*.

Now, we may not actually want to commit ourselves to Frege's theory of meaning; in particular, we may not want to commit ourselves to his view that singular terms have a customary sense as well as a customary reference and that in some contexts they refer to their customary sense. But even if we reject this view we can agree that a term *a* is validly substituted for a term *b* in a context *C* only when they refer to the same thing *in that context*. If we agree with this obvious truth, we shall have some understanding of why the form of substitution discussed earlier is invalid. In the context of 'the intention of killing Smith' the expression 'killing Smith' does not appear to refer to an *action*; in fact, it is not clear that it functions as a term referring to anything at all. What is clear is that the expression occurs as part of a complex term that refers to a certain intention or mental state. The question how a complex term of this kind, containing an expression that refers to an action when standing alone in most other contexts, manages to refer to a mental state is well worth investigating. But even in the absence of such an investigation we should hesitate to say that the mere identity of doing *A* and doing *B* should justify the substitution of the terms 'doing *A*' and 'doing *B*' in a peculiar context like 'the intention of doing *A*'. The identity of doing *A* and doing *B* certainly does not show us that the expressions 'doing *A*' and 'doing *B*' *have the same reference* in that context.

Why, we might ask, is it natural to include an action-locution like 'doing *A*' in a term used to denote an intention? My account of intention suggests at least a partial answer. If, in a context like 'Jones did *A* with the intention of doing *A*', the term 'the intention of doing *A*' refers to a particular mental state of the person Jones, then if I am right about intention, that term has the same reference as 'the mental state conventionally expressed in words by a Jonesian utterance of "I *will* do *A*" '. Though having (as matters stand) the same reference, these terms are far from synonymous, for one is explicitly metalinguistic while the other is not. Nevertheless, the co-extensiveness of these terms suggests a plausible analysis of 'the intention of doing *A*' as used in the contexts we have been discussing.

It would appear that the idea conveyed by 'Jones did *A* with the intention of doing *A*' could also be conveyed by 'Jones did *A* with the intention that he do *A*'; in fact, these formulas would seem to be mere stylistic variants of one another. In view of this close relationship, we could regard 'Jones did A intentionally' as elliptical for either formula. Let us therefore consider the latter formula and focus our attention specifically on the term 'the intention that he (Jones) do A'. This term does not refer to any words, and it does not refer to an action. On the other hand, it does contain words that customarily concern an action. Since a locution like 'Jones said that he (Jones) will do A' is similar in these respects, it would seem reasonable to analyze both locutions in a similar way. Since 'the intention that he (Jones) do A' is a singular term presumably referring to a mental *state*, Davidson's analysis of 'saying that' comes immediately to mind. According to him, 'S says that snow is white' is tacitly about an utterance or statement that is identified by reference to the words exhibited after the word 'that'. In line with this, we could say that 'the intention that he (Jones) do A' refers to a mental state that is picked out (or identified) by reference to the predicate *exhibited* after the 'that'. In fact, we could contend that 'the intention that he (Jones) do A' may be *explicated* as meaning 'the intention expressible in words by that. I (Jones) will do A', where the words 'I (Jones) will do A' function as verbal decoration denoted by the word 'that'. Note that the usual term 'the intention that he (Jones) do A' results from the longer equivalent when two relatively minor operations are performed: the 'I' is replaced by 'he', and the inner period and the words 'expressible in words by. . .will' are deleted.[67]

Although the explication just given no doubt has alternatives, it seems perfectly reasonable and it has the advantage of allowing us to explain, without reference to Fregean senses, just why we cannot expect to substitute co-referring singular terms in the context of locutions such as 'the intention of hitting Mary'. Neither the name 'Mary' nor the presumed action-description 'hitting Mary' occurs referentially in the locution 'the intention of hitting Mary' because those symbols are merely on display there, a part of the decoration. The only reference they have is their customary reference; but when they are merely on display in a formula, they are not used to *refer* to anything *in that formula*. Since these terms (or symbols) do not occur referentially in the context of 'the intention of hitting Mary', they do not, in that context, possess the distinctive features of referring terms: they are not subject, there, to the substitutivity of identity or to the operation of existential generalization.

If sound, the claims made in preceding paragraphs suggest that, properly understood, a sentence like 'Jones hit Smith with the intention of hitting

Smith' may reasonably be considered *totally extensional*. To understand such sentences fully, we must, however, consider the distinctive meaning of the preposition they contain. As I pointed out, the word 'with' has many different senses. If you hit a person with a stick, you use the stick as a weapon; but if you hit him with a certain intention, you do not use your intention as a weapon.

An Approach to 'Doing Something with an Intention'.   As we have seen, the 'with' in '*S* did *A* with the intention *I*' is a predicate modifier. If we ask how it modifies an action predicate, the answer would seem to be 'By a kind of adjunction: it adds to what is said in the predicate'. *S* did *A* with the intention *I*, it seems, just in case *S* did *A and* something special is true of his intention *I*. To clarify the meaning of the relevant 'with' in '*S* did *A* with the intention *I*', we should identify what this 'something special' is.

One possibility is that the agent *S* has the intention *I* when or while he does *A*. But this interpretation cannot be correct, for it is easy to imagine cases in which I unwittingly and thus unintentionally do something that, at the time, I fully intend to do. Suppose that I intend to kill a certain mouse that lives in my garage. Looking for the mouse, I throw aside a barrel, which strikes the mouse and kills it. Having thrown the barrel, I have killed the mouse, but I do so unwittingly: I do not realize that I have killed it. I did, however, intend to kill it, though I did not kill it intentionally.

It seems obvious that, if I do something intentionally, I do it *because* of my intention: my intention must play an important causal role in the genesis of my action. Nevertheless, it does not seem satisfactory simply to equate '*S* did *A* intentionally' with '*S* did *A* and *S*'s doing *A* was caused by *S*'s intention to do *A*'. An objection to this unqualified analysis, pointed out, in effect, by Chisholm,[68] is that having a certain intention may, in appropriate circumstances, generate a sequence of events that terminates (perhaps unknown to the agent) in the intended state of affairs. Thus, Jones, having formed the intention of killing his wife, becomes so agitated that he loses control of his car and drives into his wife, who just happens to be walking in the area. But although he intended to kill her, and killed her as a consequence of intending to kill her, he did not kill her intentionally: he killed her accidentally.

This kind of objection is not really decisive, however. Even though the man's intention may have generated a sequence of events that ended in the death (or killing) of his wife, it does not seem reasonable to regard his intention as *the* cause of her death. As I remarked in Chapter I, the relation of causing is not, generally speaking, transitive: If e_1 causes e_2 and e_2 causes e_3, we cannot always infer that e_1 causes e_3; we can do so only under special conditions. I did not, it is true, offer a precise or detailed description of such conditions in Chapter I, and I shall not attempt to do so here. Nevertheless, it seems obvious that, however such conditions might generally be described, they are not satisfied in the case just considered: the outcome depended too heavily on the presence of fortuitous circumstances. Thus, although a group of factors — the man's having a certain intention and temperament, his driving a car, and his wife's being in a certain unexpected place — undoubtedly generated the wife's death, we cannot reasonably single out the man's intention as the cause of that outcome.

In spite of all this, it does not seem advisable to accept the causal analysis in question: the mere notion of causing will not yield the clarification we need. A more satisfactory analysis emerges if we consider the obvious point that, if a person does something with a certain intention, he does it to realize that intention (at least among other things). As I argued in earlier sections of this chapter, the process by which we realize our intentions is largely, though not entirely, one of reasoning: we work out a plan of action that, if carried out, will (we believe) realize our intention, and then do what the plan requires. The analysis I wish to propose concerns this process in the following way: we do A with the intention i just when (1) we do A and (2) the fact that we do A is *psychologically explainable* by the fact that we have the intention i. The kind of explanation relevant here is what I called 'purposive explanation' in Section 5 of this chapter. The key idea is that, when we give such an explanation, we show how the agent's intention fits into a plan of action that results in the action by a sequence of events at least closely related to those envisioned in that plan.[69]

Suppose that Jones slaps Smith with the intention of insulting him. In this case Jones's plan of action, which could be part of a larger plan, might be as follows:

> I will insult Smith.
> If I slap him here and now, he will be insulted.
> No means of insulting him here is perferable to that of slapping him.
> So, I'll slap him right now.

The volitional thought 'So I'll slap him right now' is the sort of thing that, as I have argued, might be considered an act of will; and Jones's act of slapping Smith could be expected to result from it. The same general picture is applicable when it is said that Jones slapped Smith with the intention of slapping him; the difference is merely that the plan of action relevant to this case may consist of a single practical assertion, namely 'I'll slap him right now'. Such an assertion is not itself an intention; it is an expression of intention. Since an action or movement is directly caused by an expression like this, we can say that, strictly speaking, a motivating intention is not itself a cause. This is not incompatible with saying that when, referring to a person's intention, we explain why he intentionally does a certain thing, we are giving a kind of causal explanation.

My claim is that we do A with the intention i when (to put it roughly) our action is psychologically *explainable* by reference to that intention – not when our action *results* from an appropriate psychological process involving that intention. I reject the latter possibility mainly because I wish to deny that if, say, Jones hits Smith to avenge an insult and Jones's act of hitting Smith is identical with his act of angering Mary, then Jones angers Mary with this intention. Since the process of reasoning that issues in Jones's act of hitting Smith also issues in his act of angering Mary (assuming that they are the same act) I could not avoid this consequence by a purely causal account, no matter how it might be qualified. But my explanatory account does not face this difficulty, for the line of reasoning that 'rationalizes' Jones's act of hitting Smith would throw no explanatory light on the question of why he angered Mary.

It may be helpful at this point to have a close look at the sentence 'Jones stabbed Smith with the intention of killing him'. This sentence would naturally be used to give Jones's purpose in stabbing Smith. A purpose, as I argued in the last section, is an intention that one hopes to realize *by* adopting certain means. If Jones stabbed Smith for the purpose of killing him, he clearly intended to stab him. He intended to do this, presumably, *because* he intended to kill him and believed that, by stabbing him, he would kill him. Since the particular steps he took are explainable by a plan of action featuring the intention of killing Smith, it would be reasonable to say that he stabbed him with the intention of killing him.

For the sake of contrast, suppose that Jones's act of stabbing Smith were identical with his act of frightening Mary. Although he stabbed Smith with the intention of killing him, it would be extremely misleading to say that he therefore frightened Mary with the intention of killing Smith. This last claim would be extremely misleading because it would suggest that Jones's purpose in frightening Mary was to kill Smith. Such an idea is not, of course, intrinsically absurd. If Smith and Mary were seriously ill and deeply in love, the spectacle of Mary being frightened might be amply sufficient to stop Smith's feeble heart. But there is no need to attribute such an idea to Jones.

The remarks I have been making about the significance of 'with' in the context 'S did A with the intention I' do not require any amendment in my account of the logical structure of that context. Thus, I can still maintain that 'Jones hit Smith with the intention of hitting Smith' has the form of '$WAjsi$', where 'i' abbreviates a complex term. What I must acknowledge is that the complex predicate '. . .hit. . .with' is true of Jones, Smith, and Jones's intention to hit Smith (in that order) just in case Jones hit Smith and the fact that he did so is psychologically explainable, in the way I indicated, by reference to Jones's intention.

Although the analysis I have suggested requires a commitment to certain mental *states* (namely, intentions) it does not require a similar commitment to actions. It is, of course, consistent with such a commitment. A philosopher holding one of the three theories of action discussed in the last chapter need not *analyze* 'S did A with the intention I' as involving a reference to (or quantification over) events; he can perfectly well admit that it has the form of '$WAsi$' and contains a two-place predicate '. . .did A with. . .' true of a person and a certain intention. What he must say is that this predicate is true of a person and an intention just when (a) the person is the agent of an act of doing A and (b) the fact that he is so is psychologically explainable by reference to that intention. A commitment to actions or events requires no particular approach to the *logical analysis* of 'S did A with the intention I'.

Another Approach to 'Doing Something with an Intention'. If a philosopher does not accept events, he will probably not be happy with states or conditions. The question arises, therefore, 'How might such a philosopher interpret a sentence like "Jones hit Smith with the intention of hitting Smith"?' A natural approach is this. Since the 'with' in the specimen sentence has a significantly different function from the 'with' in 'Jones hit Smith with Mary's hammer', we cannot simply assume that both sentences should be analyzed as having the general form of '$WHjsi$'. As we have seen, the 'with' introducing the term 'the intention of hitting Smith' points to an explanatory relationship, and this relationship can be emphasized by interpreting 'Jones hit Smith with the intention of hitting Smith' as meaning 'Jones hit Smith and the fact that he hit Smith is psychologically explainable by the fact that he intended to hit Smith'.

Although this interpretation might seem objectionable in certain respects, it assigns the appropriate logical properties to 'Jones hit Smith intentionally', which is elliptical for 'Jones hit Smith with the intention of hitting Smith'. Thus, we may infer from 'Jones hit Smith intentionally' that Jones hit Smith and the The Avenger hit The Scapegoat (if Jones is The Avenger and Smith is The Scapegoat) but we may not conclude that, if Jones hit Smith and thereby angered Mary, Jones angered Mary intentionally. This last conclusion is ruled out by the opacity of the predicate 'intended to hit Smith'. Of course, instead of merely declaring that this predicate is opaque, we should offer an analysis of its structure that would clearly rule out the unwanted substitutions. But there are a number of ways of doing this.

Many philosophers would no doubt want to reject this approach to 'S did A intentionally' on the ground that it renders the statement fundamentally nonextensional. Although it is far from clear that nonextensionality is really objectionable, one should, in any case, be very cautious in rejecting an analysis on *this* ground. As we have seen, many expressions that appear to be nonextensional turn out to be fully extensional when their logical structure is exposed. Thus, even if nonextensionality must be avoided at all costs, the *apparent* nonextensionality of the context 'the fact that. . . is psychologically explainable by the fact that. . .' would provide a very poor basis for rejecting the suggested interpretation of 'S did A intentionally'. To reject this interpretation with good philosophical conscience, one must have some idea of the logical structure of the statement form 'The fact that Q is psychologically explainable by the fact that P'.

A philosopher who rejects events and causal relations in favor of substances and causal laws or principles (see Chapter I, pp. 41–44) might have to settle for a fundamentally nonextensional language. I shall not try to dispute this point in this book. On the other hand, having mentioned Davidson's extensional analysis of 'S said that P' in this section, I think it is worth pointing out that his analysis can easily be extended to provide a fully extensional interpretation of 'The fact that Q is psychologically explainable by the fact that P' or, more briefly, 'The fact that P psychologically explains the fact that Q'.[70] In accordance with Davidson's original analysis, we interpret the sentence following each 'that' as a mere token or orthographic display to which the 'that' refers. To avoid a commitment to facts, we then eliminate the words 'the fact' in favor of the predicate 'is true': in simple cases 'the fact that. . .' may be replaced by 'that is true and that. . .'. Since the sentence 'The fact that P psychologically explains the fact that Q' contains two 'that's with different referents, we can distinguish these 'that's by subscripts and put their referents in the appropriate order on a separate line. If we follow this procedure, we can say that 'The fact that there was a short circuit causally explains the fact that there was a fire' has the form of (1):

(1)   that$_1$ is true & that$_2$ is true & CE (that$_1$, that$_2$).
        There was a short circuit. There was a fire.

I have written the sentences 'There was a short circuit' and 'There was a fire' below the formula (1) to indicate that they do not function as subformulas occurring within it. They are merely on display in the neighborhood, serving as the referents, respectively, of the two demonstratives that do occur in it.

If we adopt the strategy of interpreting 'Jones hit Smith with the intention of hitting Smith' as 'Jones hit Smith, and the fact that Jones intended to hit Smith psychologically explains the fact that Jones hit Smith', we can say that 'Jones hit Smith intentionally' is elliptical for a statement with the form of (2):

(2)   Jones hit Smith & that$_1$ is true & that$_2$ is true & PE (that$_1$, that$_2$).
        Jones intended to hit Smith. Jones hit Smith.

Note that the formula (2), which does not include the two sentences occurring below it, is fully extensional and has the implications appropriate to 'Jones hit Smith intentionally'. It is extensional, because the 'that's it contains are open to substitution and existential generalization. Thus, if a name for one of the exhibited sentences is put in place of the appropriate 'that', a true statement results. As for the appropriateness of the implications, (2) entails 'Jones hit Smith', 'Jones hit someone', 'The Avenger hit The Scapegoat' (if Jones = The Avenger and Smith = The Scapegoat), but it does not entail 'If Jones hit Smith just in case Jones frightened Mary, then Jones frightened Mary intentionally'.[71]

It is worth observing that, if 'Jones hit Smith intentionally' is elliptical for a sentence having the form of (2), then 'Jones hit Smith intentionally' does *not* formally entail 'Jones intended to hit Smith'. Nevertheless, the following conditional is true:

> (3)   If Jones hit Smith intentionally, then Jones intended to hit Smith.

This statement is not formally deducible from (2), but it is derivable from the conjunction of (2) and the premiss 'that$_2$ = "Jones intended to hit Smith" '. Since (2) implies 'that$_2$ is true', the extra premiss just mentioned allows us to obtain the desired conclusion. Though obviously true, this extra premiss is empirical, so that the conclusion cannot count as a logical consequence of (2). On the other hand, since the needed premiss is always true when (2) is verbally expressed, the implication between (2) and 'Jones intended to hit Smith' might be considered a *pragmatic* necessity.

If we are convinced, as I am, that (3) should be considered a logical truth, we can easily amend the suggested analysis to get this result. On first approximation we can say that 'Jones hit Smith intentionally' has the sense of 'Jones hit Smith and Jones intended to hit Smith and the fact that Jones intended to hit Smith psychologically explains the fact that that Jones hit Smith'. But since the first two conjuncts of this analysis guarantee that the sentences following the demonstrative 'that's are true, we can simplify matters by saying merely the following:

> (4)   Jones hit Smith & Jones intended to hit Smith & *PE* (that$_2$, that$_1$),

where the subscripted 'that's refer to the second and first conjuncts in the formula. This amendment not only accounts for the apparent quasi-intensionality of 'Jones hit Smith intentionally' but it obviously renders the conditional (3) logically true.

In view of what I have been arguing in this section it would appear that at least two rival analyses of '*S* did *A* with the intention of doing *A*' are possible. Although neither analysis commits one to the existence of action-events, both are consistent with such a commitment. The first analysis does, however, commit one to states of intending. If a commitment to events and states is regarded as metaphysically objectionable or perhaps needless, the second analysis is no doubt preferable. It yields a fully extensional approach to '*S* did *A* intentionally', and it accounts for the formal entailments that statements of that form intuitively possess. Since there are, as I explained in

Chapter I, obvious advantages in avoiding a commitment to events (and other metaphysical exotica), the second analysis strikes me as preferable. Yet apart from metaphysical considerations, either analysis would appear to be satisfactory.

7. CONCLUDING REMARKS

My general aim in this chapter has been to develop an account of what might be called the conscious springs of purposive behavior. To this end I have argued that such behavior typically results from a process of reasoning, more or less explicit, involving premises distinctive of the agent's beliefs and intentions. Since this kind of reasoning is directed to action rather than truth, it is generally called 'practical reasoning' or, sometimes, 'deliberation'. Thus far I have said very little about the logical structure of such reasoning. This will be my principal subject in the chapters to follow.

NOTES

[1] H. A. Prichard, 'Acting, Willing, and Desiring', in A. R. White, *The Philosophy of Action* (Oxford, 1968), p. 61.

[2] David Hume, *A Treatise of Human Nature* (L. A. Selby-Bigge, ed.) (Oxford, 1941), Bk. II, Sect. III, p. 399.

[3] Gilbert Ryle, *The Concept of Mind* (London, 1949), pp. 62–69.

[4] Prichard, in White, p. 64.

[5] Immanuel Kant, *Critique of Practical Reason* (tr. L. W. Beck) (New York, 1956), p. 15.

[6] See Davidson, 'Actions, Reasons, and Causes', in White, p. 81. Davidson writes as if the agent's belief concerns the action he is performing rather than the action he will perform. But since the belief in question is a partial cause of the relevant action, the agent must have the belief before he thus acts. Consequently, it seems best to interpret Davidson as saying the belief concerns the action the agent *will* perform.

[7] R. G. Collingwood, *The New Leviathan* (Oxford, 1942), p. 97.

[8] Wilfrid Sellars, 'Thought and Action', in Keith Lehrer (ed.), *Freedom and Determinism* (New York, 1966), pp. 105–139.

[9] Davidson, in White, pp. 83f.

[10] See Chapter I, p. 11. In a footnote (see White, p. 87) Davidson makes it clear that he thinks the relevant notion of causing requires certain qualifications that he has not spelled out. Evidently, he believes that a primary reason causes intentional behavior in some special way.

[11] Davidson, in White, pp. 79f.

[12] J. L. Austin, 'Three Ways of Spilling Ink', *Philosophical Review* 75 (1966), p. 437

[13] *Ibid.*

[14] See Aristotle's discussion in Bk. III of his *Nichomachean Ethics.*

[15] Hume, Bk. II, Sect. III, pp. 413–418.

[16] Hume, p. 414.

[17] Hume, p. 415.

[18] Hume, p. 413.

[19] See Peirce, 'The Fixation of Belief', in Charles Hartshorne and Paul Weiss (eds.), *Collected Papers of C. S. Peirce*, vol. 5 (Cambridge, Mass., 1934), pp. 365–384.

[20] This formula is idealized and does not take account of the fact that intentions, like beliefs, may be more or less firm. A weak intention is less likely than a strong one to issue in appropriate behavior.

[21] Ryle, pp. 134f.

[22] I have defended essentially this view in my book *Knowledge, Mind, and Nature* (New York, 1967), pp. 213–218.

[23] My account of intention is indebted to Wilfrid Sellars; see especially his 'Thought and Action'.

[24] See Sellars, *ibid.*

[25] See Sellars, 'Thought and Action', pp. 108f.

[26] Collingwood, p. 97.

[27] My account of volition is indebted to Sellars's discussion in 'Thought and Action'. Sellars conceives of volitions as 'act of intending'; I do not. But our difference here is essentially terminological.

[28] Sellars held this view, apparently, in an early essay, 'Some Reflections on Language Games', in *Science, Perception, and Reality* (London, 1963), pp. 321–358.

[29] G. E. M. Anscombe, *Intention* (Oxford, 1958), p. 52.

[30] See Sellars, *Science, Perception, and Reality*, Ch. 5, and *Science and Metaphysics* (London, 1968), Ch. 3; P. T. Geach, *Mental Acts* (London, 1957), pp. 75–106; and Bruce Aune, *Knowledge, Mind, and Nature*, Ch. 7.

[31] I am here conceiving of a person's statement as an utterance that is produced in an assertive frame of mind and that is classifiable as something having logical consequences, a negation, and so on. Obviously, the term 'statement' is not always used this way in philosophy or in everyday life.

[32] W. V. O. Quine, 'Ontological Relativity', in *Ontological Relativity and Other Essays* (New York, 1969), pp. 26–68.

[33] I have expressed my view of Quine's thesis at length in my essay 'Quine on Translation and Reference', *Philosophical Studies* 27 (1975), 221–236.

[34] For a particularly good discussion of the notion of logical form, see Paul Ziff, 'The Logical Structure of English Sentences', in *Understanding Understanding* (Ithaca, N.Y., 1972), pp. 39–56.

[35] J. L. Austin, *Philosophical Papers* (Oxford, 1961), p. 228.

[36] W. V. O. Quine, *Word and Object* (Cambridge, Mass., 1960), p. 12.

[37] Northrop Frye, *The Well Tempered Critic* (Bloomington, Ind., 1963), Ch. 1.

[38] George A. Miller, Eugene Galanter and Karl H. Pribram, *Plans and the Structure of Behavior* (New York, 1960), pp. 195–214.

[39] Ryle, Ch. 5.

[40] For an elaboration of the points made in this paragraph, see my book, *Knowledge, Mind, and Nature*, pp. 218–223.

41 See the excellent essay by J. O. Urmson, 'Motives and Causes', in White, pp. 153–165.
42 See Carl G. Hempel, 'Aspects of Scientific Explanation', in *Aspects of Scientific Explanation and Other Essays in the Philosophy of Science* (New York, 1965), pp. 488f.
43 See *ibid.*
44 Anscombe, p. 79.
45 This point has been emphasized by Hempel; see pp. 463–486.
46 Davidson, 'Mental Events', in L. Foster and J. W. Swanson (eds.), *Experience and Theory* (Amherst, Mass., 1970), p. 100.
47 See Miller *et al., Plans and the Structure of Behavior*, Ch. 4.
48 See Hempel.
49 See Urmson.
50 Ryle, p. 89.
51 See D. S. Schwayder, *The Structure of Behavior* (London, 1965), p. 96.
52 See, e.g., G. E. M. Anscombe, 'War and Murder', in James Rachaels (ed.), *Moral Problems* (New York, 1975), pp. 285–297. The example I introduce here was suggested by Michael Bratman, who attributed it to Davidson.
53 P. J. Fitzgerald, 'Voluntary and Involuntary Acts', in White, p. 129.
54 See Joel Feinberg, 'Action and Responsibility', in White, p. 117, and H. L. Hart and A. M. Honore, *Causation and the Law* (Oxford, 1959), pp. 134ff.
55 Rudolf Carnap, 'Two Concepts of Probability', in H. Feigl and W. Sellars (eds.), *Readings in Philosophical Analysis* (New York, 1949), p. 330.
56 Davidson, 'Agency', in Robert Binkley *et al.* (eds.), *Agent, Action and Reason* (Toronto, 1971), p. 7.
57 Davidson, 'Actions, Reasons, and Causes', in White, p. 81.
58 See Quine's discussion of transparent and opaque readings of belief sentences in *Word and Object*, pp. 146–151.
59 According to the analysis I shall present, when 'Jones hit Smith intentionally' is used in the straightforward sense not equivalent to 'Smith is such that Jones hit him intentionally', the position occupied by 'Smith' is *not* open to existential generalization, that is, '$(\exists x)$ (Jones hit x intentionally)' is not a logical (= formal) consequence of it. On the other hand, when 'Jones hit Smith intentionally' does have the sense of 'Smith is such that Jones hit him intentionally', the statement '$(\exists x)$ (Jones hit x intentionally)' does follow. For further discussion, see Notes 67 and 71 below.
60 Quine, 'Referene and Modality', in *From a Logical Point of View* (Cambridge, Mass., 1953), p. 139.
61 An alternative to this formula, suggested by Stephen Schiffer, is 'Jones hit Smith intending to hit Smith'. I prefer 'Jones hit Smith with the intention of hitting Smith' because I find it easier to deal with. It should be understood, though, that I am using the sentence in such a way that the intention of hitting Smith may be just one of the intentions (and not necessarily the purpose) Jones had in hitting him.
62 Davidson would not, of course, apply his analysis of adverbial modification to (3). He would analyze (3) in accordance with his syncategorematic approach to intention-descriptions. See above, pp. 53 f.
63 Wilfrid Sellars, *Science and Metaphysics*, p. 169.
64 Davidson, 'On Saying That', in D. Davidson and J. Hintikka (eds.), *Words and Objections* (Dordrecht, Holland: Reidel, 1969), pp. 158–174.
65 *Random House Dictionary of the English Language*, College Edition (New York,

1968).

[66] See Gottlob Frege, 'On Sense and Reference', in Max Black and P. T. Geach (eds.), *Translations from the Philosophical Writings of Gottlob Frege* (Oxford, 1960), pp. 56–78.

[67] According to this analytic strategy, what Quine would call the 'transparent' reading of 'Jones hit Smith intentionally' – namely, 'Smith is such that Jones hit him intentionally' – may be formalized by '$WHjsIsHh$', where the expression '$IsHh$' is read as 'the intention concerning s that is expressible in words by that. I will hit him'. On this approach the positions occupied by 's' in the formula '$WHjsIsHh$' are both open to existential generalization; consequently, we may infer '$(\exists x)$ (Jones hit x intentionally)' ($=$ '$(\exists x)(WHjxIxHh)$') from 'Jones hit Smith intentionally', where the latter sentence is interpreted as having the form of '$WHjsIsHh$'.

[68] R. M. Chisholm, 'Freedom and Action', in Lehrer (ed.), *Freedom and Determinism* p. 37.

[69] The vagueness in this clause seems unavoidable. Here are two contrasting cases. I intend to frighten Smith and decide to do so by making a threatening gesture. My eyesight is poor, however, and I approach a rack full of coats, taking it to be Smith. I make the threatening gesture. Smith, at the other end of the room, sees me making the gesture to the coatrack and, thinking I have gone mad, becomes frightened. It seems doubtful that I frightened Smith intentionally: my decision to make the threatening gesture does not cause Smith's fright by the appropriate sequence of events. On the other hand, suppose that I intend to kill Smith and, as a means of killing him, decide to stab him with an icepick. I then lunge with the icepick, but I miss my target, striking his neck with my clenched fist. A blood vessel breaks in Smith's neck, and he dies. In this case it seems that I do kill Smith intentionally, although I do not kill him in the way I intended to kill him: the sequence of events connecting my decision to stab Smith with Smith's death would seem to be close enough to the envisioned sequence to render my killing intentional. These contrasting cases suggest that the notion of doing something with an intention is a little too vague to be pinned down by any precise formula.

[70] An extensional analysis is also possible on Sellars's approach to 'that' clauses. He could say that 'The fact that snow is white is F' is eliminable in favor of 'The ˙snow is white˙ is true and the ˙snow is white˙ is F', which is equivalent, in his system, to 'All ˙snow is white˙s are true and all ˙snow is white˙s are F'. The fundamental similarity between Sellars's approach and Davidson's is illustrated by the fact that Sellars's illustrating predicate "snow is white" can evidently be defined by Davidson's demonstrative 'that'. The definition would be: '(x) (x is a ˙snow is white˙ if x is a semantic counterpart of that', where the 'that' refers to the token flanked by the dot quotes. For details about Sellars's approach, see *Science and Metaphysics*, pp. 60–90.

[71] According to this analytic strategy, the so-called transparent use of 'Jones hit Smith intentionally' – namely, 'Smith is such that Jones hit him intentionally' – may be analyzed as 'Jones hit Smith and the fact (concerning Smith) that Jones intended to hit him psychologically explains the fact (concerning Smith) that Jones hit him. On this interpretation all positions occupied by 'Smith' are referentially transparent and thus open to existential generalization; consequently, '$(\exists x)$ (Jones hit x intentionally)' is validly inferred from the transparent use of 'Jones hit Smith intentionally'.

According to the analytic strategy suggested on page 106, the transparent use of 'Jones hit Smith intentionally' may be interpreted as 'Jones hit Smith & concerning Smith, Jones intended to hit him & PE (that$_2$, that$_1$)', where 'that$_2$' refers to the occurrence of 'Jones intended to hit him' and 'that₁' refers to the occurrence of 'Jones hit Smith'. This interpretation also renders transparent all occurrences of 'Smith' and thus permits us to infer '$(\exists x)$ (Jones hit x intentionally)' from the so-called transparent use of 'Jones hit Smith intentionally'.

Chapter III

DELIBERATION

Deliberation is a form of reasoning aimed at action rather than truth. We want to know what to *do* in some situation or other, and if our deliberation is successful, we become committed to a plan, policy or course of action. Although groups as well as individuals may engage in deliberation, I shall be concerned here only with the deliberation of individual people. My remarks in the last chapter indicate a basic line I shall take in dealing with the subject, but I shall begin by considering Aristotle's view. Not only was he the first important philosopher to discuss the subject in any detail, but his conclusions are still highly influential. After examining the main points of his view, I shall move on to consider some recent discussions of the subject; then, toward the end of the chapter, I shall develop further details of my own view.

1. ARISTOTLE ON DELIBERATION

It is often supposed that Aristotle's view of practical reasoning is expressed in what he says about the so-called practical syllogism. In Book VII of the *Nicomachean Ethics* he says this:

[In the practical syllogism] one of the premises, the universal, is a current belief, while the other involves particular facts which fall within the domain of sense perception. When [the] two premises are combined into one. . . the soul is thereupon bound to affirm the conclusion, and if the premises involve action, the soul is bound to perform this act at once. For example, if [the premises] are: 'Everything sweet ought to be tasted' and 'This thing before me is sweet' ('this thing' perceived as an individual particular object), a man who is able [to taste] and is not prevented is bound to act accordingly at once.[1]

Although this passage is entirely consistent with the natural view that the conclusion of a practical syllogism is a statement or proposition — in this case 'This thing ought to be tasted' — some philosophers interpret Aristotle as saying that the conclusion is really an action, the action of tasting.[2] If this interpretation were correct, however, the practical syllogism could hardly be a form of inference, for the conclusion of an inference must be some kind of statement or proposition — something that can be *inferred* from the given premisses.

The correct interpretation of Aristotle's remarks about the practical syllogism does not seem to me crucially important for his account of practical reasoning, since his explicit remarks on deliberation, given in Book III of his *Ethics*, present a very different, far more complicated picture. The key passage is this:

> We deliberate not about ends but about the means to attain ends. . . . We take the end for granted, and then consider in what manner and by what means it can be realized. If it becomes apparent that there is more than one means by which it can be attained, we look for the easiest and best; if it can be realized by one means only, we consider in what manner it can be realized by that means, and how that means can be achieved in its turn. We continue that process until we come to the first link in the chain of causation, which is the last step in the order of discovery. . . . Moreover, if in the process of investigation we encounter an insurmountable obstacle, for example, if we need money and none can be procured, we abandon our investigation; but if it turns out to be possible, we begin to act.[3]

As for his 'we begin to act', Aristotle implies that the action is the result of choice:

> Every man stops inquiring how he is to act when he has traced the initiation of action back to himself and to the part of himself. . .that exercises choice.[4]

Clearly, these remarks imply a view of practical reasoning far more complicated than anything suggested in this passage about the practical syllogism. Schematically, his view would appear to cover such reasoning as this:

(1)   [Would that E were realized.]

(2) M_1 will bring about E.

(3) M_2 will bring about E.

(4) M_1 is easier or better than M_2.

(5)   Doing A is the only way to bring about M_1.

(6)   It is possible for me to do A.

(7)   So, I'll do A.

The conclusion here is supposed to be a choice (Aristotle's word is *proairesis*), and I have thus expressed it by the English sentence that seems most natural for this. Although I would regard the conclusion (7) as having a direct relation to action (given that it concerns something the agent can do there and then) Aristotle seems to think that its relation to action is somewhat indirect, first generating a desire that elicits the action: 'the object of choice is something within our power which we desire as the result of deliberation. . . : we arrive at a decision on the basis of deliberation, and then let the deliberation guide our desire'.[5] His view here is not, however, clear, since he also says 'we may define choice as a deliberate desire for things that are within our power.[6]

Although the schematic argument set out here is merely intended to be an example of the sort of thing evidently covered by Aristotle's account of deliberation, it seems reasonable to interpret him as saying that deliberation is a form of reasoning that terminates − or at least has a rational or formal terminus − in a choice. As some commentators have pointed out, however, 'choice' is probably not the best word to describe what Aristotle had in mind in using the Greek *proairesis*.[7] Burnet says that '*proairesis* is really what we call the will'; and Hardie, who explicitly adopts Prichard's theory of action, apparently holds a similar view.[8] I hesitate to pronounce upon this scholarly matter, but I think that 'choice' is not a good way of describing the upshot of every deliberation as Aristotle conceives of it. If an agent should find that there is only one way to realize this end (a possibility Aristotle seems to recognize in the key passage above) he may terminate his decision without actually making a choice in the strict sense of the word. As I see it, choosing strictly involves the consideration of alternatives; and if a person thinks there is only one way to achieve his end, he might not consider any alternatives at all. He may simply decide to adopt the available means to the end he 'takes for granted' in his deliberation.

Actually, in the schematic form of reasoning given above, the conclusion reached − namely, 'So I'll do A' − does not seem to represent a choice anyway, for no alternative to doing A is mentioned there. In deciding to do A the agent may, of course, be said to have *tacitly* chosen to bring about M_1 rather than M_2, but no explicit choice between alternatives seems to be represented anywhere in the inference.

2. DECISION AND CHOICE

As I am using the words, every choosing is a deciding, but not every deciding is a choosing. Generally speaking, to decide to do something is to make up your mind to do it, where making up your mind involves giving at least minimal consideration to the question of what you are going to do. More than minimal consideration is evidently not necessary for choosing and deciding, for choices and decisions can be made capriciously − that is, without any careful consideration of reasons pro or con. If no consideration of ends of alternatives occurs at all, however, no choice or decision is properly made: at best, an intention is formed. To decide or choose is, of course, to form an intention, but not all intentions are formed by way of a decision or choice. It is only when an intention is formed in a special way − when it results from at least a minimal process of deliberation or 'decision making' − that a decision is properly made.

As I conceive of it, explicitly choosing to do A is explicitly deciding to do A in preference to some alternative action. Schematically, the deliberation leading to a decision that is a choice ideally includes steps like these:

(1)   I will bring about the end E.

(2)   Doing M will bring about E.

(3)   Doing M^* will bring about E.

(4)   I cannot do both M and M^*.

(5)   Shall I do M or shall I do M^* (or shall I do neither)?

(6)   I will do M^*.

Most actual deliberations including steps like these would include others as well, since no reasons for preferring M^* to M are represented here. Such reasons are not, of course, necessary, for a choice need not be well considered: it may, in fact, be wildly irrational. If, however, a choice is explicit, it must spring from an explicit consideration of alternatives − and this feature is well represented here. I speak of an explicit choice because, in line with my claims in the last chapter, I think we can also speak of implicit ones. A choice is implicitly or tacitly made either when an intention is formed in accordance with the idea that certain actions are alternatives or when, having actually considered certain alternatives, the agent makes movements in accordance with the idea (the intention) of making them. I commented on the difficult notion of doing something merely 'in accordance with' an idea or premiss in the last chapter, and I shall therefore say no more about it here.

My view of choosing is incompatible with the claims some well-known writers have recently made about choice, and it may be helpful to consider at least one such claim before proceeding further. Richard Taylor has claimed, for example, that to choose one thing rather than another is often simply to take one thing rather than another. As he put it:

> Think of a man. . .walking through the cafeteria, who pauses before an array of a great variety of juices and then reaches for a glass of orange juice. Here, certainly, is a perfect example of an act of choice; namely, the actual act, which consists of taking one thing from among others that were offered, and doing so under circumstances in which those alternatives were, or were at least believed to be, equally available.[9]

Taylor is right in saying that such an act could justifiably be called 'choosing something', but this by itself is not really incompatible with the view I am espousing.

According to my view, an overt act may be considered an act of choice in a derivative sense if it is the result or overt expression of a mental act of choice. The question to be considered, therefore, is this: 'Did the agent described by Taylor actually choose, in my sense, to take the orange juice?' The answer seems to be 'Yes' — at least in the sense that the man *implicitly* made such a choice. For Taylor's case to count as a plausible example of overtly choosing something, it must be assumed, first, that the man intended to take the orange juice — that he did not take it unwittingly, inadvertently or by mistake. It must also be assumed that the man regarded the other juices before him as alternatives: evidently, he had the intention of taking one glass of juice, and the glasses before him were the alternatives relative to this aim. If his aim, however implicit, were different — for example, to take two glasses of juice — he would be faced with a different set of alternatives. Consequently, in describing the man as having chosen a certain glass of orange juice, we are tacitly making at least the following assumptions:

(1)   He intended to take just one glass of juice.

(2)   He was aware, however dimly, of a number of alternatives relative to this intention.

(3)   He actually intended (meant) to take the orange juice; he did not take it by mistake, etc.

(4)   He took the orange juice in preference to the other glasses
        of juice that were before him.

In making these assumptions we are clearly supposing that the man's mind
was not a complete blank as far as the juices before him were concerned. The
thought of taking one or the other glasses must at least have crossed his mind,
and this thought must have been related to his beliefs about what is before
him, his preferences regarding juice and his leading intention to take *a* glass
of juice. As we saw in the last chapter, however, beliefs and intentions can
give rise to a particular form of behavior only when they are brought into
logical contact with one another by some kind of reasoning. Such reasoning
may be very scrappy — elliptical and enthymematic — but in the present case
it would seem to 'accord' with some such pattern as this:

(1*)   I'll have a glass of juice.

(2*)   Here is some orange juice, and here are some juices of other
        kinds.

(3*)   I'll take an orange juice.

(4*)   This one will do; I'll take it.

If the agent did not reason in accordance with this or a related pattern,
explicitly having at least elliptical versions of some of the thoughts represented here, it seems to me that it would, strictly speaking, be a mistake to
say that he *chose* the orange juice.

3. DELIBERATION AND ENDS

Aristotle says that 'we deliberate not about ends but about means to attain
ends'.[10] Viewed one way, this claim is obviously correct: we do not deliberate about the ends we already have. On the other hand, we certainly do
deliberate about whether to adopt certain ends. A student may have as his
end earning the B.A. degree, and with this end in mind he may deliberate
about how he is to earn this degree. Should he apply to State University, or
should he try for admission to an Ivy League college? Yet his end of earning
the B.A. degree might itself have been arrived at by deliberation; he may have
adopted it in the course of deciding what his life's work shall be. Ends of this

kind are not, of course, ultimate; one seeks to realize them only as a means to realizing some further end. Since any form of Aristotelian deliberation requires some end to be 'taken for granted' — at least for the purposes of a given deliberation — it follows that some end or other will have to be ultimate in the sense described. The alternative to acknowledging this is to adopt the absurd position that a man may have an unending hierarchy of ends. Acknowledging the existence of ultimate ends does not require us to hold that such ends cannot be justified; we merely have to hold that they cannot be justified by a form of Aristotelian deliberation.

But just what are ends? Are they things we desire to obtain, or what? Aristotle suggests that ends are what we wish for: 'we wish to be healthy and choose the things that will give us health'.[11] Again, he says that 'the end is the object of wish'; and the object of a wish is 'whatever seems good to us'.[12] These remarks suggest that, for him, our ends are what we wish for or, perhaps, think good for us. If this is indeed his conception of an end, it is clearly inadequate — at least for the purposes of his theory of deliberation.

When we wish to be beautiful, wise or immortal, we may know we are wishing for the unattainable, and it would be silly for us to deliberate about how to attain such wishes. On the other hand, when we wish for something we do not regard as unattainable, our wishes seem to be the same as wants or desires. Yet wants and desires are not generally sufficient to generate the kind of deliberation we have been discussing. As we saw in Chapter II (see pages 57–60, we commonly want or desire many things we have no intention of pursuing: we want an expensive, fattening dinner and we want to avoid seeing the dentist, but these may not be wants on which we are consciously prepared to act. The same holds for things we merely 'think good for us': we may know we should get more exercise, but for one reason or another we do not have the attainment of exercise as one of our conscious ends. It may, of course, be true that, when we have the end of realizing E, we want or desire to realize it, at least 'under some description'. But there is clearly more to an end than a mere want or desire.

As I have interpreted Aristotle, the conclusion of a line of deliberation is a decision; and a decision, unlike a want or desire, *commits* us to doing something. If, on deciding to do A, I fail to do it on the appropriate occasion, then, unless I have changed my mind or do not realize that the occasion is the appropriate one, I am subject to criticism: I am being *practically* inconsistent; I am not doing what I have, as it were, agreed to do. In this respect a decision is like a promise: appropriate behavior is required so long as the 'mandate' is in effect.[13] Since wants and wishes do not involve this kind of commitment, they seem patently insufficient to generate a line of reasoning that terminates in a decision. Purposes differ from wants and wishes in this regard: being leading intentions, they are ideally suited for generating a commitment to act; in fact, they involve such a commitment themselves. It seems to me that Aristotelian ends are best understood as purposes.

My conception of ends (or basic practical premisses) is out of line with the claims of thoughtful philosophers concerned with practical reasoning, and it will again prove useful to comment on opposing views. In his 1963 article 'Practical Inference' G. H. von Wright proposed the following as a primary pattern of practical inference:

> A wants to attain x.
> Unless A does y, he will not attain it.
> Therefore, A must do y.[14]

The first thing to say about this pattern is that it has nothing to do with what I have been calling practical inference unless the variable 'A' in it is replaced by 'I', 'we', or some name or description that the person using the pattern takes or refers to himself or to the group he represents. Von Wright does not view it this way, however. In fact, he seems to think that it is only inferences in the third person that conform exactly to the pattern; first-person inferences related to the pattern are to be understood according to his evident interpretation of Aristotle's remarks on the practical syllogism. As he puts it:

In the case of inferences in the first person...the premisses are a person's *want* and his *state of knowing or believing* a certain condition to be necessary for the fulfillment of that want. The conclusion is an *act*, something that the person does.[15]

Von Wright's claim here seems confused. First, wants and states of believing are not premisses, and an act such as the moving of a hand is not the conclusion of an inference. An act may be caused by the onset of a complex state of believing-P-and-wanting-E; and the act may even be shown to be justifiable or reasonable in relation to such a state. But the transition from wanting E and believing A to doing something is not an inference that could be said to be valid or invalid. Second, even if this first point were mistaken and the transition from the want and belief to the act were properly regarded as an inference, the reasoning would not in any way conform to the schema von Wright sets out. An act of, say, moving a hand is not of the form 'I must do y' or any related form.

If there is a first-person inference corresponding to the pattern von Wright discusses, it no doubt has the form:

>   (1)   I want to attain x.
>   (2)   Unless I do y, I shall not attain x.
>   (3)   Therefore, I must do y.

In view of what he says about the corresponding third-person inference, von Wright is committed to the view that the conclusion here expresses what he calls 'practical necessity'. But, clearly, the necessity in question is at best relative. It is not that, absolutely speaking, the agent must do y; it is merely that he must do y *if* he is to satisfy his want. A conclusion of this kind not only fails to correspond to the action of doing y; it does not even commit the agent to doing y.

David Gauthier, discussing von Wright's view, would apparently disagree with me on this point. Speaking of essentially the same argument form as I have set out above (his argument form differs from mine only in having a premiss in the optative mood 'I would attain x' in place of 'I want to attain x'), Gauthier says:

> But the conclusion does have *practical* force. For if the agent fails to carry out the action, he must, on pain of self-contradiction, reject one of the premisses. If the agent genuinely accepts that he would attain x, and that unless he does y he will not attain x, then he is committed to doing, or at least attempting to do, y, and that commitment is logical.[16]

Gauthier is simply wrong here. Consider the argument:

>   (1)   I want to be rich tomorrow (or I would that I were rich to-
>   morrow).
>   (2)   Unless I kill my uncle, I shall not be rich tomorrow.
>   (3)   Therefore, I must (or I 'need to') kill my uncle.

It is preposterous to suppose that anyone who accepts (1) and (2) is logically committed to killing anyone at all.

If we construct an argument similar to the above but with a conclusion in which the 'necessity' is clearly exhibited as relative, we can easily see why the conclusions of such arguments imply no commitment to act. Consider the following:

(1)   I want to attain x.

(2)   Unless I do y, I shall not attain x.

(3)   Therefore, I must do y if I am to attain x.

Now think of the argument about killing one's uncle. Its conclusion, made fully explicit, would be this:

(4)   I must kill my uncle if I am to be rich tomorrow.

Since this conclusion is merely hypothetical, it clearly does not commit one to doing anything at all. In fact, the natural step for a reasonable man to take on deriving (4) is to ask himself: 'Shall I try to satisfy my want or not?' Most of us would answer this question by saying 'No'; we should be faced with just another want that we can find no reasonable or acceptable way of satisfying.

Although Gauthier is simply wrong about the inference he discusses, a related inference is, I think, valid. If, instead of merely wanting or perhaps wishing for a certain result, a man actually intended to achieve that result, then he would have a valid logical basis for deciding to do what he sees as necessary for that result. In other words, from the premisses

(1)   I *will* achieve E.

(2)   Doing A is necessary for achieving E.

one may validly infer

(3)   I *will* do A.

My reasons for holding that this inference is valid will be developed in the next chapter, where I explicitly consider what is involved in speaking of the validity of a practical inference. At present my concern is simply to emphasize that the model for practical reasoning suggested by Gauthier and by von Wright in his 1963 article cannot be correct. To this I should in fairness add that von Wright no longer holds the view of practical inference expressed in his 1963 article; in his recent book *Explanation and Understanding* he has argued that the first premise of a practical inference expresses an intention rather than a mere want, and that the conclusion, 'when expressed in words, is "I shall do a (now)" or "I shall do a no later than at time t" '.[17]

If I am right that statements of wanting or wishing cannot be used, together with premisses expressing beliefs, to derive practical conclusions that commit one to certain actions, then the Aristotelian suggestion that our ends are merely things we wish for or desire cannot be correct, at least in the context of practical inference. I now want to suggest that the only kind of practical premiss that, taken together with statements expressing beliefs, can imply a practical conclusion directly committing one to act is one that expresses or formulates an intention. In connection with this suggestion observe that the only kind of answer that directly answers the practical question 'What shall I do. . .?' has the form 'I will do A'. Statements like 'I want to do A' or 'I ought to do A' or 'Doing A is the best, most reasonable thing for me to do' or even self-addressed imperatives like 'Do A!' do not *directly* answer such a practical question, because one can always ask oneself the further question 'Shall I do what I want to do?' or 'Shall I do what I ought to do?' or 'Shall I do what is the best, most reasonable thing to do?' or even 'Shall I do what I have just "told" myself to do?' Since these further questions can always meaningfully arise when the suggested answers are given to the practical question in point, those answers do not themselves imply a commitment to act. As far as I can see, the only kind of answer that allows no room for a further practical question about doing something A is 'I will do A'. This answer is an expression of intention, and it carries a *practical* commitment to act.

To say that 'I will do A' but not 'I want to do A', 'I ought to do A', or 'Doing A is the best, most reasonable thing for me to do here' carries a direct commitment to act is not to deny that these other statements may formulate *good reasons* for the action of doing A. But merely to have a good reason for doing something is not to be committed to doing it: a mere good reason may be used to justify an action, to show that it is reasonable, but it does not, in any logical sense, require one to perform that action. It can be said, of course, that a logically conclusive reason for doing something may commit one to doing it, but then desires and beliefs that something is good, reasonable, or even in some sense obligatory would not be logically conclusive reasons in the suggested sense. The grounds for this are simply that, given such reasons, the question whether to act on them can still meaningfully arise. But a reason like 'I will do A' allows no room for a question like 'Shall I do A?' to arise, because it has already answered that sort of question.

I have been concerned in this section to establish two basic points that bear upon Aristotle's account of deliberation or practical reasoning proper. The first is that we *may* deliberate about ends, at least if they are not ultimate ends. In line with this we may say that many if not most ends mentioned in the first premises of Aristotelian lines of deliberation are not ultimate ends; they are the sort of end that might naturally have been adopted as the result of prior deliberation. Thus, the physician's end of curing his patient, though 'taken for granted' in the context of his deliberation about how to treat his patient, is something that he might well deliberate about in another context — for example, in the context of deciding what to do about (or how to behave toward) some tyrant or mass murderer.

My second point is that the ends in question cannot be merely things that the agent wishes or desires to occur; to provide deductive support for a decision, which carries a commitment to act, they must be things that he *intends* to occur. If we take 'I will do A. . .' as illustrating the standard form of the premises that formulate or express intentions, we can then say that the basic practical premise that, occurring either explicitly or implicitly, properly begins a line of Aristotelian deliberation has the form of 'I will bring about such and such'.

If we take both these points into account, we can say that a line of Aristotelian deliberation may have a form as complicated as this:

(1)   I will bring about E.

(2) M_1 will bring about E.

(3) M_2 will bring about E.

(4)   Bringing about M_1 is, for me, easier or better than bringing about M_2.

(5)   So, I will bring about M_1.

(6)   I can bring about M_1 by doing A.

(7)   Doing A is something I can do here and now.

(8)   So, I will do A (here and now).

The argument just given is clearly not the most complex form of deliberation that, following Aristotle's account, we might engage in; but it is slightly more complicated than the form we previously considered in connection with his remarks quoted on page 113 above.

4. THE QUESTION OF VALIDITY

According to Aristotle, it is the mark of a practically wise man that he deliberates well rather than badly. But excellence in deliberation may be assessed in more than one way. We might consider, for example, how imaginative or ingenious a given line of deliberation is. Presumably, a practically wise person will be good at thinking up ways of achieving his ends that would not occur to a callow youth. Although Aristotle mentions other respects in which a line of deliberation may be good or bad, one stands out as particularly important — namely, its formal validity or lack of it. No matter what virtues a line of deliberation may possess, if it is not formally valid (at least implicitly) it cannot be considered good as a *form of inference*. In this respect deliberation is no different from forms of nonpractical or 'assertoric' inference.

If we look at the schema on page 113 above, which conforms to Aristotle's explicit remarks about deliberation, we can see that it must be invalid, because practical arguments of that form may have acceptable premisses but unacceptable conclusions. An example of such an argument is this:

(1)   [Would that I had enough money for a vacation next week.]
(2)   Successfully robbing a bank will give me enough money for a vacation.
(3)   Successfully murdering my rich uncle will give me enough money for a vacation.
(4)   Successfully murdering my uncle is easier or better than successfully robbing a bank.
(5)   Stabbing my uncle in the back is the only way for me to murder him.
(6)   Stabbing him in the back is something I can do.
(7)   So, I *will* stab my uncle in the back.

We cannot simply say that the argument just given is invalid for the usual reason — namely, that it, or some argument with the same form, has true premisses but a false conclusion. This would be unsatisfactory because it is doubtful that 'statements' like (1) and (7) actually possess truth-values. What we can say is that the argument is invalid because each of its premisses could be perfectly acceptable to a rational agent when the conclusion is patently unacceptable to him.

The question may arise, however: 'How do we know that a *rational* agent may find (7) unacceptable but (1) through (6) acceptable?' A precise general answer to this question cannot be given until we have a theory of validity for practical inference. The following informal remarks may nevertheless be help-ful. Note that premisses (2) and (3) describe two ways of achieving the end mentioned in (1). Although premisses (4) and (5) affirm that one of these ways is 'easier or better' than the other and that the easier or better way is something the agent can actually do, no reason is given for thinking that either of these described means is really a good one, or something that must be done if the end of taking a vacation is to be achieved. As far as these premisses are concerned, there might be some other means — say, working for a week or asking a rich indulgent aunt for a loan — that would be easier or better than either robbing a bank or killing an uncle. Furthermore, the stated means of realizing the end may very well have extremely unfortunate consequences — for instance, spending long years in prison. Thus, even though we do not yet have an account of practical validity, we can see that the argument form in question is invalid. It is objectionable on purely formal grounds.

My somewhat dogmatic claim that the argument form above is invalid would not be acceptable to all philosophers; in fact, Anthony Kenny has recently worked out a theory of practical inference according to which that form of argument is patently valid.[18] Although the logic of practical infer-ence is the topic of the following chapter, it will be useful to say something about Kenny's theory here, for the peculiarities of his theory will teach us something important about the nature of deliberation.

According to Kenny, the fundamental purpose of practical reasoning is to find satisfactory means of achieving our ends.[19] The following form of inference is fully in line with this purpose and should, he thinks, be con-sidered valid:

> I will (somehow) bring about E.
> If I do A, I shall bring about E.
> Therefore, I will do A.

It is easy to see that this form of inference is closely related to the Aristotelian form criticized above. In that form two means for achieving a given end were cited, one 'easier or better' than the other; the conclusion represented a decision to adopt the easier or better one. In the example Kenny declares to be valid, only one means of achieving the end is cited, and the conclusion represents a decision to adopt it. Both forms of inference are clearly subject to the same basic objection — namely, that although a given means is sufficient for an accepted end, it may be so objectionable in other respects that only a fool or a monster would ever decide to adopt it.

Kenny is well aware of this kind of objection, however. His strategy for avoiding it is to claim that a practical conclusion is to be regarded as satisfactory only in relation to a given set of premisses. If a set of premisses is enlarged by further practical premisses, a conclusion originally inferred could be disallowed if it conflicts with one of the new premisses. Thus, if we add to the set of premisses mentioned in the Aristotelian example a premiss like 'I won't do physical harm to my uncle', the conclusion 'So I'll stab my uncle in the back' might be disallowed. As Geach put it, Kenny's theory implies that practical inference is 'defeasible' in character; further principles can always render a practical conclusion unsatisfactory or inoperative.[20]

Before commenting critically on Kenny's theory, we should expound it in formal terms. In his view practical inference is based on a logic of satis-factoriness, which also covers imperatival inference. To formalize this general logic Kenny divides all sentences into two classes: assertoric and impera-tive.[21] Following R. M. Hare's strategy in *The Language of Morals*, Kenny claims that corresponding imperative and assertoric sentences do not differ in meaning (sense or reference) but in mood: their phrastics are the same but their neustics or 'tropics' (as Kenny calls them) differ. An assertoric sentence has the form 'Ep' and the corresponding imperative has the form 'Fp', where 'Ep' is short for 'Est-p' and 'Ep' is short for '$Fiat$-p'. The basic rule of Kenny's logic appears to be this:

$$\text{The inference} \quad \frac{Fq}{\text{So, } Fp} \quad \text{is valid in practical logic (or } P\text{-valid)}$$

just in case the corresponding inference $\dfrac{Ep}{\text{So, } Eq}$ is valid in

assertoric logic (or A-valid).

What this tells us is that a practical conclusion 'Fp' is derivable from a prac-tical premiss 'Fq' just in case the phrastic of the *premiss* (that is, 'q') is derivable, in assertoric logic, from the phrastic of the *conclusion* (that is, 'p'). This rule thus justifies practical inferences of the following simple sort:

$$\frac{F(\text{I do } A \text{ or I do } B)}{\text{So, } F(\text{I do } B)} \qquad \frac{F(\text{If I do } A, \text{ then I do } B)}{\text{So, } F(\text{I do } B)}$$

Practical inferences involving both assertoric and imperative premisses require a more complicated rule. Kenny states the rule as follows:

The assertoric premisses must be replaced by the corresponding imperative sentences: the inference is valid in imperative [or practical] logic if the goal fiat can be derived in assertoric logic from the conjunction of the other premisses and the conclusion (e.g., '*Fp*; *E* (*Cqp*); so *Fq*' is valid in practical reasoning because '*E* (*KCqpq*)' entails '*Ep*').[22]

It is easy to misunderstand this passage, for the first premiss is misleading. Kenny's idea is this:

$$
\begin{array}{ll}
& Fp \\
\text{An inference} & Eq \\
& \underline{Er} \\
& \text{So, } Fs
\end{array}
\quad \text{is } P\text{-valid just when } E\underline{(q \,.\, r \,.\, s)} \text{ is } A\text{-valid.} \\
\qquad\qquad\qquad\qquad\qquad\qquad\qquad\qquad \text{So, } Ep
$$

Thus, since '*E* (I bring about *E*)' may be derived in assertoric logic from '*E* [I do *A*. (If I do *A*, then I bring about *E*)]', the following is a valid practical inference:

$$
\begin{array}{l}
F \text{ (I bring about } E) \\
\underline{E \text{ (If I do } A, \text{ then I bring about } E)} \\
\text{So, } F \text{ (I do } A).
\end{array}
$$

One of Kenny's aims, in developing this theory, was to provide a formal justification for inferences that accord with what he regards as the fundamental purpose of practical inference – namely, that of finding satisfactory means of achieving our ends. The pattern of inference displayed immediately above accords with this aim, for it tells us that if we have an end *E* and know that doing *A* is sufficient for *E*, then we may adopt the fiat '*F* (I do *A*)'. As I mentioned earlier, however, a practical conclusion inferred this way is not acceptable absolutely; it is acceptable only in relation to the stated premisses. If those premisses are augmented by further fiats, the conclusion originally inferred may be ruled out. Formally, this requires an amendment to Kenny's rules as formulated above. We must add that a practical conclusion is inferable from a set of premisses *S* only when the phrastic of the conclusion is consistent with the phrastics of all premisses in *S*. This amendment, which Kenny clearly accepts, makes it clear that, as far as his logic is concerned, a fiat (or practical conclusion) is acceptable only in relation to a given set of premisses: we cannot detach such a conclusion from the premisses supporting it.

It seems to me that this last feature of Kenny's theory renders it seriously inadequate for the basic task of practical reasoning. This task is to locate practical conclusions that (given one's interests and so forth) are worthy of being acted upon. But the mere fact that a practical conclusion is derivable, by Kenny's logic, from premisses we accept is patently insufficient to show that it has this feature. For one thing, if a set of premisses specifies two incompatible means to a given end, Kenny's logic allows us to infer incompatible fiats. Thus, if doing A is physically incompatible with doing B, the premisses 'F (I bring about E)', 'E (I do $A \supset$ I bring about E)', and 'E (I do $B \supset$ I bring about E)' warrant both conclusions, 'F (I do A)' and 'F (I do B)'. For another thing, if a single fiat 'F (I do C)' is inferable from a set of premisses we accept, we cannot thereby accept the fiat and proceed to act on it, since it may be possible to enlarge our premiss set with a statement containing a phrastic that is inconsistent with the phrastic of that fiat. These points show that, at the very least, we need an additional practical rule for arriving at decisions (or fiats) that, *all things considered*, are worthy of being acted upon. Without such a higher order rule Kenny's logic is of little use for purposes of serious practical reasoning. Yet Kenny does not provide a rule of this kind.

There is, however, another difficulty with Kenny's theory, which ultimately bears upon the one just mentioned. Kenny believes that the logic of practical reasoning is not 'parallel' to the logic of assertoric reasoning. In his view, if an assertoric premiss 'Ep' entails an assertoric conclusion 'Eq', then the corresponding practical inference from 'Fp' to 'Fq' should *not* be considered valid. As Kenny says:

The inference from 'You will vote for the Labour candidate' to 'You will vote for somebody' is perfectly valid. Yet there seems to be something wrong with the inference from 'Vote for the Labour candidate' to 'Vote for somebody': the first exhortation has hardly been obeyed by someone who obeys the second by voting for the Conservative candidate.[23]

In accordance with his belief that valid practical inference is not parallel to valid assertoric inference, Kenny holds that inferences conforming to the following simple patterns must be declared invalid:

$$\frac{F(\text{I do } A)}{\text{So, } F(\text{I do } A \text{ or I do } B)} \qquad \frac{F(\text{I do } A \cdot \text{I do } B)}{\text{So, I do } A.}$$

The first thing to say about Kenny's contention here is that it is not well supported by his arguments. Take the passage quoted above, for example. There may be various obscurities about the logic of imperatives, but it is surely mistaken to suppose that, if imperative A implies imperative B, one who obeys B must thereby obey A as well. The truth is just the opposite. If imperative A implies imperative B, then one who obeys A must also obey B; if he does not obey B, he will not have obeyed A. Thus, if you don't vote for somebody, you will not vote for the Labour candidate. To take another example Kenny discusses: If you are required to kill all the conspirators and Brutus is one of the conspirators, you will have to kill Brutus: if you do not kill him, you will not obey the order to kill them all.

Quite apart from these examples, it seems clear that in deliberation we are constantly concerned with the question of what we *must* do if we are to realize our ends. Thus, in discussing the claims of von Wright and Gauthier we noted that the following form of practical inference must be considered valid:

> I will attain E.
> Unless I do A, I cannot attain E.
> Therefore, I will do A.

Another form of inference that is pretty obviously valid is this:

> I will do A if P.
> P.
> Therefore, I will do A.

Although it is not obvious how either of these forms of inference should be represented in Kenny's notation, it is clear that they would not count as valid patterns in his logic. For this reason alone, his logic is at best incomplete or inadequate.

The need for recognizing the validity of practical inferences corresponding to valid assertoric inferences stands out if we attend to a problem mentioned earlier. Consider the following line of reasoning:

(1) F(I take a vacation next week)

(2) E(I take a vacation next week $\supset$ I have fifty dollars).

(3) E(I steal my uncle's savings $\supset$ I have fifty dollars).

(4) E(I work hard for three days $\supset$ I have fifty dollars).

(5) E(I have fifty dollars $\supset$ either I steal my uncle's savings or I work hard for three days).

(6)   *F*(I don't steal anything belonging to my uncle).

(7)   *E*(I steal my uncle's savings ⊃ ∼ [I don't steal anything belong-
        ing to my uncle]).

(8)   Therefore, *F*(I work hard for three days).

Although some of the premisses here are perhaps questionable, the argument seems clearly valid. In fact, it is easily proved valid if we may use two practical principles corresponding to valid assertoric principles. The first is to the effect that, if doing *A* is *necessary* for *E* and *F*(*E*), then we may infer *F*(*A*); the second is that if we have the disjunctive premiss '*F*(*A* or *B*)' and the fiat '*F*(not-*B*)', we may infer '*F*(*A*)'. The first principle corresponds to *Modus Ponens*, the second to the so-called Disjunctive Syllogism. Given these principles we can infer '*F*(I steal my uncle's savings or I work hard for three days)' from premisses (1) through (5); then, together with '*F*(I don't steal my uncle's savings', which follows from (6) and (7), we may infer the conclusion (8).

If we are restricted to Kenny's principles, we cannot prove that the inference is valid. The first difficulty is that no premiss affirms something to be *sufficient* for satisfying fiat (1). Given Kenny's principles, we cannot, therefore, draw any inferences relevant to (1): it is logically unrelated to our other premisses. But suppose we enlarge our premiss set by adding the premiss, which we may not be able to defend by any inference, '*F*(I have fifty dollars)'. This new premiss, taken together with (3) and (4), allows us to move directly to the conclusion (8). Of course, this new set of premisses also allows us to adopt the alternative fiat '*F*(I steal my uncle's savings)'. Thus, although we are entitled, by Kenny's logic, to infer the conclusion (8), our deliberative problem is not fully resolved: we really have a choice between two practical conclusions, and we should consider which is preferable in view of our other information. But according to Kenny's logic, our remaining premisses – that is, (5), (6) and (7) – have no logical bearing on these alternative fiats.

Now if, in view of (6) and (7), we simply adopt – on the basis of inclination rather than logic – the fiat '*F*(I do *not* steal my uncle's savings)', we may proceed to infer '*F*(I work hard for three days)' from an enlarged set of premisses. But even though the premiss (5) tells us that one of the alternative fiats between which we have chosen *must* be satisfied if we are to satisfy our accepted higher-order fiat '*F*(I have fifty dollars)', Kenny's principles give us no basis for not contemplating further enlargements of our premiss set. Thus, even though we have done some careful thinking and have reached what is, on other principles, a fully justified conclusion, Kenny's rules provide a very uncertain basis for adopting (8): according to him, our conclusion (8) must still be regarded as essentially tentative.

Although I shall argue the point fully only in the next chapter, it seems to me that any system of practical logic that, like Kenny's, does not make a place for practical inferences corresponding to *Modus Ponens* and Disjunctive Syllogism cannot be considered satisfactory. I also think — in view, partly, of the logically tentative status of practical conclusions inferred by Kenny's rules — that his system would not be satisfactory even if it were supplemented by the principles I regard as indispensable for valid practical reasoning. A fundamentally different approach to practical inference is thus necessary, in my opinion; I shall attempt to work one out in the next chapter.

5. DELIBERATION AND CHOICE

An important question raised by my discussion of Kenny's theory can be dealt with in this chapter, however. It is this: 'If Kenny's rules are rejected, what should be said about the formal validity of practical inferences conforming to the pattern Kenny emphasized?' Consider:

> I will bring about E.
> If I do A, I shall bring about E.
> Therefore, I will do A.

Should we regard this as a valid pattern? The answer, I think, is 'No'. Arguments of this form should be regarded as simply invalid; considered as deductive inferences, they commit a fallacy corresponding to that of Affirming the Consequent.

I have said that such *inferences* are fallacious. Can transitions in thought corresponding to the above pattern be considered as anything other than inferences? The answer to this question seems to be 'Yes'. To appreciate the rationale for this answer, we must consider again the general nature of deliberation.

Throughout this section I have regarded deliberation as a process of practical inference. There is no doubt whatever that most deliberation involves practical inference, and in some cases the decision reached is a

deductive consequence of the reasons considered. The following, I believe, is
a simple case of this:

> I will pass the examination next Tuesday.
> I can pass that examination only if I study.
> So, I will study.

The deliberation exhibited here constitutes a practical argument, and the
reasons given are thus appropriately considered premises. But not all deliberation terminates in a decision that appears to be a deductive consequence
of the reasons given. Striking examples of this occur when the decision
reached represents a choice between alternatives. An agent may deliberate
about how to achieve some purpose P. Alternative courses of action come to
mind, all of which would be sufficient for realizing that purpose. One alternative may, as Aristotle put it, seem 'easier or better' than the others; and if
no better alternative comes to mind, the agent may decide to adopt that
course of action in preference to the others. Although his decision, his choice,
is clearly motivated by reasons, it seems clear that his decision is not a
deductive consequence of any reasons he actually considered. His choice
seems, in fact, to be a logically 'free' step: it accords with his preferences, but
it is not *inferred* from anything at all.

If not all decisions are actually inferred from the reasons that prompt
them, we must be careful not to interpret the 'So' in 'So, I'll do A' as an
infallible sign that an inference is being made. It is no doubt tempting to
accept such an interpretation, but we can reasonably reject it in favor of the
view that 'So, I'll do A' sometimes merely indicates that a decision is made *on
the basis* of certain reasons without thereby being deduced, or otherwise
inferred, from those reasons. We can then say that the transition in thought
from 'I will bring about E' and 'If I do A, I shall bring about E' to 'So, I will
do A' need not be interpreted as a practical *inference*; in some cases, at least,
it may be viewed as a process of making a decision 'on the basis' of certain
reasons.

To understand what making a decision *on the basis of* certain reasons
consists in, we must say something about the concept of preference. If a
person intends to bring about an end E and knows that he will bring about E
if he does something A, he should at least consider, if he is rational, whether
he prefers A to non-A. After all, apart from bringing about E, the action
A may have extremely repugnant consequences. A minimal account of

preference, which relates it to intentions, has been sketched by Wilfrid Sellars.[24] Sellars represents intentions in a canonical notion, and it will be useful to adopt his notion in explaining his ideas on preference. As I mentioned in Chapter II, a slightly stilted way of expressing an intention or volitional attitude is to use the prefix 'it shall be the case that'. We may abbreviate this prefix by the letter 'S' and regard statements of the form '$S(p)$' as meaning 'It shall be the case that p'. For purposes of our discussion, such statements will represent intentions.

According to Sellars, if an agent S prefers a state of affairs A to a state of affairs B, then, if he considers both A and B to be relevant to his interests but incapable of being jointly realized, he will intend '$S(A \& \sim B)$' if the question arises, '$S(A \& \sim B)$ or $S(B \& \sim A)$?' If, under these conditions, S does intend '$S(A \& \sim B)$', we can say that he prefers A to B. To this Sellars adds that 'S prefers A to B' is nevertheless compatible with 'S prefers $B\&C$ to $A\&C$'.[25] As given here, Sellars's account of preference is, as he himself admits, a 'thin' one − in fact, it is at best a conditional and thus a partial definition − but it provides enough logical information so that we can come to terms with some important cases of deliberation.

Suppose, to return to the case mentioned earlier, that an agent intends to bring about an end E and knows only that doing A will bring E about. To decide on an appropriate course of action, he must at least consider whether he prefers doing A to doing $\sim A$. Suppose he prefers to do A; then, given our skeletal account of preference, he will form the intention '$S(A \& \sim \sim A)$' or, equivalently, '$S(A)$'. This will count as a decision that will implement his leading intention (or purpose) 'S(I bring about E)'. Note that the intention '$S(A)$' need not be based, in any logical sense, on the leading intention 'S(I bring about E)'; the fact that it concerns an action contributing to the realization of his leading intention or purpose could be a purely accidental one. If the agent simply found the action A intrinsically preferable to $\sim A$, the decision '$S(A)$' would not in any way be derived from his purpose; we should not, that is, have a practical *inference* that makes use of the given reasons or 'premisses'. These reasons would merely lead the agent to raise a practical question, the answer to which is not derived or inferred from anything at all. To say that the decision was *based on* these reasons would only mean that they prompted the practical question that, given the agent's preferences, led to (or perhaps causally generated) that decision.

A more complicated example, where genuine practical inference undoubtedly occurs, is worth considering in this connection. Suppose that a person intends '$S(Ei)$' and realizes that the end E can be brought about by doing either B or C. (I am here using '$S(Ei)$' as short for 'S(I bring about E)'.) Suppose also that B and C are known to be the only alternatives, so that realizing '$S(Ei)$' implies doing B or doing C but not doing both together. The question therefore arises for the person: '$S(B \& \sim C)$ or $S(C \& \sim B)$?' If he prefers B to C, he will intend '$S(B \& \sim C)$', in which case his practical reasoning, made fully explicit, might take the following form:

(1) $S(Ei)$ [premiss]
(2)   'B' implies 'Ei'   [premiss]
(3)   'C' implies 'Ei'   [premiss]
(4)   'Ei' implies '$(B$ or $C) \& \sim(B \& C)$'   [premiss]
(5)   Therefore, 'Ei' implies '$(B \& \sim C)$
        or $(C \& \sim B)$'   [from 4]
(6)   Therefore, $S[(B \& \sim C)$ or $(C \& \sim B)]$.   [1, 5]
(7) $S(B \& \sim C)$ or $S(C \& \sim B)$?   [practical question]
(8) $S(B \& \sim C)$ [expression of choice]
(9)   Therefore, $S(B)$ [from 9]

There is clearly a lot of reasoning in this example and, if valid practical inference is parallel to valid assertoric inference, all of it is valid. Thus, the entire deliberation is, in a sense, valid. But there is an important gap in the inference. The interesting inferring leads to a complex intention that merely prompts a practical question, and the answer given to this question is logically unsupported by anything stated in the premisses. As far as the preceding steps in the deliberation are concerned, the choice (8) could have been evoked by a momentary preference that is ill-considered or even positively irrational. Since the final conclusion, or decision, is inferred from this possibly questionable premiss, the actual inference supporting that conclusion is no more complicated that this:

$$\frac{S(B \& \sim C)}{\text{So}, S(B).}$$

The questionable status of step (8) leads to an important question: Under what conditions are statements of the form '$S(p)$' rationally justified? One condition under which they are justified, at least if writers like Sellars are correct, is when they are validly derivable from other S-statements.[26] This kind of justification is, of course, relative or conditional: if '$S(p)$' is validly inferred from '$S(q)$', then '$S(p)$' is justified only if '$S(q)$' is justified. Since the question whether '$S(q)$' is justified can be raised in just the way that the question about '$S(p)$' was raised, it appears that we are faced with two alternatives: Either (a) S-statements can be validly derived from statements other than S-statements — for example, from indicative premises that need no practical justification — or (b) S-statements can be justified *at least in some cases* without deriving them from anything at all. All things considered, alternative (b) seems the most promising.

As we have seen, Aristotle held that some end must always be 'taken for granted' in deliberation. He also held that all rational beings have a single ultimate end that can serve as a first principle for all their practical inference — the end, roughly, of being happy. Evidently, this fundamental end can have no practical justification, in his view, for he seems to have held that a practical justification is nothing other than a proof that something contributes toward this end. Many philosophers have seriously doubted that we all have one fundamental end, and some have even doubted that there is any end we all have or even that we ourselves have throughout our lives. For my part, these doubts are well founded, and the idea that most lower-level intentions (or ends) are justifiable only because they are derivable from one or more fundamental intentions (or ends) that cannot themselves be justified strikes me as mistaken.

Wilfrid Sellars has argued that there is a form of practical reasoning in which we adopt ends, or fairly high-level intentions, without actually inferring them from more fundamental intentions.[27] He distinguishes two stages to such reasoning. If an agent is concerned to decide whether he will bring about an end E that he values, the first stage of his reasoning is to consider the available means of bringing it about. Suppose that he concludes that E can be realized only by bringing about M by performing a minimal action A. The next stage in his reasoning is to consider whether the complex state of affairs $A\&M\&E$ is preferable to $\sim A\&\sim M\&\sim E$. Although he values E, he may find M or even A objectionable. He therefore raises the practical question '$S(A\&M\&E)$ or $S(\sim A\&\sim M\&\sim E)$?' If the first state of affairs is preferable, he will intend '$S(A\&M\&E)$', which will enable him to conclude that $S(A)$, $S(M)$, and $S(E)$. The minimal intention '$S(A)$' is, in this case, 'motivated' by the end E, but '$S(E)$' is not actually adopted prior to ascertaining the acceptability of '$S(A)$' itself.

The importance of viewing certain forms of deliberation this way becomes apparent if we consider the vague notion of wanting. Although some philosophers have interpreted simple cases of practical reasoning as sometimes having the form 'I want E; E can be achieved only by doing A; therefore, I will do A', the relation between wants and rational action is, as we have seen, considerably less direct. In any normal sense of the word 'want', a person may want many things he has no intention of pursuing. Not only may wants conflict with wants, but they may conflict with well-considered intentions to act. No matter how strongly a rational person may want something, the question can (indeed, should) always arise: 'Shall I take steps to satisfy my want?' In settling such a question he should first consider the consequences of acting in various ways to satisfy his want. The identification of these consequences corresponds to what Sellars calls 'the first stage' of rational deliberation. The second or 'summative' stage involves bringing the relevant alternative courses of action together to be evaluated as wholes. The question may then be asked: 'Shall I bring about this complex state of affairs or shall I bring about that one?' To answer this question is to *decide* what to do; it is to choose a course of action. The result of such deliberation is not a mere want but a settled intention to act.

In spite of the interest of this form of reasoning as a contrast to the kind discussed by Aristotle and others, it is clear (a) that its inferential structure is extremely simple and (b) that it turns on a choice that, as far as anything explicitly contained in the reasoning is concerned, is purely capricious. The logical structure of the reasoning can be represented as follows:

(1)   I value E (to a certain degree x)
(2)   Realizing E implies realizing M, and realizing M implies doing A.
(3) $S(E\&M\&A)$ or $S(\sim E\&\sim M\&\sim A)$?   [practical question]
(4) $S(E\&M\&A)$ [choice]
(5)   Therefore, $S(A)$.

The statements (1) and (2) do not really function as premises from which the conclusion (5) is ultimately derived; they merely serve to raise a practical question. Since (4) is not supported by anything in the argument, it is logically capricious; and the only actual inference in the argument is the trivial move from (4) to (5).

This brings us back to the question of how a step like (4) can be justified.

One way of answering this is to appeal to the principle of so-called Bayesian Deliberation.

6. BAYESIAN DELIBERATION

In the argument just considered the premisses (1) and (2) have no evident *logical* bearing on the acceptability of the choice (4). But, clearly, they are relevant to its acceptability. If the agent were to defend his choice without trying to deduce it from some higher-order intention, he might well emphasize that he valued E, that he thought he could realize E only by doing A, and that, all things considered, he preferred the state of affairs $E\&M\&A$ to the alternative $\sim E\&\sim M\&\sim A$. Even though these reasons do not, as a matter of formal logic, warrant the inference of (4), it seems obvious that there is some *normative* relation between these reasons and (4) by virtue of which (4) is justifiably adopted. The basic principle of Bayesian deliberation specifies such a relation.[28] One way of formulating the principle is to say that, relatively speaking, an agent is justified in performing any action in circumstances C that has, for him in C, *maximum expected desirability* or *MED*. To understand this principle we must understand what is meant by 'maximum expected desirability'.

The *MED* of an action A for an agent S in circumstances C depends fundamentally on three things: (a) the agent's assessment of the desirability of doing A in C relative to the desirability of what he regards as appropriate alternative actions; (b) the agent's view of the consequences of the action A and its alternatives, and his estimate of the relative desirability of these consequences; and (c) the agent's beliefs about various conditions or contingencies that bear upon the consequences of the actions he regards as his alternatives. Since the *MED* of an action thus depends on the agent's subjective estimate of his practical situation, his justification for intending to perform such an action (or for performing it) is essentially relative. An inference from 'Doing A has, for me, *MED*' to 'S(I do A)' is, we may grant, a justifiable one, but the premiss may be based on what we regard as a poor estimate of the situation, and the action of doing A may be incompatible with moral or other standards that we hold but that the agent rejects. Since my concern in this chapter is with the justification of intentions relative to the interests and so forth of a given agent, I shall not try to consider what may be deemed relevant to the assessment of an intention as 'absolutely speaking justifiable'.

Let us consider a case where an agent has raised the practical question '$S(A\&\sim B)$ or $S(B\&\sim A)$?' but where he has no available premises from which to *deduce* an appropriate answer. More specifically, suppose that the agent is a philosopher who is committed to giving a lecture in Chicago on a certain day, and that he is trying to decide whether to take the train or take an airplane: he believes that adopting one of these alternatives is necessary for arriving in Chicago at the proper time. His task is to determine which of these alternative acts has *MED*. If their expected desirability should turn out, on examination, to be the same (an unlikely outcome), he could on Bayesian grounds do either with equal justification; if their expected desirability is unequal, one of the acts will have *MED* (since there are only two alternatives). He will then choose the one with *MED*.

Now, the desirability of both alternatives is likely to depend, for the agent, on various contingencies. If he is an experienced traveler, the desirability of taking the plane is certain to depend on the weather conditions at the Chicago airport.[29] If the airport is fogged in, he can expect a substantial delay in landing: he will no doubt have to spend a tedious time circling the field. On the basis of his available information about flight delays, we might construct a *desirability matrix* that will allow him to compute the relative desirability of taking the plane or taking the train depending on the weather conditions in Chicago. A simple matrix of this kind will have the following form:

$$\begin{array}{c} \\ \text{Plane} \\ \text{Train} \end{array} \overset{\displaystyle \text{Good weather} \qquad\qquad \text{Bad weather}}{\begin{bmatrix} \quad - \quad & \quad - \quad \\ \quad - \quad & \quad - \quad \end{bmatrix}}$$

If the man is able to estimate how desirable he expects taking the plane in good weather to be, how desirable it would be to take it in bad weather, and how desirable it would be to take the train under both conditions, he might represent these estimated desirabilities by numerical values – taking 1 to represent the highest degree of desirability and 0 to represent the lowest degree. He might, then, fill in the above matrix as follows:

$$\begin{array}{c} \\ \text{Plane} \\ \text{Train} \end{array} \overset{\displaystyle \text{Good weather in Chicago} \quad \text{Bad weather in Chicago}}{\begin{bmatrix} \quad 0.9 \quad & \quad 0.2 \quad \\ \quad 0.4 \quad & \quad 0.3 \quad \end{bmatrix}}$$

Although this matrix may represent the *desirability* of either proposed action depending on the weather at the Chicago airport, it does not represent the *estimated desirability* of the outcomes, because it does not take into account the agent's expectations about the weather. To deal with these expectations, we must construct another matrix, called a 'probability matrix'. Suppose the agent thinks that the chances of having bad weather in Chicago are (at that time of year) 7 out of 10. Since this probability is, as he supposes, independent of either envisaged mode of travel, his probability matrix will have the same entries for either act:

$$
\begin{array}{c}
 & \text{Good weather in Chicago} & \text{Bad weather in Chicago} \\
\text{Plane} & 0.3 & 0.7 \\
\text{Train} & 0.3 & 0.7
\end{array}
$$

To compute the *expected desirability* of each outcome, the corresponding entries of both matrices are multiplied together. The results are as follows:

$$
\begin{array}{c}
 & \text{Good weather...} & \text{Bad weather...} \\
\text{Plane} & (0.9)(0.3) = 0.27 & (0.2)(0.7) = 0.14 \\
\text{Train} & (0.4)(0.3) = 0.12 & (0.3)(0.7) = 0.21
\end{array}
$$

To determine the expected desirability of each act, add the figures representing the expected desirability of each outcome of each act. For example, the ED of taking the plane is equal, in the case considered, to the ED of taking the plane when the weather is bad in Chicago plus the ED of taking it when the weather there is good. Simple computation shows that the ED of each act is as follows:

Plane: $0.27 + 0.14 = 0.41$
Train: $0.12 + 0.21 = 0.33$.

Since the ED of taking the plane is higher than that of taking the train, the principle of Bayesian deliberation requires the agent to choose the former alternative.

I have used the principle of Bayesian deliberation to deal with an extremely simple practical problem, but it is clear that the principle will allow us to deal with problems of great complexity. I shall not consider any really difficult cases, or cases where the agent cannot make the kind of desirability and probability estimates illustrated by the case I have given. My interest is in the basic structure of deliberation, and the refinements of Bayesian decision theory can be studied elsewhere.[30]

My claim has been that the principle of Bayesian deliberation can be used to justify decisions (or S-statements) even when those decisions cannot be deduced from other decisions, or intentions, that the agent accepts. But what shall we say about the following inference, which might come at the end of a line of deliberation in which the question 'S(I do A) or S(I do B)?' is raised:

(1)   Doing A has, for me in these circumstances, MED.

(2)   Therefore, S(I do A in these circumstances)?

Can we regard this inference as logically valid? The answer, I think, is 'No'. If we regard the principle of Bayesian deliberation as acceptable, then *we* can maintain that an agent adopting premiss (1) is *rationally entitled* to the practical conclusion (2). But if someone does not accept the Bayesian principle, his acceptance of (1) would in no way commit him to (2): if he disavows (2) while accepting (1), he might strike us as a stupid or peculiar man, but he would not be logically inconsistent.

How might we represent a commitment to the Bayesian principle? One way of doing it is to adopt Wilfrid Sellars's treatment of what he calls 'action on policy'.[31] According to Sellars, to have a rational policy of doing a certain kind of thing in a certain kind of circumstance is to have the disposition or propensity to form conditional intentions that accord with that policy. If, in line with this, one has the policy of deliberating in accordance with the Bayesian principle, one would have the propensity to form conditional intentions of which the following is a representative example:

(BI)   I will do A in C if doing A has, for me in C, MED.

Together with this conditional intention ('BI' abbreviates 'Bayesian Intention'), the premiss 'Doing A has, for me in C, MED' will *logically imply* the conclusion 'I will do A in C' if, as I have contended, the following form of inference is logically valid:

I will do A if P.

P

Therefore, I will do A.

In the next chapter I shall offer detailed reasons why this form of inference should be regarded as logically valid.

The principle of Bayesian deliberation thus provides a means of eliminating the logical gap in practical inferences of the kind Sellars discusses. If a person has the policy of deliberating in accordance with the Bayesian principle, he will have another intention or S-premiss that will enable him to deduce S-conclusions from premisses concerning his assessment of the relative desirability of the courses of action open to him. If he does not have such a policy, he will not (I assume) be able to derive any S-conclusions from his beliefs about what courses of action are maximally desirable, but if he chooses to do what in fact has, for him in his circumstances, *MED*, then *we* may regard his choice as a reasonable one to make. Thus, even choices that are, logically speaking, capricious in the sense of being unsupported by a valid practical inference may still be justifiable if they are formed when the agent has made, or might well have made, a suitable assessment of his practical situation.

In line with this, the principle also provides an answer to the general question raised earlier of how an intention or S-statement may be rationally justified if it cannot be validly derived from some more fundamental intention the agent already has. The answer, roughly and in brief, is that an intention may be regarded as rationally justifiable if it stands in a suitable relation to the agent's desires and beliefs.

It is worth considering in this connection a significant analogy between the justification of an intention and the justification of a belief. In both cases justification can be provided by inference — that is, one may justify a belief by validly deriving it from some other accepted belief, and one may justify an intention by deriving it from some other intention. This kind of justification is, of course, relative: the conclusion is shown to be acceptable only on the assumption that the premiss is acceptable. Since the acceptability of the premiss may be questioned in turn, it is tempting to suppose that, if any belief or intention is ultimately justifiable, some belief or intention must be self-justifying.[32] It seems to me, however, that this temptation is thoroughly misguided: beliefs and intentions, no matter what their character or subject matter, are *never* self-justifying.[33]

My view here does not have the consequence that beliefs and intentions are not ultimately justifiable; it merely implies that a belief or intention may be justifiable without being justified by some other belief or intention.[34] This claim seems obvious: after all, 'justifiable' does not mean 'justified'. Of course, if something is justifiable, it must be capable of justification; but to give a justification for something, we do not actually have to justify every premiss we use in our justification: it is generally sufficient to use premisses known to be justifi*able*. I might add to this that a person can be said to know something, or be justified in believing it, even when *he* cannot justify what he knows or believes. In the case of elementary beliefs such as 'That is a dog', one can be justified in holding them by virtue, essentially, of having been taught to identify the appropriate objects by competent people. When this condition is met, one's belief might be justifiable even if one *cannot* offer any reasonable justification for one's belief. The ability to give a justification requires a skill that all knowers need not possess; in some cases, at least, a person's belief may be considered justified merely by virtue of the relation it bears to the person's past training (or past 'experience') and to the situation that evokes it. On analogy with this, certain intentions may be considered justified merely by virtue of the relation they bear to a person's beliefs and desires. If they stand in the appropriate Bayesian relation to such beliefs and desires, then he is justified in having them, whether he can offer any justification for them or not.

7.   CONCLUDING REMARKS

I have been concerned in this section with the basic structure of deliberation or practical reasoning. The distinctive feature of such reasoning is that it terminates in a decision or choice rather than in a statement of fact. I have argued that a decision may or may not be deduced from the premisses employed. When it is not so deduced − as in cases where the decision is a choice − there is no question of the reasoning being formally valid, but the conclusion may nevertheless be warranted, or rendered acceptable, by the premisses. My contention was that such reasoning may be evaluated by the principles of Bayesian decision theory. When, on the other hand, the conclusion of a line of deliberation is deduced, or deducible, from the premisses, the reasoning may be considered formally valid. In the next chapter I shall be specifically concerned with the basic principles of formally valid practical reasoning.

NOTES

[1]   Aristotle, *Nichomachean Ethics*, trans. Martin Ostwald (New York, 1962), 1147a,

p. 183.
2 For references and discussion, see W. F. R. Hardie, *Aristotle's Ethical Theory* (Oxford, 1968), pp. 240–257.
3 Aristotle, 1112b-1113a; Ostwald, pp. 61f.
4 *Ibid.*, 1113a, pp. 62f.
5 *Ibid.*
6 *Ibid.*
7 See Hardie, p. 163.
8 *Ibid.*, p. 170.
9 Richard Taylor, *Action and Purpose* (Englewood Cliffs, N.J., 1966), p. 76.
10 Aristotle, 1112b; p. 61.
11 *Ibid.*, 1111b; p. 59.
12 *Ibid.*, 1113a; p. 63.
13 As Castañeda calls it; see his *The Structure of Morality* (Springfield, Ill., 1974), p. 36. G. E. M. Anscombe's discussion of mistakes in performance rather than in thought is relevant to what I am calling 'practical inconsistency'; see her *Intention* (Oxford, 1958), pp. 56f.
14 G. H. von Wright, 'Practical Inference', *Philosophical Review* 72 (1963), p. 172.
15 *Ibid.*, pp. 168f.
16 David Gauthier, 'Comments', in Robert Binkley *et al.*, *Agent, Action, and Reason* (Toronto, 1971), p. 104.
17 G. H. von Wright, *Explanation and Understanding* (Ithaca, N.Y., 1971), p. 229.
18 Anthony Kenny, 'Practical Inference', *Analysis* 26 (1966), 65-73.
19 *Ibid.*, p. 67.
20 P. T. Geach, 'Dr. Kenny on Practical Inference', *Analysis* 26 (1966), pp. 76f.
21 Within the class of imperatives Kenny distinguishes fiats from directives. The logic he proposes is meant to apply only to fiats; directives evidently have a more complicated logic. See pp. 68f.
22 *Ibid.*, p. 75.
23 *Ibid.*, p. 67.
24 Wilfrid Sellars, 'Thought and Action', in Keith Lehrer (ed.), *Freedom and Determinism* (New York, 1966), pp. 113–117.
25 *Ibid.* Sellars adds a qualification to his definition of '*S* prefers *A* to *B*', which I have not discussed, and he also defines two additional concepts pertaining to preference.
26 *Ibid.*, pp. 110f. Sellars's view is discussed in detail in the next chapter.
27 *Ibid.*, pp. 131–138.
28 See Richard Jeffrey, *The Logic of Decision* (New York, 1965), Ch. 1.
29 The following example is similar to one discussed by Jeffrey; see *ibid.*
30 A very useful book is Howard Raiffa, *Decision Analysis: Introductory Lectures on Choices Under Uncertainty* (Menlo Park, Calif., 1970). A textbook covering a larger field is R. Duncan Luce and Howard Raiffa, *Games and Decisions* (New York, 1957).
31 See Sellars, 'Thought and Action', pp. 136ff.
32 See R. M. Chisholm, 'Theory of Knowledge', in Chisholm *et al.*, *Philosophy* (Englewood Cliffs, N.J., 1964), pp. 232–344. See especially pp. 261–275.
33 See my book, *Rationalism, Empiricism, and Pragmatism* (New York, 1970), pp. 141–153.
34 See my article, 'Remarks on an Argument by Chisholm', *Philosophical Studies* 23 (1972), 327–334.

Chapter IV

THE LOGIC OF PRACTICAL REASONING

The aim of this chapter is to clarify the formal logic appropriate for practical reasoning. Several theories of practical reasoning have been proposed in recent years, of which Kenny's theory, discussed in the last chapter, is a representative example. Although in criticizing Kenny's theory I raised no doubts about the need for a special logic, involving special operators like Kenny's 'Fiat(. . .)', I shall argue that practical reasoning can be interpreted as requiring no more than ordinary 'assertoric' first-order logical principles. My view here is not based on general considerations or on philosophical ideology. I think there is a good *prima facie* case for a special logic of practical inference, and any dissenting view, such as mine, requires careful, detailed defense. I shall therefore proceed by considering important alternative views and develop my own position in the process of criticizing them.

1. SELLARS'S THEORY OF PRACTICAL INFERENCE

One of my principal objections to Kenny's theory was that, according to it, valid practical inferences do not correspond to valid assertoric inferences. In opposition to this idea, I contended that certain intuitively valid practical inferences do correspond to valid assertoric inferences. In particular, I contended that, given Kenny's notation, we should at least count the following argument forms as valid:

$$F(A \text{ or } B) \qquad\qquad \underline{F(A \& B)}$$
$$\underline{F(\sim\!A)} \qquad\qquad\quad \text{So}, F(A).$$
$$\text{So}, F(B).$$

A distinctive feature of Sellars's system is that *all* valid practical inferences correspond to valid assertoric inferences. For this reason alone, Sellars's system seems highly promising.

In line with what I have been arguing in the past couple of chapters, Sellars contends that the logic of practical inference is essentially a logic of intentions. Basic practical premisses are, for him, expressions of intention, and he represents them in the canonical notion I used (somewhat carelessly) in presenting his ideas on preference. Although I have spoken mainly of intentions to *do* this or that, it seems obvious that one may also intend *that* something be the case or *that* a certain state of affairs obtain. The object of this latter kind of intention is not, in general, an action on one's part, but it always implicitly involves the idea of such an action. Thus, to intend that one's children are properly educated is at least to intend to do what one deems necessary for their proper education. Since the intention to *do A* can be interpreted as the intention *that* one does *A*, all intentions can be expressed or formulated by a single canonical form.[1] In this early work, at least, Sellars represented this form by 'SHALL (*P*)', but I shall represent it by the simpler '*S(P)*', which I shall understand to mean 'It shall be the case that *P*'.[2]

According to Sellars, statements of the form '*S(P)*' are neither true nor false.[3] He holds this view because *S*-statements express intentions. If a person says, using grammarian's English, 'I *will* study this afternoon', he expresses the intention of studying in the afternoon. If he does not study in the afternoon, it would be odd to say that his intention was false; a more natural way of speaking would be to say that his intention was not *realized* or *fulfilled*. The fact that we do not think of intentions as true or false places certain restrictions, Sellars thinks, on the allowable form of *S*-statements. For one thing, an *S*-statement cannot, he contends, have an external negation: a sentence like '∼*S(P)*' is ill-formed. If a person who had the intention of doing *A* changed his mind and formed a contrary intention, he might think 'I won't do *A*', and this latter statement should be formulated as '*S(∼A)*', for the person would have an intention — namely that of *not* doing *A*. In expounding Sellars's theory I shall say that *S*-statements have *incompatible counterparts* rather than negations. The incompatible counterpart of '*S(P)*' is '*S(∼P)*'. Such statements clearly have incompatible semantic values: if the first is realized or fulfilled, the second is unrealized or unfulfilled, and *vice versa*.

Another limitation on *S*-statements, for Sellars, is that they cannot meaningfully be joined to other statements by the familiar connectives 'or', 'and', 'if...then...', and 'if and only if'.[4] Sellars's reason for this, evidently, is that the connectives, as we currently understand them, connect statements having truth-values; they express 'truth functions'. If '*S(P)*' does not have a truth-value, then '*Q* or *S(P)*' would not, given our current understanding of the connective 'or', make clear sense. Of course, we do commonly say such things as 'I *will* do *A* or I *will* do *B*', and it may be tempting, therefore, to define generic connectives that would assign an appropriate semantic value to a compound depending on the semantic values of the constituent statements. Although Sellars has not, to my knowledge, explicitly commented on this idea, he would presumably reject it on the grounds (a) that introducing such generic connectives would require an unnecessary complication of our basic logic, and (b) that the content of such claims as 'I *will* do *A* or I *will* do *B*' does not seem to differ from that of 'I *will* do *A* or *B*', where this is understood to mean '*S*(I shall do *A* or I shall do *B*)'. As for mixed cases like 'I will do *A* or grass is green', Sellars would presumably contend that they do not make clear sense anyway — at least on any straightforward reading.

This brings me to the subject of what *S*-statements imply, or what may validly be derived from them. According to Sellars, the implications of *S*-statements are all based on a single axiom, which may be formulated as follows:

$$\text{`}S(P)\text{' implies `}S(Q)\text{' just when `}P\text{' implies `}Q\text{'.}$$

Although I have expressed the axiom as a biconditional, it is more perspicuously expressed, Sellars contends, as a third-level principle telling us that the metalinguistic statement ' "*S*(P)" implies "*S*(Q)" ' implies and is implied by the metalinguistic statement ' "*P*" implies "*Q*" '. Concerning this axiom Sellars says:

There is. . .no need for a special 'logic of intentions' other than that formulated by the third-level principle [just given]. . .together with certain conceptual truths about the function of 'shall'.[5]

Since he also says 'I am so using "implies" that "*P* implies *Q*" is equivalent to "*Q* may be inferred from *P*" ', his idea is that a statement of the form '*S*(Q)' may be inferred from one of the form '*S*(P)' just in case the corresponding indicative of the form '*Q*' may be inferred from the corresponding indicative of the form '*P*'. To put it in another way:

$$\frac{S(P)}{\text{So, } S(Q)} \text{ is valid just when } \frac{P}{\text{So, } Q} \text{ is valid.}$$

It is clear that, according to Sellars's conception of practical inference, every valid practical inference corresponds to a valid assertoric inference. In fact, his conception implies that a necessary and sufficient condition for a practical inference to be valid is that a corresponding assertoric inference is valid. This means two things. First, to discover whether a given practical inference from '$S(P)$' to '$S(Q)$' is valid, we have only to consider whether a corresponding inference from the indicative 'P' to the indicative 'Q' is valid. If this latter inference is valid, then we know that the practical inference is valid. But we also know, and this is the second important point, that if the inference from the indicative premiss to the indicative conclusion is *not* valid, then the corresponding practical inference is *not* valid either. Thus, if Sellars is right, ordinary assertoric inference is both necessary and sufficient for evaluating *every* inference from an S-premiss to an S-conclusion. This seems to imply that, for Sellars, the logic of practical reasoning is entirely deriva- tive from the ordinary logic of indicatives; in a sense, at least, it does not really constitute a distinct or separate subject.

Since I too want to contend that there is no distinct subject of practical reasoning, it might appear that Sellars's approach ought to be acceptable to me. But Sellars's particular account involves complications and obscurities that distinguish it from the view I accept.

The first complication is owing to Sellars's use of 'implies'. As I pointed out, Sellars uses 'P implies Q' as meaning 'Q may be inferred from P'. Since principles of inference may, for him, be material as well as formal, he conceives of implication in a very broad sense. As far as indicatives are concerned, he uses 'implies' as a general term to cover logical or formal implication in the narrow sense, causal or physical implication, and some- times even related forms of dependent implication.[6] As we shall see, this very broad use of the term 'implies' raises serious doubts about the soundness of his axiom and about its adequacy for a complete (though admittedly derivative) logic of intentions.

Since Sellars wishes to include causal implications within the scope of his axiom, it is natural, at least initially, to think of ' "P" implies$_i$ "Q" ' (where 'implies$_i$' represents the relation between indicatives) as having the intuitive sense that in any causally possible world 'Q' is true if 'P' is true. As far as intentions are concerned, this would have the consequence that '$S(Q)$' is inferable from '$S(P)$' just in case 'Q' is true whenever (causally speaking) 'P' is true. Although Sellars insists that S-statements, being canonical expressions of intentions, are neither true nor false, they must have some semantic values that, by virtue of his axiom, have a *systematic* relation to truth and falsity.

If we interpret 'implies$_n$' in the way suggested, this relation is easy to specify. Normally, we think of intentions as being realized (fulfilled) or unrealized (unfulfilled) rather than as true or false. Since S-statements express intentions, it is thus natural to think of them as having the values R (for realized) and U (for unrealized). These values have an obvious relation to truth and falsity: 'S(I shall go skiing)' is realized just in case 'I shall go skiing' is true; and it is unrealized just in case 'I shall go skiing' is false. This suggests that ' "$S(P)$" implies$_n$ "$S(Q)$" ' (where 'implies$_n$' refers to the implication relation between intentions) just in case '$S(Q)$' is realized in any causally possible world in which '$S(P)$' is realized. If this interpretation is accepted, then to say that one intention implies another is only to say that if the first intention is realized, the second is realized as well − it is not to say or even suggest that if someone *has* the first intention, he must also *have* the second intention.

But is this interpretation of ' "$S(P)$" implies$_n$ "$S(Q)$" ' really plausible? Is it, in other words, an acceptable interpretation of the relation we have in mind (however dimly) when we say that one intention implies another? I myself think it is, though it will turn out that the idea is controversial. To conceive of implication$_n$ this way is to conceive of the logic of intentions as a logic of realization. Kenny, we may recall, conceived of practical logic as a logic of satisfactoriness, the aim of which is to find a satisfactory means of realizing our ends. According to the present conception, the aim or practical logic is to discover what *must* be done if our ends are to be realized. Thus, if we have the end '$S(P)$', then if 'P' implies$_i$ 'Q', our end can be realized only if the end '$S(Q)$' is realized − only if, that is, the indicative 'Q' is true. If 'Q' means 'I shall do A', then our leading intention in this case can be realized only if we (that is, I) do A − or, in other words, only if the derivative intention 'S(I shall do A)' is realized. Since, given the implication$_i$ between 'P' and 'Q', the intention 'S(I shall do A)' *must* be realized if the end '$S(P)$' is realized, the implication$_n$ between '$S(P)$' and 'S(I shall do A)' *gives us a good reason* for adopting the latter intention. This accords nicely with the pragmatics of valid inference: If 'C' is inferable from 'P' and we have 'P' as a premiss, we have a good reason for accepting the conclusion 'C'.

Another consideration in favor of the suggested interpretation of 'implication$_n$' is this. If '$S(P)$' implies$_n$ '$S(Q)$', then anyone who intended '$S(P)$' would be inconsistent if he intended anything inconsistent with '$S(Q)$'. As we have seen, Sellars contends that S-statements do not have external negations; for him, the 'denial' of '$S(P)$' is '$S(\sim P)$'. Given this, we must say that, if '$S(P)$' implies$_n$ '$S(Q)$', anyone who intended '$S(P)$' and '$S(\sim Q)$' would be inconsistent in the relevant sense. But under what conditions, intuitively speaking, should two *intentions* be considered inconsistent? The answer would seem to be that they have this property just in case they *cannot* be jointly realized. Thus, the set of formulas { '($S(P)$', '$S(\sim Q)$'} is (logically or causally) inconsistent just in case the set { 'P', '$\sim Q$'} is (logically or causally) inconsistent. But this latter set is inconsistent just in case 'P' implies$_i$ 'Q'. Consequently, 'P' implies$_i$ 'Q' under precisely the same conditions as '$S(P)$' implies$_n$ '$S(Q)$', which is exactly as it should be if Sellars's axiom is true.

Although Sellars's axiom is clearly acceptable on the interpretation just given, it does not seem adequate, on that interpretation, for a complete logic of intentions. For one thing, it merely allows us to deduce S-consequences from single premises. Obviously, however, inferences of the following sort should be considered valid:

$S(P)$	$S(P \lor Q)$	$S(P)$
$S(Q)$	$S(\sim P)$	$S(\sim(P \,\&\, Q))$
$S(P \,\&\, Q)$	$S(Q)$	$S(\sim Q)$

To validate these inferences we must reformulate Sellars's axiom so that an intention may be derived from any number of S-premises. It is very easy to do this, however. We need only say:

'$S(P_i)$',...,'$S(P_n)$' implies$_n$ '$S(C)$' just when 'P_1',...,'P_n' implies$_i$ 'C'.

As reformulated, the axiom is capable of exactly the same kind of justification as before.

Another inadequacy in Sellars's axiom is that, even as reformulated, it does not seem adequate to validate inferences involving conditional intentions. A simple pattern of reasoning whose validity Sellars insists upon is this:

I *will* do A if P.
P.
So, I *will* do A.

Sellars does not regard this simple inference as logically basic; he contends that it is derivable from his fundamental axiom. Yet that axiom (at least as I have interpreted it) makes no provision for practical inferences having mixed premises. It tells us that we can derive S-statements from a set of premises consisting of S-statements, but it does not tell us that we can derive an S-statement from a set of premises consisting of both S-statements and indicatives, where the indicatives are essential to the inference.

In spite of this Sellars offers a derivation of the pattern above from his axiom.[7] His first step is to interpret the conditional intention 'I *will* do A if P' as '$S(P \supset$ I shall do $A)$', which may be read 'It shall be the case that if P, I shall do A'. His aim is then to show that inferences of the canonical pattern

$$S(P \supset \text{I shall do } A)$$
$$\underline{P}$$
$$\text{Therefore, } S(\text{I shall do } A)$$

can be validated by his axiom. His next step is to introduce the concept of dependent implication, or implication relative to an assumption. According to this concept,

$$X \text{ implies } Y \text{ relative to } A \textit{ iff } X \& A \text{ implies } Y.$$

With this concept in hand Sellars then argues that since '$P \supset$ I shall do A' implies 'I shall do A' (relative to 'P'), we may conclude from his axiom that '$S(P \supset$ I shall do $A)$' implies '$S(\text{I shall do } A)$' relative to 'P'. But this last relative implication is true just in case 'P' and '$S(P \supset$ I shall do $A)$' independently imply '$S(\text{I shall do } A)$'. In view of Sellars's reading of 'X implies Y' as 'Y may be inferred from X' we must therefore agree, he thinks, that the pattern of practical inference in question is valid.

If this derivation is to be acceptable, the 'implies' of Sellars's axiom must cover dependent implication as well as independent logical and causal implication. The justification I gave for his axiom is not applicable, however, when 'implies' is interpreted so broadly. The question thus arises: 'Is his axiom really acceptable when "implies" is understood in this broad sense?' It seems to me that the answer to this question is far from obvious. To see this, note that his axiom will now allow us to derive the following questionable forms, where 'Q' stands in place of an appropriate future-tense indicative:[8]

$$\text{I} \quad \frac{\begin{array}{c} S(P) \\ P \supset Q \end{array}}{Q} \qquad \text{II} \quad \frac{\begin{array}{c} P \\ S(P \supset Q) \end{array}}{Q} \qquad \text{III} \quad \frac{\begin{array}{c} S(P) \\ P \supset Q \end{array}}{S(Q)}$$

If these forms are not regarded as valid (and they certainly do not look valid, at least *prima facie*) then Sellars's axiom cannot be regarded as valid when 'implies' has the broad sense in question.

Since the form Sellars wishes to validate – namely,

$$\text{IV} \quad \frac{P}{S(P \supset Q)}, \text{ where '} Q \text{' is an appropriate indicative –}$$
$$S(Q)$$

cannot be derived from his axiom unless his 'implies' covers dependent implication, it follows that Sellars is confronted with an important choice: He must either accept the forms I, II and III as valid, or he must restrict his 'implies' to independent implication and then find some other means of validating the form IV. It is not clear which choice he is prepared to make, since both alternatives can be supported by various things he has said.

Consider form III, for example. Although Sellars has not, to my knowledge, commented directly on this form, it would appear that he would want to reject it in view of his treatment of a class of arguments that might be taken as instances of it. The following schematic argument, which might have 'Unless I do A, I can't bring about E', 'If I am to bring about E, I must do A', or 'A necessary condition of my bringing about E is that I do A' in place of premiss (2), illustrates my point:

(1)   I *will* bring about E.
(2)   I can bring about E only by doing A.
(3)   Therefore, I *will* do A.

To validate arguments of this kind Sellars interprets premiss (2) as a causal implication.[9] Put in canonical form, the argument schema thus becomes:

(1') S(I shall bring about E).
(2')   'I shall bring about E' implies 'I shall do A'.
(3')   Therefore, S(I shall do A).

Since, by virtue of premiss (2), the indicative corresponding to (1') causally implies the indicative corresponding to (3'), the argument may be validated by his original axiom. Evidently, it is because of arguments of this kind that he wishes his sense of 'implies' to cover what he calls 'causal implications'.

Premiss (2) as well as the related statements I mentioned above are, of course, modal statements that are logically stronger than mere material conditionals. In applying truth-functional logic, however, we are frequently able to render such statements by material conditionals and thereby validate many familiar arguments containing them. If we could do the same for the arguments above, we could simplify our system of practical logic and define practical validity without reference to causal possibilities. Since Sellars does not interpret premiss (2) as a material conditional and attempt to validate the inference as an instance of the form III, the presumption is that he does not think of this form as valid. If so, he should reject any interpretation of his axiom that validates this form.

Sellars has made remarks, however, that favor the other alternative — namely, that of accepting the forms I, II and III as valid. In one essay he said: '. . .an intending is *more than* but *includes* a thinking that something will be the case' and 'that in the verbal expression of intentions which *makes* it an expression of intention *does not suspend this commitment* [to its being the case that. . .]'.[10] Along with certain earlier remarks, this suggests that he might want to accept the following inference as valid:[11]

$$V \quad \frac{S(P)}{P}$$

This inference does not seem capable of validation by his axiom, though it would account for the validity of such forms as I. But he has also said that 'shall' (where it serves to express intention) 'can be said to be a *manner* rather than a *content* of thought'.[12] Since the validity of an inference would seem to depend on the content of the relevant thoughts (or statements) Sellars might then regard not only form V but form VI as valid:

$$VI \quad \frac{P}{S(P)}$$

Obviously, if both forms V and VI are valid, the forms I, II, III and IV are valid as well, and his axiom would no doubt hold for dependent implication.

Although it might seem absurd to suppose that forms V and VI are valid, a reasonable case can be made in their favor. There is, first, the consideration that Sellars produced — namely, that the volitional thought 'I *will* do A' seems to differ from the indicative thought 'I shall do A' not in content but in manner of affirmation. As far as the corresponding statements are concerned, the first differs from the second in expressing a volitional attitude toward a state of affairs that both affirm will obtain. This consideration seems to be supported by the observation that 'I *will* do A' logically implies

'I shall do A' just in case the set {'I *will* do A', 'I shall not do A'} is inconsistent, and that 'I shall do A' implies 'I *will* do A' just in case the set {'I shall do A', 'I *won't* do A'} is inconsistent. And these sets do seem inconsistent. Intuitively, it would appear that an intention is inconsistent with an indicative thought just in case the intention could not possibly be realized if the thought were true. This condition is clearly met for the intentions and indicative thoughts in question.

This conception of the conditions under which intentions and indicative thoughts are inconsistent suggests a semantical approach to mixed inferences that is related to the one I introduced in attempting to justify Sellars's axiom. We simply postulate a positive semantic value 1 and a negative semantic value O defined as follows:

> X has the value 1 *iff* either (a) X is an indicative and has the value T or (b) X is an S-statement and has the value R. Otherwise, X has the value O.

We can then say that an inference is valid just in case its conclusion has the value 1 whenever its premisses have the value 1.

It may be objected, of course, that this conception of validity cannot really be acceptable for the logic of intentions, because it validates such questionable forms of inference as I, II and III. But it is not really clear that there is anything wrong with these forms of inference. Take III, for example, which Sellars seems to reject. Exactly what is objectionable about this form of inference? One suggestion is that it has the consequence that an unfulfilled intention will imply anything at all, including inconsistent intentions. Thus, if '$S(P)$' is unrealized, then 'P' is false, '$P \supset Q$' is true for any 'Q' whatever, and '$S(Q)$' follows. I fail to see anything objectionable about this, however; it is merely an example of the so-called paradoxes of material 'implication'.

If a person has the premisses '$S(P)$' and '$P \supset Q$', he should be willing to accept the conclusion '$S(Q)$' whether he happens to like it or not. The case is fundamentally the same as that in which a person has the premisses 'P' and '$P \supset Q$': if he accepts these premisses, he should be willing to accept the conclusion whether he likes it or not. (Of course, if his dislike of the conclusion is strong enough in either case, he should pull in his horns and reject one of the premisses.) On the other hand, if a person has the premiss '$S(P)$' and knows that it will not be realized — that is, if he knows that $\sim P$ — then, although he can then accept '$P \supset Q$' for any 'Q' whatever, he should not be distressed, since two of his premisses are presumably inconsistent – namely, '$S(P)$' and '$\sim P$'. And it is a familiar principle of standard logic that anything may be derived from an inconsistency.

One thing shown by this last example is that the acceptability of the form III actually rests on the acceptability of the form V, which allows us to infer 'P' from '$S(P)$'. As we have seen, Sellars might well accept this form of inference on the grounds that 'an intending is *more than* but *includes* a thinking that something will be the case'. To accept this form of inference is not to claim that if a person has a certain intention, the corresponding thought or belief that something will be the case must be true. It is merely to claim that if his intention has an appropriate semantic value (which it seems natural to take as R) then the corresponding thought or belief will have an appropriate semantic value (namely, T). This seems to be a plausible basis for accepting V as a valid form of inference. If it is accepted, however, the forms I and II should not appear objectionable, for each is easily validated by V.

The form III may still seem doubtful, but since it may be inferred from VI, I shall comment on the latter. In an unpublished manuscript Sellars accepts the inference from 'P' to '$S(P)$' in cases where 'P' does not concern an action that the agent believes to be within his power.[13] Sellars calls the principle behind the inference 'the So-be-it Principle', and says that if a person believes that something will certainly be the case, it would be perfectly reasonable for him to conclude 'So be it. . .' or 'It shall be the case that. . .'. Sellars evidently thinks, however, that the So-be-it Principle is not applicable when the premiss concerns something the agent believes is within his power. Yet it seems to me that, if the principle is applicable at all, it is applicable in both cases: after all, the principle is a purely formal one, and there is no *formal* test or mark by which to determine whether a premiss concerns an action that an agent believes he can perform.

Consider the simple indicative, 'I shall raise my hand in two minutes'. If I really believe that this premiss is true – if I actually accept it – I might just as well accept the conclusion 'I *will* raise my hand in two minutes'. To adopt the principle in these cases is not to adopt a fatalistic attitude toward my future actions; at most, it is to adopt such an attitude toward what I believe will be the case. If I am an anti-fatalist who believes that no person's action can ever be predicted with certainty, I shall find the So-be-it Principle useless in connection with voluntary actions: I shall deny that an appropriate premiss can ever be well-founded.

Further support for the So-be-it Principle arises from the extreme oddity of certain conjunctive statements. As we have seen, Sellars holds that no S-statement can meaningfully be joined to an indicative by an ordinary sentential connective. But Sellars seems to be clearly wrong about this point. Surely statements like the following are perfectly familiar and perfectly unobjectionable:

(1)   I *will* flunk that student — even though his mother is a trustee.

(2)   I *will* take on the job if, and only if, the pay is satisfactory.

(3)   He doesn't need the job, but I *will* offer it to him anyway.

Yet these statements are naturally formalized with S-statements in the scope of connectives:

(1′) S(I shall flunk that student) & (His mother is a trustee).

(2′) S(the pay is satisfactory $\supset$ I shall take the job) & S(the pay is not satisfactory $\supset$ I shall not take the job).

(3′) $\sim$(He needs the job) & S(I shall offer the job to him).

It seems to me that any logic that does not allow for statements like these cannot be fully adequate for practical inference. Fortunately, the semantical approach recommended above deals with such statements as a matter of course.

But if we do allow S-statements to be joined to indicatives by ordinary sentential connectives, what shall we say about the following?

(4)   I *will* go tomorrow but I shall not go tomorrow.

(5)   I shall stay home tomorrow but I *won't* stay home tomorrow.

It seems to me that both statements are best regarded as inconsistent. If this is right, however, then, since the inconsistency of (4) supports the validity of the form V and the inconsistency of (5) supports the validity of the form VI, we have an additional reason for accepting the semantical interpretation according to which they are valid.

It may be helpful to emphasize at this point that 'I *will* go tomorrow' does not mean 'I intend to go tomorrow' and 'I *won't* stay home tomorrow' does not mean 'I do not intend to stay home tomorrow'. To be sure, when a person says 'I *will* go tomorrow', he *expresses* the intention of going tomorrow — just as he *expresses* the belief that pigs are carnivorous when he says 'Pigs are carnivorous'. And although the statements

(6)   I intend to go tomorrow but I shall not go tomorrow

(7)   I believe pigs are carnivorous but they are not carnivorous

are undoubtedly odd or peculiar in a pragmatic sense, they are not *logically*
inconsistent. But (4) and (5) do seem logically inconsistent; they are not just
objectionable on pragmatic grounds. For this reason, the argument forms V
and VI seem valid even though the forms

$$\text{VII} \quad \frac{\text{I intend to do } A}{\text{I shall do } A} \qquad \text{VIII} \quad \frac{\text{I shall do } A}{\text{I intend to do } A}$$

are patently invalid.

In pondering the apparently problematic argument forms I have been
discussing, we should keep in mind that the vernacular 'shall' and 'will' of
volition do two distinct jobs: they serve to express the speaker's intention,
and they indicate futurity. It is because of this that the canonical interpretation of 'I *will* do A' is 'S(I shall do A)' and the canonical interpretation of
'Tom *shall* come' is 'S(Tom will come)', where 'shall' and 'will' are used in
the old-fashioned grammarian's sense. This point is worth keeping in mind,
because the S-operator in the canonical counterparts to ordinary expressions
of intention will always be applied to indicative statements in the future
tense. When the formal machinery of Sellars's theory is put to work in
formalizing practical discourse, anomalies can be expected to arise, for the
S-operator will inevitably be applied to indicatives in the present or past
tenses. Thus, since 'I shall pay Jones the dollar I have owed him for years'
implies 'I have owed Jones a dollar for years', the statement 'S(I shall pay
Jones the dollar I have owed him for years)' implies 'S(I have owed Jones a
dollar for years)'. Obviously, this last S-statement does not correspond to any
vernacular expression of intention, and it is odd to think of it as expressing
any intention at all.

It is obvious that this kind of difficulty is merely a symptom of a more
general difficulty reminiscent of the so-called Good Samaritan Paradox in
deontic logic. Sellars can, no doubt, avoid this kind of difficulty by placing
restrictions on his logical principles. In fact, in one essay Sellars suggested
that, to avoid paradox, restrictions will probably have to be placed on the
scope of the S-operator.[15] Thus, in a formula like '$S(A \& B)$' the operator
'S' may have to be understood as applying to one rather than the other
conjunct of the inner formula. But instead of complicating his system in this

way, which would seem to cast serious doubt on his leading idea that the logic of intentions is really derivative from ordinary logic and not a separate subject, another alternative is possible: simply eliminate the S-operator. After all, if the semantical interpretation I have suggested for Sellars's logic of intentions is accepted, and if (as I have shown) S-statements must in any case occur within the scope of connectives like 'and', there is really no need to introduce such operators in the first place. Given the validity of the argument forms I have discussed – in particular, given the validity of forms V and VI – we can easily see that the volitional 'shall' and 'will' of everyday discourse are *logically* indistinguishable from the 'shall' and 'will' of mere futurity. Since arguments containing the latter words may be assessed for validity by the principles of ordinary logic, the same will be true of the statements containing 'shall' and 'will' that Sellars formalizes with the help of his S-operator. If we take seriously Sellars's remark that the volitional 'shall' represents a '*manner* rather than a *content* of thought', then this view is an entirely natural one to take.

Sellars might, of course, want to insist that expressions of intention are neither true nor false, and that this fact requires us to provide a special logic for them. I agree that we do not think of intentions or their verbal expressions as being true or false, but this does not seem worth insisting upon for systematic logical purposes. After all, if the obvious semantic values for S-statements are R and U, then the close relation of these values to T and F removes any formal or logical need for distinguishing them. It is, of course, obvious that 'realized' is not synonymous with 'true', but then 'and' is not synonymous with 'in spite of the fact that' – even though they are properly regarded as logically indistinguishable. Another natural but ultimately unimportant point observed by Sellars is that S-statements or expressions of intention cannot have an external negation – that '$\sim S$(I shall go)' or '$\sim$(I *will* go)' does not really make sense. But from a semantical point of view, the position of the negation sign turns out to be insignificant. We can read '$\sim S(P)$' in the very same way as '$S(\sim P)$': both formulas have the value U (or F) just in case the formula '$S(P)$' has the value R (or T). Furthermore, there is really no need to stipulate that S-operators cannot be iterated (though Sellars himself has not offered this stipulation). If the values R and T (or U and F) are not distinguished, then the value of '$SS(P)$' would be indistinguishable from the value of '$S(P)$'; the extra S-operator is mere decoration. These consequences may seem very surprising to anyone who has really struggled with the logic of volitional statements, but unless something is fundamentally wrong with the semantical approach I have suggested here, they are ultimately unavoidable.

It may be helpful to conclude this discussion with a concrete example of how a practical inference may be validated by ordinary indicative logic. The example may be set out schematically as follows:

(1)   I *will* bring about E.
(2)   Unless I do A, I can't bring about E.
(3)   Therefore, I *will* do A.

If this argument is to be regarded as valid, premiss (2) must be understood as implying

(4)   I shall bring about $E \supset$ I shall do A,

where the 'shall' represents mere futurity. Given my thesis that the volitional 'will' is logically indistinguishable from the 'shall' of mere futurity, the conclusion (3) follows from (1) and (4) by *Modus Ponens*.

Another example, which illustrates the advantages of this simplified approach to practical inference, was mentioned earlier. I remarked that in Sellars's system the conclusion '*S*(I have owed Jones a dollar for years)' is a logical consequence of the premisses:

(1)   *S*(I shall pay Jones the dollar that I have owed him for years).
(2)   'I shall pay Jones the dollar I have owed him for years' implies 'I have owed Jones a dollar for years'.

Yet if we restrict ourselves to ordinary indicative logic, treating 'will' and 'shall' as logically indistinguishable in their first-person uses, we could simply say that the only relevant conclusion derivable from the premiss (2) and the expression of intention 'I *will* pay Jones the dollar I have owed him for years' is the simple indicative, 'I have owed Jones a dollar for years'. It seems to me that this is a far more natural response to the premisses in question.

2. BINKLEY'S THEORY OF PRACTICAL REASONING

My approach to practical inference is incompatible with an interesting and complicated theory worked out by Robert Binkley.[16] Binkley's aim is to define a general concept of validity applicable to both practical and theoretical (that is, assertoric) reasoning. The system he develops is complicated, and I shall make no effort to discuss it in detail. For the purposes of this chapter, it is sufficient to describe his general approach and then focus critical attention on the key features of his system that distinguish it from the system (or non-system) that I have been defending.

Binkley's theory actually provides two approaches to the study of valid reasoning. As Binkley observes, our thought is reflected in language in two ways. There is, first, the *linguistic vehicle* by which our thought is verbally expressed. When we judge that snow is white, our judgment may be expressed by the English words 'Snow is white'; and when we decide to do something, our decision may be expressed by a locution like 'I will do such and such'. Binkley's canonical vehicles for judgments and decisions are similar to those adopted by Sellars: ordinary indicatives for judgments, and expressions like '$\$(p)$' for decisions. But there is, second, the verbal *description* of our thought, statements to the effect that we judge that p or decide to bring it about that q. Binkley's notation for these so-called descriptions is '$J(p)$' and '$D(p)$'.

Given the distinction between vehicles and descriptions, Binkley remarks:

We may approach [the study of practical and theoretical reasoning] by way of the vehicle and study, say, imperative and indicative logic; or we may approach [it] by way of description, and a modal logic of judgment and decision.[17]

Binkley's actual procedure in his published paper and in an unpublished address is to take both approaches at once.[18] He constructs a formal system, called '*IC*' in his more recent address, which he conceives as describing the logic of an ideal reasoner. He then contends that an actual argument or form of reasoning involving linguistic vehicles may be considered valid just when it corresponds to a line of reasoning involving descriptions that is valid in *IC*. If we let '$v(t_i)$' represent the vehicle of a judgment or decision t_i and 'T_i' represent the description of an unspecified individual as having t_i, then we can say that the argument

$$v(t_1)$$

$$\vdots$$

$$\frac{v(t_{n-1})}{v(t_n)}$$

is valid just when the description 'T_n' follows from the descriptions 'T_1', ..., 'T_{n-1}' in the system *IC*. Thus, the practical argument

$$\$(p_1)$$
$$\vdots$$
$$\frac{\$(p_{n-1})}{\$(p_n)}$$

is valid just when the description '$D(p_n)$' is derivable in *IC* from the premises '$D(p_1)$', ..., '$D(p_{n-1})$'. This gives formal expression to the idea that the practical argument exhibited above is valid just when an ideal reasoner would decide to bring it about that p_n on the basis of deciding to bring it about that p_1 ... and deciding to bring it about that P_{n-1}.

In the essays referred to Binkley does not give us axioms or rules of inference specifically applicable to practical and assertoric reasoning. To evaluate such reasoning we must therefore attend to the definition just given and determine whether the given reasoning corresponds to an appropriate description valid in the system *IC*, which constitutes a modal logic of judgment and decision applicable to an ideal reasoner.

A key idea underlying Binkley's approach is that 'valid reasoning is reasoning it would be irrational to reject'.[19] Since he holds that a piece of reasoning is explicitly rejected when we assent to the premises but withhold assent to the conclusion, his idea is that a line of reasoning is invalid just when it would be irrational to accept the premises but not accept the conclusion. The notion of irrationality here is specified by reference to the behavior of an ideal reasoner. If an ideal reasoner would not accept the premises and withhold assent from the conclusion, then and only then is the inference valid. Binkley's canonical description for the withholding of assent to a judgment or decision is '$W(\theta)$'; he represents the vehicle of an act of withholding assent to θ by '$?(\theta)$'. His notation may be summarized by the following table:

Description	Vehicle
$J(p)$	p
$D(p)$	$\$(p)$
$WJ(p)$	$?(p)$
$WD(p)$	$?(\$[p])$

Although I shall not discuss the axioms of Binkley's system *IC*, the complexity of his approach can be illustrated by stating his axioms.[20] The system *IC* consists of a set of axioms holding for actual thinkers (the system *AC*) together with axioms holding only for ideal thinkers. In presenting the following axioms I shall omit certain complications that, though interesting and important, are not relevant to my concerns in this chapter.[21]

The System AC

Propositional calculus plus:

$(AC\text{-}1)$ $WT \supset \sim T$

$(AC\text{-}2)$ $WWT \equiv T$

$(AC\text{-}3)$ $DD(p) \equiv D(p)$

$(AC\text{-}4)$ $DWD(p) \equiv WD(p)$

The System IC

The system *AC* plus the following rule and axiom schemata:

$(IC\text{-}R)$ If 'p' is a theorem of *AC*, then '$J(p)$' and '$D(p)$' are theorems of *IC*.

$(IC\text{-}1)$ $\sim T \supset WT$

$(IC\text{-}2j)$ $J(p) \supset WJ(\sim p)$

$(IC\text{-}2d)$ Same for decision

$(IC\text{-}3j)$ $J(p \supset q) \supset (J[p] \supset J[q])$

$(IC\text{-}3d)$ Same for decision

$(IC\text{-}4)$ $J(p) \supset WD(\sim p)$

The fundamental or crucial difference between Binkley's system and my nonsystem stands out if we consider the key argument forms that, allowing *S*-operators, I would regard as valid but that Binkley disallows. (My contention, again, was that such operators are not actually needed for practical inferences and that problems can be avoided if we dispense with them.) Consider the argument forms:

$$(\text{I})\quad \frac{p}{S(p)} \qquad (\text{II})\quad \frac{S(p)}{p} \qquad (\text{III})\quad \frac{S(e)}{\frac{e \supset m}{S(m)}} \qquad (\text{IV})\quad \frac{S(p \supset q)}{\frac{p}{S(q)}}$$

In Binkley's system these arguments are invalid, but related arguments are valid:[22]

$$
\text{(I*)} \quad \frac{p}{?(\$[\sim p])} \qquad\qquad \text{(II*)} \quad \frac{\$(p)}{?(\sim p)}
$$

$$
\text{(III*)} \quad \$(e) \qquad\qquad\qquad \text{(IV*)} \quad \&(p \supset D[q])
$$

$$
\frac{e \supset D(m)}{\$(m)} \qquad\qquad\qquad \frac{P}{\$(q)}
$$

I shall discuss these argument forms in turn, comparing Binkley's counterpart with the one I favor.

The form (I*) corresponds to what Binkley called, in his first paper, the axiom of resignation – namely, '$Jp \supset WD\sim p$'.[23] Commenting on this axiom, Binkley said: 'once a rational man reaches a judgment about the happening of some event, he will withhold decision to bring about the opposite event; he will resign himself to the inevitable'. This sentiment is related to the one I expressed in calling the form (I) the So-be-it Principle. My contention was that, if you are convinced that some statement P about the future is true, you are rationally entitled to conclude 'So be it: $S(P)$'.

A possible reason for rejecting the form (I) is that, even though you are totally convinced that p, you may not want to be *committed* to '$S(p)$'. Suppose that your friend Jones is extremely ill and will certainly die within a week. You know this. You also know that he will die within a week if you now smother him with a pillow. But you do not want to be the agent of his death; you don't want him to die at all. Of course, knowing that he will die, it would be absurd to form the intention 'S(Jones will not die)'. But if, in line with the form (I), you form the intention 'S(Jones will die)', you would thereby be committed to bringing about his death. Surely this is objectionable; the form (I) cannot be allowed. But Binkley's form (I*) causes no trouble here; it merely requires you, if you are rational, to withhold the decision 'S(Jones does *not* die)'. As we have seen, this is perfectly reasonable, because the decision is totally pointless in view of what you know.

This objection to the form (I) is fundamentally confused. In the first place, the intention 'S(Jones will die)' does *not* thereby commit me to taking an active part in bringing about Jones's death. It may be true that *if* I smother Jones, he will die; but this does not provide a valid basis for concluding 'S(I shall smother Jones)'. As we have seen, arguments of the form

S(I shall bring about E)

If I do A, I shall bring about E.

Therefore, S(I shall do A)

are invalid. Of course, if my smothering of Jones were *necessary* for his death, I could validly infer 'S(I shall smother Jones)'. But in the present case *no* action on my part is necessary for Jones's death: the assumption is that Jones will die no matter what I do. Thus, in adopting the intention 'S(Jones will die)' on the basis of the So-be-it Principle I am *in no sense* committed to harming him at all.

Another defect with the objection is that the So-be-it Principle does not actually *require* you to adopt the intention '$S(p)$' when you have the premiss 'p'. In fact, you are never required actually to adopt an intention when it is implied by premisses you accept: you are merely entitled to that intention on logical grounds, and you would be inconsistent if you adopted any intention incompatible with it. One reason why you do not have to accept such an intention is that you never have to draw any conclusions at all: you don't have to reason, infer, or even contemplate the possible consequences of your premisses. A person who refuses (for a time) to draw any conclusions from his premisses may be irresponsible, perverse, or even insane — but he is not thereby *inconsistent*. And it is inconsistency that is the bane of a logical mind; the aim of such a mind is to be consistent, not actually to draw the countless conclusions implied by every one of his premisses. Thus, while one may allow that if you actually adopted the intention of harming a person, you would be *practically* inconsistent (as I put it in Chapter III[24]) if you did not act in accordance with this intention, one should emphatically reject the idea that the form (I) requires you actually to adopt such an intention if you have an appropriate indicative premiss.

I have emphasized this last point because it brings out my fundamental disagreement with Binkley. His view seems to be that it would be unreasonable to withhold one's assent from a conclusion if it were implied by premisses one accepts. But he offers no real support for this doubtful idea, which should not be confused with the patently sound idea that it is unreasonable to withhold one's assent from a conclusion one has actually inferred from premisses one accepts. Binkley simply claims that withholding assent to a conclusion implied (whether one realizes it or not) by one's premisses is irrational, arguing that it is incompatible with the idea of what he calls a

Sage. A Sage, as Binkley defines him, is Socratically omniscient and Stoically omnificent. Binkley says:

The Socratically omniscient thinker combines comprehensiveness of knowledge with avoidance of error by never judging where he does not know, and by knowing that he does not know when he does not. . . . And on the practical side, the Stoically omnificent agent combines comprehensiveness of action with avoidance of frustration by never deciding to do a thing without doing it, and by deliberately not doing those things that he does not do. . . . I add in each case the requirement that he withhold those mental acts that he does not perform ($\sim \theta \supset W\theta$). The Sage is then the man who possesses both this omniscience and this omnificence. . . . Irrationality, finally, is to be condemned on the grounds that being irrational is incompatible with being a Sage.[25]

But I can't think of any good reason why we should endeavor to be Sages. Given our inherent limitations of mind and body, we could never hope to be Sages anyway.

As I see it, our aim in being logical is complex. When we draw indicative conclusions from indicative premises, we want to be assured that our conclusions are true if our premises are true; we want to minimize our chances of accepting sets of statements some of which *must* be false. When we infer practical conclusions from practical premises, we want to be assured that our conclusions will be realized if our premises are realized; we want to minimize the chance of adopting plans of action that cannot possibly succeed. Formal logic, whether assertoric or practical, never requires us to *do* anything; it gives us a conditional assurance about the value of certain conclusions, and it discourages us from adopting certain sets of beliefs or intentions. But the decision actually to draw a particular conclusion is a purely practical one that we can refrain from making without any fear of inconsistency.

This brings me to the argument form (II*), which corresponds to Binkley's 'axiom of hope' – namely, '$Dp \supset WJ\sim p$'.[26] Speaking of this axiom, Binkley says: 'a rational man decides to bring about a state of affairs only if he withholds judgment that it will not happen; he always acts, if not with full confidence, at least with the hope of success'. Binkley's principle here is, again, weaker than my counterpart – namely, that '$S(p)$' entails 'p' – and its weakness is owing to Binkley's peculiar conception of validity. We both agree that if you have the premiss '$S(p)$', you should not accept the idea that $\sim p$, for it is absurd to suppose that your intentions are bound to be unrealized. But unlike Binkley I am prepared to make a further claim: If you fully intend to do something, then you are *entitled* to assume that it will be done. This does not mean, again, that if you intend to do A, you are bound to succeed, or that you must believe you will succeed. As far as I am concerned, neither of the following arguments is valid:

S intends that P S intends that P
Therefore, P.   Therefore, S believes that P.

My claim, reflected in the form (II), is merely that, having adopted the premiss 'I *will* do A', you are logically entitled to conclude 'I shall do A'. This seems entirely reasonable to me; it is an obvious truth if, as I believe, 'I *will* do A' differs from 'I shall do A' not in assertive content (they involve the same claim) but in the attitude they express.

I come now to the form (III*), which is, again,

$$\$(e)$$

$$\frac{e \supset D(m)}{\$(m).}$$

Binkley rejects my counterpart to this — namely, '$S(e)$; $e \supset m$; therefore, $S(m)$' — on the following grounds:

I may decide to bring it about that my picture hangs on the wall, and also judge that my picture will so hang only if there is a nail in the wall. It by no means follows that I must rush to put a nail in the wall, for there may already be one there, or it may be that a nail will come to be there through some other agency. The most that follows is that I must restrain myself from preventing there being a nail in the wall. Before my decision to hang a picture will require a decision to pound a nail, I must judge that there will not be a nail in the wall unless I put it there.[27]

As the last sentence makes clear, Binkley is assuming that, if my counterpart is a valid form, the premisses in question would require us actually to make a certain decision. But, again, this assumption is much too strong: formal logic does not *require* us to do anything at all. The nail that *must* be in the wall if I am to succeed in hanging the picture may, indeed, already be there, or may be put there by someone else. But even if it is not necessary for *me* to drive in the nail, it is still reasonable, under the circumstances, for me to intend that it be there. After all, if the nail is already there or if it is being pounded in by another person, I could always conclude 'So be it'.

If I am right about validity and its relation to practical commitment, it is not, therefore, necessary to reject the form (III) in favor of the more complicated form (III*). To this I should add that, if I am right, the form (III*) should not be regarded as valid anyway — even though one who adopts the premiss '$S(e)$' and '$e \supset D(m)$' is *justified* in adopting the intention '$S(m)$'. As I see it, the premisses entail 'S(I shall decide to bring about m)', but this does not formally entail the conclusion '$S(m)$'. On the other hand, if, in line with the form (III), one adopts the conclusion 'S(I shall decide to bring about m)', one is *practically committed* to accepting '$S(m)$'. This practical commitment is based on the idea that one who forms an intention but does not act in accordance with it is being practically inconsistent. This kind of inconsistency is not formal, a matter of deductive logic; but it does allow us to identify a sense in which one may be committed to *doing* something. Since one who makes a decision to form a certain intention (or make a further decision) may be said to be practically committed to forming that intention (or making that further decision), one who actually adopts the conclusion 'S(I shall decide to bring about m)' is thereby committed to intending '$S(m)$' and may, in consequence, be regarded as justified in adopting this intention.

I now come to the remaining argument form, (IV*). Actually, though Binkley rejects my simpler form (IV), he believes that his system allows two different ways of handling conditional decisions. In his view, the reasoning loosely expressed in the vernacular by 'I'll do A if P; P; so I'll do A' can be interpreted in two non-equivalent ways — either as

$$\frac{\begin{array}{c} \$(p \supset D[q]) \\ p \end{array}}{\$(q)} \quad \text{or as} \quad \frac{\begin{array}{c} \$(p \supset q) \\ p \\ q \supset D(q) \end{array}}{\$(q)}$$

It seems to me, however, that neither schema corresponds to the reasoning in question. The first schema does not correspond to that reasoning because its first premiss does not represent a conditional intention to perform the relevant behavior; it represents an intention to make a certain decision if p. The second schema does not possess this defect, but it contains a premiss not explicitly involved in the relevant reasoning. But quite apart from the question of how close Binkley's schemata correspond to the argument expressed in the vernacular, both should be rejected if my remarks on validity are sound. The conclusion actually entailed by the premisses in both cases is '$S(D[q])$' rather than '$S(q)$'; and although one who *adopts* '$S(D[q])$' is, for reasons outlined in the last paragraph, rationally entitled to '$S(q)$', he would not be *logically* inconsistent if he adopted '$S(D[q])$' and '$S(\sim q)$'. He would not be logically inconsistent in this case because there is no formal entailment between the so-called description 'I shall decide to do A' and the prediction 'I shall do A'.

As my comments on the forms (I*) through (IV*) make clear, my basic objection to Binkley's system is directed entirely to its semantic or pragmatic underpinnings. If, like Binkley, one thinks that an agent is irrational or unreasonable in a *logical* sense if he refuses to adopt a conclusion implied (whether he realizes it or not) by premisses he accepts, then one may find Binkley's system entirely satisfactory. But although I agree that an agent may sometimes be deemed irrational or unreasonable when he refuses to draw a certain conclusion, I regard this unreasonableness as, at most, a form of perversity, for the agent is not thereby inconsistent in any formal sense. Since my conception of validity seems more in line with customary logical practice than Binkley's unusual conception, there is at least one good reason to prefer my approach to his. Another, perhaps more compelling reason to prefer my approach is that Binkley's system is far more complicated than my non-system. It seems to me that if we can get along without a special, complicated formal logic for practical reasoning, we should certainly do so. Since my approach requires no special formal logic at all, there is thus very good reason to prefer it to Binkley's.

3. CASTAÑEDA'S GENERAL THEORY OF THE LANGUAGE OF ACTION

In a series of papers written over a period of nearly twenty years Hector-Neri Castañeda has worked out a remarkably rich and complicated general theory of the language of action. This theory has been brought together in Castañena's recent book, *The Structure of Morality*.[28] Apart from a logic of intentions, Castañeda's formal theory deals with arguments involving normative statements as well as various kinds of mandates or imperatives. Since statements of the form 'It is obligatory (right, permitted) that p' are normatives in Castañeda's sense, his theory includes a so-called deontic logic. His theory is, thus, far more general and in some respects far more complicated than the rival theories of Sellars and Binkley.

A basic feature of Castañeda's system, which I shall eventually try to ignore, is that the premisses and conclusions of practical arguments are conceived of not as statements but as 'thought-contents' or, as he calls them, *noemata.*[29] It is convenient to regard *noemata* as the objects of thought represented or perhaps 'conveyed' by various sentences. For systematic logical purposes, sentences can be divided into four classes:

(1)   Ordinary indicatives, such as 'Snow is white'.
(2)   Normatives, such as 'It is wrong to steal'.
(3)   Imperatives, such as 'Jones, do A!'
(4)   Resolutives, such as 'I will do A'.

According to Castañeda, the *noemata* corresponding to indicatives and normatives are propositions; those corresponding to imperatives are mandates (or imperatives); and those corresponding to resolutives are intentions.

An imperative sentence, as Castañeda defines it, formulates a possible appropriate answer to a question like 'What shall I (or we) do?' asked in interpersonal discourse.[30] Such an answer may convey a command, an order, a request, or a piece of advice. The commands and so forth thus conveyed are examples of mandates (or imperatives) in Castañeda's technical sense. The *noemata* conveyed or represented by the following sentences are thus mandates:

'S, do A!' (a command or order)
'S, please do A' (a request)
'S, you'd better do A' (a piece of advice)
'S, I beg you, do A' (an entreaty).

According to Castañeda, *noemata* of these kinds, together with propositions and intentions (=what an agent may intend), constitute appropriate premisses or conclusions of practical arguments.

One of Castañeda's fundamental contentions is that mandates are 'embellishments' of a more basic conceptual structure called a 'practition'.[31] A practition, for Castañeda, is a structure distinctive of an intention or a family of mandates. The practition common to the mandates conveyed by the sentences 'S, do A!', 'S, please do A', 'S, you'd better do A', and 'S, I beg you, do A' can be identified by the italicized parts of the following:

S was ordered (commanded) *to do A.*
S was requested (told, asked) *to do A.*
S was advised *to do A.*
S was begged (entreated) *to do A.*

The common italicized part here, '*S*. . .to do *A*', represents the common practition; and by neglecting the three dots, Castañeda forms a canonical representation of that practition – namely, '*S* to do *A*'. (He sometimes also neglects the 'to', thus representing the mandate by the simpler '*S* do *A*'.) The practition so identified differs from the mandates in question by not representing the *attitudes* those mandates involve – the attitudes expressed by 'please', 'you'd better', the parenthetical 'I beg you', and so on. These words or phrases represent the embellishment of the practition involved in each mandate.

According to Castañeda, the practitions involved in all mandates are second-person or third-person practitions; he calls such practitions 'prescriptions'.[32] Thus, since we can say 'You, do *A*!' just as well as '*S*, do *A*' we can have the second-person practition 'You to do *A*' (or 'You do *A*') as well as the third-person practition '*S* to do *A*' (or '*S* do *A*'). The practitions corresponding to resolutives such as 'I will do *A*' are always first-person; they may be represented by 'I to do *A*' or 'I do *A*'. Castañeda calls such practitions 'intentions'. Although an intention is normally expressed in words by a future tensed sentence like 'I *will* do *A*', Castañeda prefers the artificial 'I (to) do *A*', which is reflected in the sentence 'I intended to do *A*'.

The distinctions Castañeda draws concerning practical assertions may be represented by the following simplified table:

Vehicle	*Noema*	*Practition*
'*S*, do *A*!'	*S, do A!*	*S* (to) do *A*
(an imperative sentence)	(a mandate)	(a prescription)
'I will do *A*'	*I (to) do A*	I (to) do *A*
(a resolutive)	(an intention)	(an intention)

To simplify my discussion of Castañeda's system, I shall ignore his distinction between vehicle and *noema*. I shall regard practical premisses and conclusions as mere vehicles, and I shall interpret practitions as vehicles with the relevant attitudinal embellishments deleted. The distinctions I ignore are not really important for a discussion of the purely formal, or logical, features of Castañeda's system; their interest is essentially metaphysical.

Castañeda's basic practical logic concerns practitions. As he says: 'The differences . . . in types of mandate do not belong to logic, but to the *uses* of our attitudes toward prescriptions'.[33] This remark recalls my claim in Section

1 of this chapter that the difference between the indicative 'I shall do A' and the expression of intention 'I will do A' is not a formal one, to be taken account of in formal logic, but a nonlogical matter of the attitudes expressed. Castañeda does not agree with me on this particular point, however. He contends (for reasons to be discussed in due course) that 'I shall do A' and 'I will do A' are significantly different in formal respects: the latter represents a practition while the former does not.

According to Castañeda, the key difference between the practition 'X (to) do A' and the corresponding indicative 'X does A' lies in the mode of 'copulation' of their subjects and predicates.[34] He represents this difference in his formalism by putting the subject or argument of the practition in brackets. Thus, for him, the logical form of an atomic practition is

$$A[x],$$

while that of the corresponding indicative is

$$A(x).$$

Castañeda contends that the *pure* logic of practitions is formally the same as, or isomorphic to, the logic of propositions. As he says:

the systematization of prescriptive implications is formally a rather trivial matter. Any systematization of the logic of propositions allows of being taken either as the logic of propositions, as originally intended, or as the logic of pure prescriptions.[35]

(It will be recalled that prescriptions are merely second- or third-person practitions; his point is really a general one, holding for the pure logic of practitions.) In line with his general claim here, Castañeda allows the variables in practitions to be bound by quantifiers, and he also allows the negation, conjunction, disjunction and so forth of practitions. Apart from the special mode of copulation involved in atomic practitions, there is thus no syntactical difference between his pure logic of practitions and ordinary first-order logic.

The peculiarity of the pure logic of practitions is thus semantical. Castañeda insists that practitions are neither true nor false. He admits, however, that they have semantical values analogous to truth and falsity, and that the structure of their semantical interpretation is essentially the same as that of ordinary indicatives, so that the standard consistency and completeness proofs for first-order logic can be adapted to his logic of practitions. The positive value corresponding to T (or Truth) is J (or Justified) and the negative value corresponding to F is N (for Not Justified). Since the words 'Justified' and 'Not Justified' can be interpreted in more than one way, Castañeda prefers to designate these special values by 'Jth' and 'Nth'.[36]

For essentially the reasons I gave in criticizing Sellars's theory (see especially page 155) Castañeda contends that an adequate logic for practical reasoning must be an extension of the pure logic just described; it must allow compound expressions containing both practitions and indicatives, and it must cover mixed inferences as well as those that merely involve practitions. Thus, the practitional core of the mandate 'Erase all the boards' must be acknowledged to have both indicative and practitional components, for it has the form '$(x)(B(x) \supset E[\text{you}, x])$'. And apart from covering the sort of mixed arguments involving intentions that I discussed in earlier sections of this chapter, an adequate logic for the entire language of action must cover (Castañeda contends) imperatival arguments such as the following:

(A)   Everybody take the course.
        Therefore, John, take the course.
(B)   Students, all of you, take the course.
        You, John, are a student.
        Therefore, John, take the course.
(C)   John, open the door.
        Hence, someone, open the door.

Castañeda's mixed logic of practitions allows the following sentential combinations, where A and B are either indicatives or practitions:

$$\sim A, \quad A \& B, \quad A \vee B, \quad A \supset B, \quad A \equiv B, \quad (x)A, \quad (\exists x)A$$

He also holds that any formula containing a practition is a practition; thus, '$A(a) \vee B[c]$' is a practition (or represents one). The formal semantics for his mixed system is essentially the same as the one I suggested (on page 153) for an extension of Sellars's system — namely, that every formula has either a positive (or designated) value 1 or a negative value 0 defined as follows:

> A has the value 1 *iff* either (i) A is an indicative and has the value T or (ii) A is a practition and has the value J. Otherwise, A has the value 0.

As far as the elementary mixed logic of practitions is concerned, Castañeda says this:

Take negation and conjunction as the primitive connectives. Then the following value-tables yield the whole [elementary] system of implications between *noemata*, whether propositions or practitions:

Table 3 - 1

p^*	$(\sim p^*)$	p^*	q^*	$(p^* \& q^*)$
1	0	1	1	1
0	1	1	0	0
		0	1	0
		0	0	0

As is customary, a formula having only '1's in its last column is a tautology, and if a formula of the form '$\sim((X_1 \& X_2 \& ...\& X_n) \& \sim Y)$' expresses a tautology, the argument-form '$X_1, ..., X_n \therefore Y$' is valid.[37]

To this account Castañeda offers a semantical interpretation of quantifiers that is a generalization of the usual interpretation. This gives him a general mixed logic of first-order practitions.

Although I did not explicitly introduce quantifiers into my suggested extension of Sellars's system, it is clear that the difference between that system so enriched and Castañeda's mixed system rests very largely on the basic semantical values assigned to the nonindicative (or practical) formulae. Thus, if practitions were given the value 1 just when their corresponding indicatives have the value T, then even though we might not want to speak of practitions as true or false, the corresponding formulae '$A(c)$' and '$A[c]$' would always have the same generic values (namely, 1 or 0) and the following arguments would be valid:

$$\frac{A[c]}{A(c)} \qquad \frac{A(c)}{A[c]}.$$

Yet if these and all similar arguments were valid, there would be no significant logical, or formal, difference between indicatives and corresponding practitions; and the practical part of Castañeda's system would reduce to the indicative part, leaving no special logic of practical reasoning.

Since Castañeda is committed to the view that there is a special logic of practical inference not reducible to ordinary indicative logic, he must insist that indicatives and their corresponding practitions sometimes differ in generic semantic value. Specifically, he must insist that an indicative '$A(c)$' might have the value 0 when the practition '$A[c]$' has the value 1, and *vice versa*. And, in fact, he argues for this point, at least in effect, claiming that a certain practition would not be justified in a certain context when its corresponding indicative is true. Given his definition of 'Justified', we may grant the soundness of this last contention; but we may nevertheless raise the question, 'Why should we regard practitions as having the basic values of *Jth* and *Nth* rather than some other values that, like my *R* and *U*, are closely related to truth and falsity?' Unless we have good reason to adopt Castañeda's preferred values, or values similar to the ones he prefers, we shall not have good reason to accept his complicated and unusual system.

As far as I know, Castañeda has not offered clear, specific reasons for accepting his preferred values of *Jth* and *Nth*. He does, however, have a reason for adopting these values: Evidently, it is that these are the most plausible values for a unified practical logic that is sufficiently general to cover not only intentions but the full range of mandates. (I neglect, for the moment, his interest in the logic of normatives, which leads him to merge his mixed system with a modal, deontic logic.) Thus, Castañeda holds that statements expressing commands, requests and pieces of advice may occur as premises or conclusions of practical arguments; and he would no doubt argue that such statements could not reasonably be interpreted as having the positive value 1 whenever their corresponding indicatives happen to be true. Clearly, one who offers the advice 'Jones, you'd better do *A*' is not generally entitled to assume that 'Jones will do *A*' is true; and if one believes that Jones will do *A*, it would generally be silly rather than reasonable to advise him to do it.

It has, of course, been argued that imperatives do not have logical implications, and that the following sequences cannot represent genuine arguments:

Erase all the blackboards.	If Tom calls, go home.
This is one of them.	Tom calls (or has called).
Therefore, erase this.	So, go home.

As Castañeda points out, however, the usual basis for this claim is extremely weak, expressing an arbitrary and narrow-minded decision to use the term 'logical implication' only in connection with statements (or formulas) that have truth values.[38] Obviously, we can turn the tables on one who takes this stubborn position by defining a special sense of 'implication' that holds for imperatives, and then contending that, according to other definitions we introduce, certain sequences of imperatives unquestionably are arguments and

are valid or invalid as the case may be. But an arbitrary move of this kind
would be philosophically uninteresting. The important question at issue is
not how we merely propose to use the words 'implication', 'argument', and
'validity', but whether it is philosophically important or worth our while to
provide such definitions and to elaborate the relevant semantical interpretation. This is the question I now want to investigate.

As we normally conceive of it, a valid form of argument corresponds to a
valid pattern of reasoning — a pattern in which some kind of conclusion is
inferred from certain premisses. But do we ever, in fact, *infer* imperatives
from practical premisses? Obviously, Castañeda thinks we do, but I find the
idea extremely doubtful. Consider the following, which, like the specimens
on pages 171 and 173, Castañeda regards as valid arguments:

<table>
<tr><td>If he comes, give him the book.</td><td>Don't invite him, or be</td></tr>
<tr><td>He is coming.</td><td>nice to him.</td></tr>
<tr><td>So, give him the book.</td><td>(But) invite him.</td></tr>
<tr><td></td><td>Hence, be nice to him.</td></tr>
</table>

It is hard to believe that sequences like these ever occur outside a philosophical article or monograph. To my knowledge, people in the real world never
reason according to such patterns. They commonly have reasons for issuing
this or that mandate, but the mandates they issue never seem to be the
conclusions of deductive arguments.

As far as I can tell, any genuine inferring that may occur in connection
with the issuing of a mandate can be accounted for by the theory of deliberation discussed in the last chapter. Suppose I say to Smith, 'Do A if p'. I then
learn, or come to realize, that it is true that p. I thus know that the conditions are now appropriate for Smith to do A. But suppose I doubt that Smith
is aware of the truth of 'p'. Since I want (intend) him to do A under the
present conditions, I might reason as follows:

(1)   I have commanded Smith to do A if p.
(2)   My command will be obeyed only if Smith does A when p.
(3) S(my command will be obeyed).   [Expression of intention]
(4) S(Smith does A when p).   [2, 3]
(5) p.
(6)   Therefore, S(Smith does A).   [4, 5]
(7)   If I say 'Smith, do A' he will (probably) do A.

(8)   All things considered, saying 'Smith, do A' is now preferable
        to not saying 'Smith, do A'.   [Expression of preference]
(9)   So, S(I say 'Smith, do A').   [Expression of intention]
(10)   Smith, do A!

Here the transition from (9) to (10) does not represent an inference but the
implementation of a choice or intention. (I have used Sellars's S-operator here
merely for convenience; as I argued in Section 1 of this chapter, it is not
really necessary.)

Now consider the possible reasoning of an agent who hears a command
addressed to him. Suppose he hears the command 'Jones, do A!' He might, in
the circumstances, reason as follows:

(1)   He commanded me to do A.
(2)   If I am to obey his command, I must do A.
(3)   To do A, I must do B.
(4)   Shall I obey his command or not? [Practical question]
(5)   Obeying his command is, in the circumstances, preferable to
        not obeying it.
(6)   I will obey his command.   [Choice]
(7)   Therefore, I will do A.   [2, 6]
(8)   Therefore, I will do B.   [3, 7]

Here the transition from (5) to (6) is a nonlogical one; it is not an inference.
But from (6) and the preceding information, the conclusion (8) is validly
drawn; and the implementation of this decision leads to a course of action
necessary for obeying the command in question.

The general point illustrated by these examples is that mandates, no
matter who issues them, are adequately taken account of in practical reasoning by corresponding indicatives to the effect that someone or other is
commanded, advised, entreated to do a certain thing. To be successful, the
relevant reasoning obviously requires certain truths about imperatives and
what must be done to obey or follow them. For example:

> S obeys Q's command to do $A \supset S$ does A.
> S follows Q's advice to do $A \supset S$ does A.
> Q begs S to do A & S does what Q begs him to do $\supset S$ does A.

But formulae like these do not have the status of axioms in some special formal logic; in fact, they are not formal principles at all, for they contain essentially descriptive predicates like 'obeys', 'follows', and 'command'. Yet given these obvious truths, which might be termed 'meaning postulates', the principles of deliberation as I have described them seem adequate for the *reasoning* that both those who issue mandates and those who receive them might *naturally* engage in.

What I have been saying here does not take account of the role of normatives in practical reasoning — that is, statements like 'S ought to do A', 'S may do A', or 'It is right to do A'. But if Castañeda is right, the basic formal logic of these statements — so-called deontic logic — is a modal logic, and logics of these kinds raise special problems. The view I have been expressing may thus be taken as the restricted one that, at least for analyzing nonmodal forms of practical reasoning, there seems to be no *need* for introducing a special logic of mandates or practitions: we do not actually use such a logic, and the manner in which mandates enter our reasoning can be adequately understood without it. If I am right here — if there is actually no need within nonmodal reasoning for a special logic of mandates — then there appears to be no need to interpret the formal logic of such reasoning by reference to the special semantic values of *Jth* and *Nth*. Instead of relying on these unusual values, which yield a special logic, we can use the values R and U, which are semantically indistinguishable from the standard values of T and F, and which yield the nonsystem of practical logic I have been defending.

In making this restricted claim I am not disputing a point that has no doubt strongly impressed Castañeda — namely, that certain mandates are clearly justified when certain other mandates are justified. But this fact does not require us to define a special relation of implication between mandates — any more than the fact that certain statements are clearly justified when other statements are justified requires us to define a special relation of justification-implication between them. Of course, we can define such relations if we want to. But the possibility of doing this does not show that the logical structure of our reasoning, whether practical or assertoric, cannot be adequately understood without reference to such relations.

Before coming to terms with normative statements, I want to call attention to certain peculiarities of Castañeda's mixed system. According to his principle $M4$, mandates are supposed to 'have the implications of their characteristic prescriptions [or practitions]'.[39] Consequently, the following 'arguments' should be valid in his system:

S, I beg you, do A.	S, please do A.
Therefore, S, do A!	Therefore, S, do A!

These arguments represent commands inferred from an entreaty or a piece of advice. But even if we can allow imperatival inference, these particular arguments should raise our eyebrows. On the face of it, the conclusion in both cases seems stronger than the premisses: if the premisses are justified in either case, it seems doubtful that the conclusion is *thereby* justified as well. To be confident about the matter, we must obviously have a better understanding of Castañeda's semantical values, *Jth* and *Nth*.

As it happens, Castañeda does not actually clarify these particular values; instead, he clarifies the relative values, *Justified-in-context-C* and *Not-justified-in-context-C*. And then, instead of defining validity by reference to all contexts C — that is, by saying that an inference is valid just when, *for every context C*, the conclusion is true or justified in *C* if the premisses are true or justified there — he defines a relativized notion of validity: An inference is valid-in-a-context-*C* just when the conclusion is 'automatically' assigned the value true-in-*C* or Justified-in-*C* when the premisses are all assigned one or the other of these values.[40] In line with this relative approach to validity he admits that an argument may be valid in one context but not in another. Thus, though the following argument is not generally valid, it is valid in 'appropriate contexts', which include X's having p as an end:[41]

> X wants p to be the case.
> p will be the case only if you do A.
> Hence, do A.

Evidently, the argument here must be understood as directed to X: the 'you' in the second premiss must refer to X, and the conclusion must be tacitly addressed to him.

I can see little point in regarding 'arguments' like this as *valid* in any sense at all. Clearly, they are not formally valid — that is, valid by virtue of their logical form. Of course, in a context where the agent not only has p as an end but where the speaker wants or intends to assist X in achieving his end, the advice represented by 'X, do A' may be considered justifiable, but this does not seem sufficient to warrant our saying that we are dealing with a relatively valid argument. To assess the reasonableness of such advice given the information at hand, the Bayesian strategy discussed in the last chapter would seem entirely sufficient. If we are to apply this strategy to pieces of advice (as opposed to acts of giving advice) we must, of course, identify the person for whom the advice is justified. We might say that advice A is justified for a speaker when his act of issuing it has, for him in the circumstances, MED; and it is justified for the person to whom it is directed if his act of carrying it out has, for him in his circumstances, MED. As for any practical reasoning that might naturally be employed either by the person offering advice or the person receiving it, the kind of deliberation discussed on pages 174–175 would seem to provide an acceptable general model.

In the effort, perhaps, to add objectivity to his account of practical validity, Castañeda lays down a condition in the light of which he speaks of the 'unlimited validity' of an inference.[42] The condition is this:

> (U)   When an imperative is employed in its central or basic mode it is used against the background of the total hierarchic complex of ends and conventional procedures to which both the agent and the imperative user subscribe.[43]

Castañeda's contention, apparently, is that when a practical argument is used in a context where its ingredient imperatives (or resolutives) are used in their 'central or basic mode', it will be valid in all contexts if it is valid in this one.

Castañeda's discussion of relative validity is somewhat confusing and (at first sight, at least) does not seem consistent with his earlier remarks about the logic of practical inferences. To understand his definition of 'Justified-in-context-C' we must first understand some special terms that he employs. Corresponding to any context C there is a set of propositions $C(E)$ that is closed under logical implication. These propositions are all true and, as he puts it,

(i) formulate the circumstances of the domain of the agents under consideration for a certain period of time; (ii) formulate the facts about their endorsement of, or subscription to, ends E, as well as certain of their views about certain aspects of the universe; (iii) formulate causal connections among other propositions in $C(E)$.[44]

He adds that the propositions in $C(E)$ are consistent with the proposition that the ends E are attained. He then forms the set $C^*(E)$, which consists of all the propositions in $C(E)$ together with the proposition that the ends E are attained.[45]

The part of Castañeda's definition of 'Justified-in-context-C' applying to atomic prescriptions is, then, this:

A primary imperative $X_1, \ldots, X_n$, do A is Justified-in-context-C. . . if and only if either (i) its corresponding performance proposition $X_1, \ldots, X_n$ do (*will do, or have done*) A is implied by $C^*(E)$; or (ii) neither it (the prescription. . .) nor its negation $X_1, \ldots, X_n$, *don't do A* is implied by $C^*(E)$, but it is endorsed by at least some of the persons whose ends are E and its negation is endorsed by none of the persons whose ends are E; or (iii) neither it nor its negation is implied by $C^*(E)$, nor does condition (ii) obtain, but its corresponding proposition $X_1, \ldots, X_n$ do A (*or have done A, or will do A*) is true.[46]

The other parts, or clauses, of his definition specify the conditions under which negations, disjunctions, and so forth of prescriptions and of indicatives-and-prescriptions are Justified-in-context-C.

Although this definition is not difficult to understand, perplexities enter the picture when he puts this definition to work in particular cases. On page 177 I cited an example of an argument that Castañeda regards as valid only in a special context. Commenting on this argument, Castañeda says, 'Now, if. . . the realization of p satisfied (U), then we can form the inference (2), which has unlimited validity:

(2) X wants p to be the case.
        Nothing else matters to X or me (the speaker).
        p will be the case only if X does A.
        X can do A.
        Hence, X, do A'.[47]

To this Castañeda adds, 'whenever it is assumed or taken for granted that one's end to help a state of affairs p to be the case is compatible with his [the agent's] highest ends, schema (1) [as given above on page 171] yields valid imperative inferences'.[48] These contentions by Castañeda may seem reasonable given his condition (U), his definition of 'Justified-in-context-C', and his conception of relative validity, but they seem seriously at odds with the conception of practical inference that he defends initially. As a consequence of this, his general conception of practical inference is difficult to understand.

Before attempting to define the special values *Jth* and *Nth*, Castañeda specified a tabular method for determining the validity of nonquantified mixed arguments involving practitions, and he offered a semantical interpretation of quantifiers that is a generalization of the usual interpretation (see page 172 above). His claim was that mandates are merely embellishments of practitions, and that the formal logic of practitions can be set forth as a simple generalization of ordinary indicative logic. Thus, he gave generalized

value tables for practitional connectives, and defined a practitional tautology
as a formula having only 1's in its last column and a valid practical argument
as a sequence of formulas that corresponds to a tautology. Yet if this conception of practical validity is assumed, the schema (2), given above, *should not
count as valid*: it certainly does not correspond to a truth-table tautology or
to an indicative argument valid in the logic of quantifiers. Thus, it would
seem that, in introducing the concept of relative validity, Castañeda has
either changed his mind about practical validity or strayed from his original
position.[49]

If we consider the set of propositions $C^*(E)$ corresponding to the schema
(2), we can agree that the conclusion 'X, do A' is Justified-in-that-context.
Given that the premisses are all in $C^*(E)$ and that $C^*(E)$ also contains the
premiss that the agent's wants are satisfied, the first clause of his definition
of 'Justified-in-context-C' would seem to be satisfied. But even though the
conclusion is (we may assume) Justified-in-the-context, we really have no
reason to assume that the conclusion is a *logical consequence* of the premisses. Presumably, it is a contingent fact that the set $C^*(E)$ has certain
contents, and this contingent fact cannot be used as a premiss in a deduction
showing that the conclusion 'X, do A' is a logical consequence of the premisses given in the schema (2). For my part, the schema (2) seems just as
invalid as the schema (1): in neither case, I think, do we have a valid deductive argument.

It seems to me that Castañeda's original, nonrelative approach to practical
validity is far preferable to the one that supposedly awards 'unlimited
validity' to schemata like (2). Yet his original, nonrelative approach possesses
some striking limitations. Consider the following argument, for example:

> I *will* attend the game on Saturday.
> If I don't earn some money, I shall not attend that game.
> Therefore, I *will* earn some money.

In Castañeda's system this argument presumably has the form of

$$A[i]$$
$$\sim E(i) \supset \sim A(i)$$
$$\therefore E[i]$$

But although the argument about earning money seems clearly valid, this
argument form does not satisfy Castañeda's truth-table test. Since practitions

and their corresponding performance propositions — for example, '*A* [*i*]' and '*A*(*i*)' — need not agree in semantic value, the truth-table for our argument form does not contain only '1's in its last column. It seems to me, however, that any system of practical logic that does not account for the validity of arguments like the one about earning money cannot be regarded as satisfactory. (See above, pages 153 f.)

In view of this last consideration it is perhaps fortunate that, if I am right in thinking that we do not actually make commands, requests, and so forth *as the conclusions of deductive inferences*, even Castañeda's original, non-relative approach to practical validity is not something we need to accept. Neglecting normatives, which I shall consider in the next section, I think we can deal with all genuine practical inferences by the nonsystem I discussed in the first part of this chapter. As for the justification of mandates (for certain people at certain times) the Bayesian approach seems perfectly satisfactory. In fact, that approach seems decidedly preferable to Castañeda's.

Recall the decision problem presented on pages 138 f. An experienced traveler was faced with the problem of whether to take the plane or the train to Chicago. Given his preferences and expectations concerning such things as the weather conditions at the Chicago airport, we saw that his best course of action is to take the plane. In view of this conclusion the advice 'Take the plane' would clearly be justified, but it is hard to see how it could be justified in Castañeda's approach. According to his definition (see page 179 above) the mandate 'Take the plane' would be justified just in case one of three conditions is met. Yet none of these conditions takes effective account of the kind of calculations that render this course of action preferable to taking the train. If, in addition to this case, we consider the complexity of the calculations required to justify decisions made under various conditions of *uncertainty* — and thus to justify us in advising or commanding a person to do one thing rather than another under such conditions — the inadequacy of Castañeda's approach to the justification of mandates should strike us as obvious.[50]

4. NORMATIVE STATEMENTS AND PRACTICAL REASONING

I turn now to normatives. As Castañeda points out, *oughtness* or *obligatoriness* can be taken as the basic normative concept, and *right*, *wrong*, and *permitted* can be defined in terms of it.[51] The question I am mainly concerned to consider in this section is how normative statements enter into practical reasoning, but I shall not neglect Castañeda's claim that the logical peculiarities of such statements make it strongly advisable to adopt his special logic of practitions. Although Castañeda cannot claim to have proved that such a logic is advisable, his analysis of normatives accounts for important facts and thus provides indirect support for a special practical logic. These facts concern what he regards as the fundamental property of normatives — namely, 'their involvement with grounds or reasons, with the weighing of these reasons, and with the finding of the most reasonable course of action'.[52] His analysis also allows a simple resolution of various paradoxes in deontic logic, such as the Good Samaritan paradox and Åqvist's Paradox of the Knower. I shall begin by discussing Castañeda's conception of the fundamental property of normatives.

Some writers, notably R. M. Hare,[53] have contended that a distinctive mark of normative statements is that they imply corresponding imperatives. Although Castañeda allows that certain normatives have this feature, he insists that normatives do not characteristically have it. As we have seen, he holds that normatives are primarily used for the weighing of reasons for action. His account of the logic of normatives is designed to clarify the role of such statements in deliberation, and it does this by relating normatives to the basic logic of practitions.

As Castañeda points out, any systematic treatment of normatives must come to terms with the familiar conflicts of duties. Consider the following monologue:

Inasmuch as you promised to wait for him, you ought to wait for him; but *inasmuch* as your waiting for Peter will disappoint your wife, you ought not to wait for him. Everything relevant to this case being considered, you *must* not do anything which will disappoint your wife; *so*, you must not wait for Peter; hence, don't wait for him.[54]

It is obvious, Castañeda believes, that the advice given here is consistent. Yet if it is consistent, the first sentence must be interpreted so that it does not warrant the conclusion:

(1)   You ought to wait for Peter and you ought not to wait for Peter.

Castañeda's strategy for avoiding such a contradiction is to argue that the two 'ought's in the first sentence actually differ in import; they concern different duties.[55] Thus, instead of the consequence (1), what really follows is (2):

(2)   You ought$_i$ to wait for Peter and you ought$_j$ not to wait for Peter.

Since the 'ought's involved here are different, (2) is not formally contradictory.

According to Castañeda, the 'ought's in (2) are *qualified* 'oughts'; they are qualified by the claims introduced, in the passage above, by the phrases beginning with 'Inasmuch as. . .'. In contrast with these 'oughts', the 'ought' corresponding to the 'must' in 'So, you must not wait for Peter' — that is, in the sentence immediately preceding the imperative in the passage above — is *unqualified*. Concerning this last kind of 'ought' Castañeda says:

a normative which *merely* formulates the solution to the conflict of grounds or claims: (a) presents a certain course of action as the *most* reasonable, everything (relevant) being considered, (b) is used, if publicly asserted, to tell a person or group of persons what to do, (c) is conceived of as a premise for deriving resolutions or pieces of advice, and (d) includes no reference to specific qualifications or grounds, for otherwise it would not satisfy condition (a). We shall say that the concept of *ought*, or an *ought*, is *used unqualifiedly* when a person thinks that a certain normative is the case, and the normative in question satisfies conditions (a) - (d).[56]

As I understand Castañeda, there is just one unqualified 'ought'; and if both 'ought's in (2) were unqualified, (2) would be self-contradictory.

It is clear from the quotation above that, for Castañeda, the qualified 'oughts' are logically fundamental: we are to understand the unqualified ones in terms of them. Now, Castañeda does not attempt to define these basic 'oughts'; rather, he formulates a general schema by which their truth-conditions can be specified. The schema is this:[57]

(DT.2) X ought$_i$ to do A $\equiv$ There is a consistent set B_i of both true propositions and at least partially endorsed practitions which implies the practition X to do A.

The intuitive import of this schema can be illustrated by a first-person example, where 'X' is replaced by the pronoun 'I'. Let the set B_i contain the two formulae:

$$D[I]$$
$$D(I) \supset A(I).$$

Given that '$D[I]$' expresses an end or intention, we can then say, *if* we accept

Castañeda's relativized logic of practitions, that 'A [I]' is validly derived from the set B_i with respect to the understood context C. (Recall that the corresponding set $C^*(E)$ contains the assertion that the relevant ends are fulfilled.) Using the terminology I favor, we could describe this case by letting B_i include the premisses:

> I will do D.
> If I do D, then I (must) do A.

In my nonsystem 'I will do A' follows from these premisses. Given Castañeda's schema DT.2, the statement 'I ought$_i$ to do A' should be true.

The idea behind this approach is that, if the intention to do A is implied by other intentions I have together with certain factual truths about my circumstances, the statement 'I ought$_i$ to do A' is true as well. This idea seems reasonable, at least on the assumption that the 'ought' here might well be qualified. If doing D requires doing A, then the assertion 'Inasmuch as I aim to do D, I ought$_i$ to do A' seems perfectly all right; and if, as Castañeda holds, we may detach qualified 'ought' statements from the clauses that qualify them, the statement 'I ought$_i$ to do A' would seem to be at least relatively justified.

The question arises, however: Are we really entitled to detach 'ought' statements from the clauses that qualify them? Many philosophers would insist that the proper answer to this question is 'No'; and I am inclined to agree with them. To introduce some key considerations bearing on the question, I want to present one of the paradoxes in deontic logic that is easily avoided by Castañeda's approach to 'ought' statements. The paradox I shall discuss is known as 'the paradox of the knower'; it was discovered by Lennart Åqvist.[58]

Like the so-called Good Samaritan paradox, the paradox of the knower arises from a plausible axiom of deontic logic that Castañeda formulates as follows:

> (P')   If X performs A implies Y performs B, then X is obligated$_i$ to do A implies Y is obligated$_i$ to do B.[59]

Castañeda presents the paradox of the knower this way:

Consider the case of a man, say Jones, whose job is to know what is done wrong by other people in a certain office. Suppose that Smith did A, which is wrong by the rules of the office. Then 'It is wrong$_i$ that Smith does A' and 'Jones ought$_i$ to know that

Smith (does) did A' are true. Since 'Jones knows that Smith (does) did A' implies 'Smith does (did) A', we have, then [by the principle P'], 'Smith ought$_j$ to do (have done) A', which contradicts the hypothesis that it is wrong$_j$ for Smith to do A. [60]

Since a very plausible axiom of deontic logic thus allows us to derive a contradiction from reasonable premisses, we are faced with a genuine paradox.

Castañeda resolves this paradox (and the related paradox of the Good Samaritan) by modifying the axiom (P'). In his system an obligation-statement consists of a modal operator 'O_i' prefixed to a practition; thus the vernacular 'Smith ought$_i$ to do A' is rendered as 'O_i(Smith do A)' — not as 'O_i (Smith does A)'. In line with this he adopts the axiom

(P*)   If the practition X *do A* implies the practition Y *do B*, then *It is obligatory$_i$ that X do A* implies *It is obligatory$_i$ that Y do B*.

But this axiom does not generate the paradox of the knower. Even though 'Jones knows that Smith did A' implies 'Smith did A', neither statement is a practition. Consequently, we have no basis for the conclusion that Smith ought$_i$ to have done A.

Although Castañeda's approach does avoid the paradox of the knower, that paradox may be avoided in another way. Specifically, we can reject a key premiss on which it is based — namely, that the statement 'Jones ought$_j$ to know that Smith did A' is true. As Castañeda formulated the paradox, Jones's job requires him to know what is done wrong by other people in a certain office. But this assertion is best interpreted as supporting a conditional 'ought' statement that may be expressed by the schema,

O_i (Jones knows that X does A, given that X's doing A is wrong).

For the special case of Smith, the appropriate 'ought' statement is

O_i (Jones knows that Smith did A, given that Smith's doing A was wrong).

But together with the premiss that Smith's doing A was wrong, this conditional assertion does not imply the categorical statement needed for the paradox

O_i (Jones knows that Smith did A).

As in the case of qualified (or conditional) probability statements, we are not entitled to infer a categorical conclusion by dropping the qualifying clauses.[61]

This means of resolving the paradox of the knower could, of course, be regarded as objectionably *ad hoc* if there were not independent reasons for interpreting qualified 'ought' statements as I am doing here. But such reasons are not difficult to locate. As Lawrence Powers and others have observed,[62] a truly unqualified statement of the form '$O_i(P)$' specifies a deontic ideal (of kind i): intuitively speaking, it affirms that a deontically ideal$_i$ world would include the state of affairs connoted by 'P'. Yet a statement like 'Given Q, S ought$_i$ to do A' does not have the intuitive import of the disjunction 'Either $\sim Q$ or an ideal$_i$ world would include S's doing A', which would be equivalent to the material conditional '$Q \supset \cdot S$ ought$_i$ to do A'. On the contrary, 'Given Q, S ought$_i$ to do A' seems to affirm that, other things being equal, S's act of doing A would be included in the *best$_i$* world in which 'Q' is true. If 'Q' means that the person S murdered someone, a world in which 'Q' is true would be morally imperfect. But the best, or at least the morally preferred, state of such a world might involve S's being punished — in which case we could say, 'Given that S committed a murder, S ought$_m$ to be punished'. This last assertion could be taken to express a *prima facie* moral duty, and it might be rendered more formally by the conditional 'ought' statement, 'O_{pfm} (S is punished, given that S murdered someone)', where the subscript indicates that the relevant obligation is a *prima facie* moral one.

If we adopt this approach to qualified 'ought' statements, we shall have to acknowledge that, formally speaking, there are at least two obligation operators, one dyadic and one monadic. The dyadic operator is used as I have just used it, to formulate conditional 'ought' statements; the monadic operator is used to formulate categorical statements. But categorical 'ought' statements fall into two fundamentally different classes. The first class consists of unqualified statements of basic principles such as 'One ought not to lie, steal, or cheat'; intuitively speaking, these statements express deontic ideals of various kinds. The second class consists of statements that formulate what W. D. Ross called 'absolute duties'.[63] Though these duties contrast with *prima facie* duties, they are *not* unqualified: they specify the best course of action, everything considered, for specific agents in specific circumstances. I shall have more to say about these two classes of categorical 'ought' statements in due course. For the moment, I simply want to point out that these statements should be distinguished by special monadic obligation operators.

Although Castañeda appears to treat all qualified 'ought's by a single schema (namely, DT.2 given on page 183 above), it seems clear that some of them do not specify a duty of any kind and do not fall within the province of deontic logic. Consider the statement 'If you want (intend) to be rich, you ought to pay more attention to the stock market'. As I understand it, this statement does not even suggest a duty; it merely specifies something that is presumed necessary, or perhaps virtually indispensable, for achieving your aim. Or consider 'If you want to make money, you ought to go into business for yourself'. If your rich uncle uses this sentence in giving you advice, he will not be telling you what you must do to make money; he will be identifying what he regards as the best (or a preferred) way of making it. It seems to me that such 'ought' statements cannot be clarified by any simple schema such as Castañeda's DT.2. On the other hand, they appear to have nothing to do with duties and they have no evident relevance to the subject of deontic logic.

To keep my discussion within reasonable limits I shall be concerned only with the 'ought' statements, qualified and unqualified, that represent various kinds of obligations. Castañeda's claim that these statements play an important role in deliberation is unquestionably correct; and although I cannot accept his account of 'ought' statements, I should at least indicate how, in my view, the principal kinds of obligation statements are related to expressions of intention — these being, for me, the fundamental units of practical thought. In rejecting his account of normatives I am, of course, rejecting the remaining basis for his special logic of practitions.

As I see it, the 'ought's that Castañeda considers unqualified are *absolute* 'ought's; they override conflicts of *prima facie* duties, and they represent the best, most reasonable courses of action in particular circumstances. I believe that the truth-conditions for these 'ought's can be specified by a schema that is somewhat similar to Castañeda's DT.2. Before describing this schema, however, I want to come to terms with an important, though restricted class of conditional 'ought' statements — those that specify *prima facie* moral duties. These statements deserve treatment before the corresponding absolute ones because absolute 'ought's commonly (and characteristically) override conflicts between *prima facie* duties. This is not to say, of course, that one cannot have an absolute moral duty without first experiencing a conflict of *prima facie* moral duties.

Let M_S be the set of moral principles accepted by an agent S, and let '$O_{pfm}(\ldots$given that - - -)' be a dyadic operator appropriate for statements of conditional *prima facie* moral obligations. The following schema seems satisfactory for specifying truth-conditions for a restricted class of conditional obligation statements:

(PFO) $\ulcorner O_{pfm}(X$ does A, given that $Q)\urcorner$ is true for $S \equiv \ulcorner X$ does $A\urcorner$ is logically independent of Q & $(\exists P)$ (P is in the set M_S & the conjunction of Q and $X^\frown$'obeys'$^\frown$quote$^\frown P^\frown$unquote implies, given S's meaning postulates for words like 'obeys', $\ulcorner X$ does $A\urcorner$).

The application of this principle can be illustrated by an example. If Q is 'X promised to do A', then the conjunction of Q and the premiss 'X obeys principle P (requiring X to keep his promises)' will imply 'X does A'.

An interesting feature of the schema just introduced is that it does not require us to specify the form of the agent's moral principles. As far as the schema is concerned, these principles could be formulated in a variety of ways — for example, as fiats or 'ought' statements not even qualified by *ceteris paribus* clauses. As for the possibility of conflicting *prima facie* duties, it is clear that both $\ulcorner O_{pfm}(X$ does A, given that $Q)\urcorner$ and $\ulcorner O_{pfm}(X$ does non-A, given that $R)\urcorner$ may be true when Q and R are true. Since incompatible actions are here *prima facie* required of the agent X given conditions that obtain, we can say that we have a genuine conflict of *prima facie* duties. This seems an improvement over Castañeda's schema DT.2 for qualified 'ought's (see above, page 183), for it is not clear, on his account, that the assertions '$O_i(X$ does $A)$' and '$O_j(X$ does non-$A)$' really conflict at all. A final point about the schema (PFO) is that it can easily be modified to deal with classes of nonmoral duties. Thus, we could let L_S be a set of legal principles, or laws, binding on the agent S; and then, following the pattern of (PFO), we could specify the truth-conditions (relative to S) of $\ulcorner O_{pfl}(X$ does A, given that $Q)\urcorner$. Schemata like (PFO) do not, of course, take account of the fact that the principles accepted by, or binding on, S at one time may not be accepted by, or binding on, him at another time. But this possibility can easily be accommodated by adding a temporal variable to the relevant schema.

I come now to absolute 'ought' statements. As a preliminary point, note that the schema (PFO) throws no light on the manner in which (or the degree to which) the agent is committed to the principles M_S. These principles may jointly specify a deontic ideal, but they may be weighted differently when brought to bear on an imperfect world. If, with Castañeda, we assume that an agent is capable, in principle, of resolving a conflict of *prima facie* duties, we cannot suppose that he has the same attitude to every principle in his M-set. If he is to be rational in resolving such conflicts, he must no doubt have some higher-order principle that regulates his commitment to the lower-order principles. Such a principle would naturally presuppose an ordering of the lower-order principles in terms of their relative weight or importance. To deal with conflicts among *prima facie* duties of all kinds whatever, we could contemplate an ordering of all principles generating conditional duties with, say, moral principles at the top and legal principles (or laws) coming next. Since my concern here is mainly with basic logical problems pertaining to the uses of 'ought', I shall simplify matters by considering only moral principles. The higher-order principle, or policy, that I introduce could easily be extended (at least in principle) to cover all qualified *prima facie* obligations.

Another preliminary point to keep in mind is that, if a conflict of duties is ever satisfactorily resolved by an absolute 'ought' statement, all available evidence bearing on the case must be considered. Thus, if an agent X knows that 'P' and 'Q' are true and acknowledges the truth of both '$O_{pfm}(X$ does A, given that $P)$' and '$O_{pfm}(X$ does non-A, given that $Q)$', he cannot reasonably expect to resolve his problem merely by considering the relative weight of the principles that, together with factual premises, generate these conflicting conditional obligations. He must, at the least, consider whether any other principles bear upon the case and whether he has other conditional obligations that conflict with the two he is explicitly considering. If he does not attend to these possibilities, he might overlook his most pressing conditional obligation.

In line with my general conception of practical reasoning, I shall formulate the higher-order principle appropriate for resolving conflicts between *prima facie* duties as a policy or intention. As I said, the principle will presuppose that all lower-order principles in the set M_S are ranked in order of moral weight or importance. Let $R(M_S)$ be the sequence of principles in M_S ordered this way; the ordering represents the agent's estimate of their relative moral weight at the time in question. The following schema would seem to provide, at least at first approximation,[64] a suitable higher-order principle:

(FP)   It shall be the case that X does A in C if X's doing A is required in C by some principle in $R(M_S)$ that precedes every principle in $R(M_S)$, if there are any, that requires X to do something incompatible with A in C.

Given this higher-order policy or intention, we can specify the truth-conditions for the absolute moral 'ought' by the following schema:

(AMO) $\ulcorner O_{am}(X \text{ does } A \text{ in } C)\urcorner$ is true for S at time $t \cdot \equiv \cdot S$ accepts the principle FP at t & $(\exists B)$ (B is a set of true statements containing no normatives or S-statements such that (i) B neither implies nor is implied by $\ulcorner S(X \text{ does } A \text{ in } C)\urcorner$ but (ii) the union of B and the singleton $\{FP\}$ — that is, $B \cup \{FP\}$ — does imply $\ulcorner S(X \text{ does } A \text{ in } C)\urcorner$ and is also consistent).

This last schema bears a certain similarity to Castañeda's schema DT.2, which I have commented on. It differs from his schema in not applying to nonabsolute 'ought' statements, and it is distinguished by two special restrictions. First, the only S-statement relevant to the deduction of '$S(X$ does A in $C)$' is (FP), for it is only (FP) that generates the absolute 'moral' ought. Second, since in my nonsystem of practical logic the indicative 'P' is semantically indistinguishable from '$S(P)$', we must be assured that '$S(X$ does A in $C)$' follows from (FP) and not some inappropriate factual truths; otherwise, (AMO) would imply that an agent is morally obligated to do everything he does do. Apart from these qualifications, (AMO) remains in the spirit of Castañeda's definition, for it bases the truth of an 'ought' statement on the derivation of a corresponding decision (or intention) from a set containing practical but non-normative premisses.

Although (AMO) seems adequate for solving the particular problem that prompted it, one might think it runs afoul of the obvious fact that most people have never heard of the principle (FP). Having never heard of the principle, they can hardly be said to accept it; yet obviously statements like '$O_{am}(X$ does A in $C)$' remain true for them. Since (AMO) requires that an absolute moral 'ought' statement is true for a person only if he accepts the principle (FP), we must acknowledge that (AMO) is simply untenable.

This is an important objection, which can be met only by arguing that anyone who distinguishes *prima facie* from absolute duties must be viewed as tacitly accepting (FP) or something tantamount to it. Clearly, a person who recognizes such a distinction must have *some* higher-order principle for resolving conflicts of *prima facie* duties. Although the principle may be held only for the moment, it can resolve such a conflict only by ranking one underlying principle higher than the other. This is precisely what (FP) does; different people who use it simply rank the relevant lower-order principles in different ways (and they may, of course, recognize different sets of lower-order principles). But all this is compatible with the role of (FP) in the schema (AMO). Each person's use of (FP), or each person's policy corresponding to (FP), concerns his own ordering $R(M_x)$ of his own set M_x of lower-order principles; the policy simply requires him to obey the principles that he ranks highest.

An ethical intuitionist may object that he certainly distinguishes *prima facie* from absolute duties but employs no higher-order principle at all; he might claim that, in his view, absolute duties must be identified by one's 'moral sense' or 'intuition', which does not operate by applying principles. But even if we allow that one's moral sense (assuming that it exists) reaches its verdicts without applying any principles, we do not have to agree that we as moral agents apply no principle in selecting our duties. Obviously, even the most intuitive of moral intuitionists applies a principle in selecting his absolute duties: the principle is that of doing what is required by the lower-level rule that is deemed most weighty, in the circumstances, by his moral intuition. This principle is clearly a version of (FP); the alleged moral sense simply provides a ranking (complete or partial, as the case may be) of the lower-level principles that (FP) concerns. The peculiarity of the intuitionist's view is that no single ranking of lower-order principles is tenable for all contexts; the appropriate ranking in any instance must be determined by one's moral sense or intuition. Nothing I have said here is incompatible with this idea; it certainly casts no serious doubt on the schema (AMO).

Another possible objection to the schema (AMO) is that it does not reflect the so-called universal validity of absolute moral 'ought's. It specifies merely the truth *for a particular agent at a particular time* of an absolute moral 'ought' statement; consequently, it does not do justice to the important fact that such statements are, if true for one person at one time, true for all persons at all times. I cannot deny that philosophers sometimes say that absolute moral 'ought's have this kind of 'validity', but it seems obvious that, if we are to speak of moral truth at all, we must regard it as relative to a moral system. Since different people often support significantly different moral principles (just think of current debates about abortion) it seems absurd to suppose that there is just one moral system tacitly accepted by all rational beings. Absurd or not, however, this supposition is actually consistent with the schema (AMO), so there is no need for me to dispute it here.[65] Another claim actually consistent with (AMO) is that a proper moral system must express the 'general will' of some moral community, even when such a community has only a single remaining member.[66] As far as (AMO) is concerned, this claim might well be true.

Although my approach to normatives differs significantly from Castañeda's, I fully agree with his view that there is an intimate logical relation between certain 'ought' statements and basic practical premisses. My final task in this section is to clarify this basic relation, at least as I see it. This is fairly easy to do, given the schema (AMO). My fundamental thought is that absolute 'ought' statements provide the key link between normatives and expressions of intention.

The first thing to note is that a general policy or intention plays a decisive role in generating absolute obligations. A person may acknowledge a certain deontic ideal and he may habitually employ a corresponding set of principles, which may have the form of fiats ('Thou shalt not. . .') or of unqualified 'ought' statements ('One ought to maximize human happiness'). But he incurs an absolute obligation to do a certain thing only by virtue of a possibly tacit policy or intention to implement his principles in a certain way. Thus, a general policy or intention provides the ultimate premiss from which absolute 'ought' statements are inferred. This is an important point, because absolute 'ought' statements are the ones that resolve concrete moral problems and lead to action.

The logical connection between absolute 'ought' statements and practical decisions can also be identified by reference to the schema (AMO). If a rational person is convinced that he ought (morally and absolutely) do something A in circumstances C, he will accept as true, at least for himself at the time, the corresponding absolute 'ought' statement. If he has access to the schema (AMO), he will then know that the statement 'S(I will do A in C)' is logically implied by his general policy or intention (FP) together with truths of fact. Such a statement will clearly be acceptable to him, for he will know that, given the facts of the case (whatever they may be), he must satisfy this statement (that is, realize the corresponding intention) if his general policy (FP) is to be satisfied. He may thus reason, metalinguistically: 'Since "O_{am}(I will do A in C)" is true for me, now, and since I accept (FP), the conclusion "S(I will do A in C)" is clearly acceptable for me now. Therefore, S(I will do A in C)'. This last transition from

'S(I will do A in C)' is acceptable for me now

to

S(I will do A in C)

corresponds to the move from

The statement 'Snow is white' is true

to the assertion

Snow is white.

Clearly, both moves are justified, though neither counts as an inference valid in the object language. Since the practical conclusion 'S(I will do A in C)' or 'I *will* do A in C' will lead the agent to do A when he believes he is in C, the ultimate connection between absolute 'ought' statements and rational action is implicitly represented by the schema (AMO).

5. CONCLUDING REMARKS

My principal aim in this chapter has been to support the idea, expressed in the introduction, that no special formal logic is needed for the general purposes of practical inference or rational deliberation. (This idea is, of course, consistent with the view that a system of deontic logic is needed for the special purposes of certain normative systems.) In accordance with this aim I investigated the general theories of practical inference espoused by three philosophers who evidently hold views to the contrary — namely, Wilfred Sellars, Robert Binkeley, and Hector-Neri Castañeda. (I also examined the rival view of Anthony Kenney in Chapter III.) After examining their theories in what I trust was a fair and sympathetic way, I conclude that they have not made a convincing case for a special system of practical logic. Sellars's system, at least in the papers I referred to, seems more orthodox than those of the other three, and his view that practical logic is reducible to indicative logic is fairly close to my own. Although I used his S-operator now and then to clarify the logic of practical arguments, I used it merely for convenience: like his special axiom, his S-operator is not really needed, in my view, for the job of formalizing practical inferences. As I argued, ordinary indicative logic seems perfectly satisfactory for formalizing practical inference, since basic practical assertions (that is, expressions of intention) are semantically indistinguishable from corresponding indicatives.

In the concluding pages of my remarks on Castañeda's system I laid down truth-conditions for two important classes of 'ought' statements, and I related the absolute moral 'ought' to expressions of intention. I had nothing to say about the so-called emotive meaning of the 'ought' statements I discussed, but then I did not attempt to analyze their meaning at all: I was concerned only with truth-conditions. A satisfactory account of the meaning of these statements could be consistently added to what I said, and an appropriate system of deontic logic could also be developed. The upshot of my discussion of 'ought' statements is that the formal logic of normatives can be clarified without reference to an underlying practical logic of a special sort. This supports my view that practical inference can be understood without reference to such a special logic. Formally speaking, the basic structure of practical inference is indistinguishable from that of ordinary assertoric inference: both forms of inference employ the same general principles.

NOTES

[1] Sellars's views on the logic of practical reasoning are recorded principally in two places: 'Thought and Action', in Keith Lehrer (ed.), *Freedom and Determinism* (New York, 1966), pp. 105–139, and Chapter VII of Sellars's *Science and Metaphysics* (New York, 1969), pp. 140–174. Important remarks also occur in an early essay, 'Imperatives, Intentions, and the Logic of "Ought" ', *Methodos*, 8 (1956), 227–268, a revised version of which is included in H. N. Castañeda and G. Nakhnikian (eds.), *Morality and the Language of Conduct* (Detroit, 1965), pp. 159–218.
[2] This section grew out of my article, 'Sellars on Practical Reason', in H.N. Castañeda (ed.), *Action, Knowledge, and Reality* (Indianapolis, Indiana: Bobbs-Merrill, 1974), pp. 1–25.
[3] See Sellars, *Science and Metaphysics*, p. 188. I shall refer to this book as '*SM*' in the notes to follow.
[4] 'Thought and Action', p. 115.
[5] *SM*, p. 82.
[6] *SM*, p. 181f.
[7] See 'Imperatives, Intentions, and the Logic of "Ought" ', in the volume by Castañeda and Nakhnikian, p. 190.
[8] The derivations for these forms follow the same strategy as Sellar's derivation. The derivations for I and II are based on the premiss that, since 'P' and '$P \supset Q$' imply 'Q', then '$S(P)$' and '$S(P \supset Q)$' imply '$S(Q)$'. We can therefore say that '$S(P \supset Q)$' implies

'S(Q)' relative to 'S(P)'. From this we infer that 'P ⊃ Q' implies 'Q' relative to 'S(P)', which validates form I. To validate form II we use the premiss above to conclude that 'S(P)' implies 'S(Q)' relative to 'S(P ⊃ Q)' and then to conclude that 'P' implies 'Q' relative to 'S(P ⊃ Q)'. To validate form III we simply note that 'P' implies 'Q' relative to 'P ⊃ Q' and then infer that 'S(P)' implies 'S(Q)' relative to 'P ⊃ Q'.

9 See *SM*, p. 190f.

10 See 'Thought and Action', p. 128 and 127.

11 See 'Imperatives, Intentions. . .', p. 175, where Sellars says 'it seems proper to stipulate that "Shall [*my* shortly crossing the road]" implies "I will shortly cross the road", i.e., that it contains the prediction, just as "Necessary [Tom's shortly crossing the road]" contains "Tom's shortly crossing the road" '.

12 See 'Thought and Action', p. 129.

13 In the unpublished manuscript referred to Sellars introduces two *S*-operators into his canonical language to avoid various problems. Since he has not published the manuscript and may, for all I know, have second thoughts about the views expressed in it, I have not taken account of it in this work.

14 These anomalous statements could be avoided, I believe, if Sellars allows compound statements consisting of *S*-statements and indicatives. The statement '*S*(I shall repay Jones the dollar I have owed him for years)' could then be reformulated so as not to entail '*S*(I have owed Jones a dollar for years)'. The reformulation would be 'I have owed Jones a dollar for years and *S*(I shall repay that dollar)'.

15 See *SM*, p. 181.

16 Robert Binkley, 'A Theory of Practical Reason', *Philosophical Review* 74 (1965), 423–448. Binkley gives a more recent version of his system in 'The Validity of Reasoning', an address presented to the Canadian Philosophical Association meeting at Kingston, Ontario in June, 1973.

17 'A Theory of Practical Reason', p. 425.

18 See note 16 above.

19 'A Theory of Practical Reason', p. 436.

20 These axioms are given in 'The Validity of Reasoning'.

21 The complications I omit concern the reasoner's means of referring to himself. See 'The Validity of Reason'.

22 See *ibid*.

23 See 'A Theory of Practical Reason', p. 437.

24 See p. 136.

25 'A Theory of Practical Reason', p. 447.

26 *Ibid*., p. 437.

27 *Ibid*., p. 443.

28 Hector Neri Castañeda, *The Structure of Morality* (Springfield, Illinois, 1974), henceforth referred to as '*S of M*'.

29 *S of M*, pp. 29–45.

30 *Ibid*., pp. 28, 36.

31 See *ibid*., 69–79, and also Castañeda, 'Intentions and Intending', *American Philosophical Quarterly* 9 (1972), p. 145, where the term 'embellishment' is explicitly used.

32 *Ibid*.

33 *S of M*, p. 79.

34 See 'Intentions and Intending', p. 145.

35 *S of M*, p. 85.

36 *Ibid.*, pp. 83ff.
37 *Ibid.*, p. 89.
38 *Ibid.*, pp. 82f.
39 *Ibid.*, p. 99.
40 *Ibid.*, p. 124.
41 *Ibid.*, p. 127.
42 *Ibid.*, p. 128.
43 *Ibid.*, p. 126.
44 *Ibid.*, p. 117.
45 *Ibid.*
46 *Ibid.*, p. 118. As printed in his book, Castañeda's definition does not contain the word 'or' between the clauses (i), (ii) and (iii), but Castañeda assures me this is owing to a misprint.
47 *Ibid.*, p. 128.
48 *Ibid.*, p. 129.
49 In a private communication Castañeda has told me that his conception of relative validity should be viewed as an extension of his original system designed to accommodate, e.g., arguments whose validity depends on the logic of 'wants'.
50 See Howard Raiffa, *Decision Analysis: Introductory Lectures on Choices under Uncertainty* (Menlo Park, Calif., 1970).
51 *S of M*, p. 56.
52 *Ibid.*, p. 54.
53 See R. M. Hare, *The Language of Morals* (Oxford, 1952), Ch. 11.
54 *S of M*, p. 154.
55 *Ibid.*, p. 50.
56 *Ibid.*, p. 53. The clauses (a)–(d) were indented in the original text.
57 *Ibid.*, p. 64.
58 See Lennart Åqvist, 'Good Samaritans, Contrary-to-Duty Imperatives, and Epistemic Obligations', *Noûs* 1 (1967), 366ff.
59 *S of M*, p. 80.
60 Castañeda, 'On the Semantics of the Ought-to-Do', *Synthese* 21 (1970), 459–461. For Castañeda's solution to the Good Samaritan paradox, see *S of M*, p. 81.
61 See C. G. Hempel, *Aspects of Scientific Explanation* (New York, 1965), pp. 394–403, and also Gilbert Harmon, 'Detachment, Probability, and Maximum Likelihood', *Noûs* 1(1967), 401–411.
62 See Lawrence Powers, 'Some Deontic Logicians', *Noûs* 1 (1967), 381–400, and also Bas C. Van Fraassen, 'The Logic of Conditional Obligation', *Journal of Philosophical Logic* 1 (1972), 417–438.
63 See W. D. Ross, *The Right and the Good* (Oxford, 1930), pp. 18–36.
64 The schema (FP) is actually oversimplified and does not accommodate the fact that a single moral principle may generate conflicting *prima facie* duties. (I may keep a promise to Jones only by not keeping a promise to Smith.) A more satisfactory version of (FP) is as follows: 'It shall be the case that X does A in C if (a) X's doing A is required in C by some principle P in $R(M_S)$ that precedes any other principle in $R(M_S)$ requiring X to do something incompatible with A in C and (b) if P also requires X to do something B in C that is incompatible with doing A, then either (i) there is some special sub-principle (or a highest among an ordered set of subprinciples) appropriate for resolving conflicts between acts required by P, and X's doing A, but not X's doing B, is required

by it, or (ii) there is some highest principle succeeding P in $R(M_S)$ — for example, one concerning justice or fidelity — that requires X to do A rather than B in C'. If neither (i) nor (ii) is applicable in a particular case of conflict, it may be held that, absolutely speaking, X is required neither to do A nor to do B in C. It is possible that a fully satisfactory version of (FP) will require even further qualifications. I am not discouraged by this possibility, because I am concerned less with the details of the policy corresponding to (FP) than with the use of such a policy to specify the truth-conditions for the absolute moral 'ought'.

[65] See Gilbert Harmon, 'Moral Relativism Revisited', *Philosophical Review* 84 (1975), 3–22, for a recent defense of moral relativism. Harmon's analysis of moral 'ought' statements strikes me as wide of the mark, however.

[66] See Wilfrid Sellars's discussion of community intentions and morality in his *Science and Metaphysics*, pp. 217–226.

BIBLIOGRAPHY

Anscombe, G. E. M., 1958, *Intention*, Oxford.

Anscombe, G. E. M., 1975, 'War and Murder', in *Moral Problems* (ed. by James Rachaels), New York, pp. 285–297.

Åqvist, Lennart, 1967, 'Good Samaritans, Contrary-to-Duty Imperatives, and Epistemic Obligations', *Noûs* 1, 301–379.

Aristotle, 1962, *Nichomachean Ethics* (ed. and trans. by Martin Ostwald), New York.

Aune, Bruce, 1967, *Knowledge, Mind, and Nature*, New York.

Aune, Bruce, 1970, *Rationalism, Empiricism, and Pragmatism*, New York.

Aune, Bruce, 1972, 'Remarks on an Argument by Chisholm', *Philosophical Studies* 23, 327–334.

Aune, Bruce, 1973, 'On Postulating Universals', *Canadian Journal of Philosophy* 3, 285–294.

Aune, Bruce, 1974, 'Sellars on Practical Reason', in *Action, Knowledge, and Reality* (ed. by H. N. Castañeda), New York, pp. 1–25.

Aune, Bruce, 1975, 'Quine on Translation and Reference', *Philosophical Studies*, 27, 221–236.

Austin, J. L. (ed.), 1961, 'A Plea for Excuses', in *Philosophical Papers*, Oxford, pp. 123–152.

Austin, J. L. 1966, 'Three Ways of Spilling Ink', *Philosophical Review* 75, 427–440.

Binkley, Robert, 1965, 'A Theory of Practical Reason', *Philosophical Review* 74, 423–448.

Binkley, Robert, Bronaugh, Richard, and Marras, Ausonio, 1971, *Agent, Action, and Reason*, Toronto.

Castañeda, Hector-Neri, 1970, 'On the Semantics of the Ought-to-do', *Synthese* 21, 449–468.

Castañeda, Hector-Neri, 1972, 'Intentions and Intending', *American Philosophical Quarterly* 9, 139–149.

Castañeda, Hector-Neri, 1974, *The Structure of Morality*, Springfield, Ill.

Carnap, Rudolf, 1949, 'Two Concepts of Probability', in *Readings in Philosophical Analysis* (ed. by H. Feigl and W. Sellars), New York, pp. 330–348.

Chisholm, R. M., 1964, 'Theory of Knowledge', in *Philosophy* (ed. by Chisholm *et al.*), Englewood Cliffs, N.J., pp. 232–344.

Chisholm, R. M., 1966, 'Freedom and Action', in *Freedom and Determinism* (ed. by Keith Lehrer), New York, pp. 28–44.

Clark, Romane, 1970, 'Concerning the Logic of Predicate Modifiers', *Noûs* 4, 311–335.

Collingwood, R. G., 1940, *An Essay on Metaphysics*, Oxford.

Collingwood, R. G., 1942, *The New Leviathan*, Oxford.

Collingwood, R.G., 1946, *The Idea of History*, Oxford.

Cornman, James, 1971, 'Comments', in *Agent, Action, and Reason* (ed. by Robert Binkley *et al.*), Toronto, pp. 26–37.

Cresswell, M. J., 1974, *Logics and Languages*, London.

Davidson, Donald, 1963, 'Actions, Reasons, and Causes', *Journal of Philosophy* 69, 685–700. Reprinted in *The Philosophy of Action* (ed. by Alan R. White), Oxford, (1968), pp. 79–94.

Davidson, Donald, 1967, 'The Logical Form of Action Sentences', in *The Logic of Decision and Action* (ed. by Nicholas Rescher), Pittsburgh, pp. 81–120.

Davidson, Donald, 1967, 'Causal Relations', *Journal of Philosophy* 74, 691–703.

Davidson, Donald, 1969, 'On Saying That', in *Words and Objections* (ed. by D. Davidson and J. Hintikka), Reidel, Dordrecht, Holland, pp. 158–174.

Davidson, Donald, 1970 'Mental Events', in *Experience and Theory* (ed. by L. Foster and J. W. Swanson), Amherst, Mass., pp. 79–102.

Davidson, Donald, 1971, 'Agency', in *Agent, Action, and Reason* (ed. by Robert Binkley *et al.*), Toronto, pp. 3–25.

Feinberg, Joel, 1965, 'Action and Responsibility', in *Philosophy in America* (ed. by Max Black), London, pp. 134–160. Reprinted in *The Philosophy of Action* (ed. by Alan R. White), Oxford, (1968), pp. 95–119.

Fitzgerald, P. J., 1968, 'Voluntary and Involuntary Acts', in *The Philosophy of Action* (ed. by A. R. White), Oxford, pp. 120–143.

Fodor, J. A., 1972, 'Troubles about Actions', in *Semantics of Natural Language* (ed. by D. Davidson and G. Harmon), Reidel, Dordrecht, Holland, pp. 48–69.

Frege, Gottlob, 1960, 'On Sense and Reference', in *Translations from the Philosophical Writings of Gottlob Frege* (ed. by Max Black and P. T. Geach), Oxford, pp. 56–78.

Frye, Northrop, 1963, *The Well Tempered Critic*, Bloomington, Ind.

Gauthier, David, 1971, 'Comments', in *Agent, Action, and Reason* (ed. by Robert Binkley *et al.*), Toronto, pp. 98–107.

Geach, P. T., 1957, *Mental Acts*, London.

Geach, P. T., 1966, 'Dr. Kenny on Practical Reasoning', *Analysis* 26, 76–79.

Geach, P. T., 1968, 'Some Problems About Time', in *Studies in the Philosophy of Thought and Action* (ed. by P. F. Strawson), Oxford, pp. 175–191.

Hardie, W. F. R., 1968, *Aristotle's Ethical Theory*, Oxford.

Harmon, Gilbert, 1967, 'Detachment, Probability, and Maximum Likelihood', *Noûs* 1, 401–411.

Harmon, Gilbert, 1975, 'Moral Relativism Revisited', *Philosophical Review* 84, 3–22.

Hart, H. L. A. and Honoré, A. M., 1959, *Causation and the Law*, Oxford.

Hempel, C. G., 1965, *Aspects of Scientific Explanation and Other Essays in the Philosophy of Science*, New York.

Hume, David, 1888, *A Treatise of Human Nature* (ed. by L. A. Selby-Bigge), Oxford.

Jeffrey, Richard, 1965, *The Logic of Decision*, New York.

Kant, Immanuel, 1956, *Critique of Practical Reason* (trans. by L. W. Beck), New York.

Kenny, Anthony, 1966, 'Practical Inference', *Analysis*, 26, 65–73.

Luce, R. Duncan, and Raiffa, Howard, 1957, *Games and Decisions*, New York.

Mackie, H. L., 1974, *The Cement of the Universe*, Oxford.

Miller, George A., Galanter, Eugene and Pribram, Karl H., 1960, *Plans and the Structure of Behavior*, New York.

Montague, Richard, 1974, 'English as a Formal Language', in *Formal Philosophy: Selected Papers of Richard Montague* (ed. by Richmond Thomason), New Haven, Conn., pp. 188–221.

Parsons, Terence, 1970, 'Some Problems Concerning the Logic of Predicate Modifiers',

Synthese 21, 320—333.

Peirce, C. S., 1938, 'The Fixation of Belief', in *Collected Papers of C. S. Peirce*, Vol. 5, (ed. by Charles Hartshorne and Paul Weiss), Cambridge, Mass., pp. 365—384.

Powers, Lawrence, 1967, 'Some Deontic Logicians', *Noûs* 1, 381—400.

Prichard, H. A., 1945, 'Acting, Willing, and Desiring', in *Moral Obligation*, Oxford, pp. 89—98.

Quine, W. V. O., 1953, 'Reference and Modality', in *From a Logical Point of View*, Cambridge, Mass., pp. 139—159.

Quine, W. V. O., 1953, 'On What There Is', in *From a Logical Point of View*, Cambridge, Mass., pp. 1—19.

Quine, W. V. O., 1960, *Word and Object*, Cambridge, Mass.

Quine, W. V. O., 1969, 'Ontological Relativity', in *Ontological Relativity and Other Essays*, New York, pp. 26—68.

Quine, W. V. O., 1974, 'Methodological Reflections on Current Linguistic Theory', in *On Noam Chomsky: Critical Essays* (ed. by Gilbert Harmon), New York, pp. 104—117.

Raiffa, Howard, 1970, *Decision Analysis*, Menlo Park, Calif.

Ross, W. D., 1930, *The Right and the Good*, Oxford.

Russell, Bertrand, 1927, *Analysis of Matter*, London.

Russell, Bertrand, 1946, *Human Knowledge: Its Scope and Limits*, London.

Russell, Bertrand, 1948, *An Inquiry into Meaning and Truth*, London.

Ryle, Gilbert, 1949, *The Concept of Mind*, London.

Scheffler, Israel, 1963, *The Anatomy of Inquiry*, New York.

Schwayder, D. S., 1965, *The Structure of Behavior*, London.

Sellars, Wilfred, 1963, 'Time and the World Order', in *Minnesota Studies in the Philosophy of Science*, Vol. 3 (ed. by H. Feigl and G. Maxwell), Minneapolis, Minn., pp. 527—616.

Sellars, Wilfrid, 1963, 'Some Reflections on Language Games', in *Science, Perception, and Reality*, London, pp. 321—358.

Sellars, Wilfrid, 1963, *Science, Perception, and Reality*, London.

Sellars, Wilfrid, 1965, 'Imperatives, Intentions, and the Logic of "Ought" ', in *Morality and the Language of Conduct* (ed. by H. N. Castañeda and G. Nahknikian), Detroit, pp. 159—218.

Sellars, Wilfrid, 1966, 'Thought and Action', in *Freedom and Determinism* (ed. by Keith Lehrer), New York, pp. 105—139.

Sellars, Wilfrid, 1966, 'Fatalism and Determinism', in *Freedom and Determinism* (ed. by Keith Lehrer), New York, pp. 141—174.

Sellars, Wilfrid, 1968, *Science and Metaphysics*, London.

Sellars, Wilfrid, 1973, 'Actions and Events', *Noûs* 7, 179—202.

Suppes, Patrick, 1960, *Axiomatic Set Theory*, Princeton, N.J.

Taylor, Richard, 1966, *Action and Purpose*, Englewood Cliffs, N.J.

Thalberg, Irving, 1973, 'Constituents and Causes of Emotion and Action', *Philosophical Quarterly* 23, 2—14.

Urmson, J. O., 1968, 'Motives and Causes', in *The Philosophy of Action* (ed. by A. R. White), Oxford, pp. 153—165.

Van Fraassen, Bas C., 1972, 'The Logic of Conditional Obligation', *Journal of Philosophical Logic* 1, 417—438.

Von Wright, G. H., 1963, 'Practical Inference', *Philosophical Review* 72, 159—179.

Von Wright, G. H., 1971, *Explanation and Understanding*, Ithaca, N.Y.

Wittgenstein, Ludwig, 1958, *Philosophical Investigations* (trans. by G. E. M. Anscombe), Oxford.

Ziff, Paul, 1972, 'The Logical Structure of English Sentences', in *Understanding Understanding*, Ithaca, N.Y., pp. 39–56.

INDEX

abstracta 31f., 45f.
accordian effect 5, 24
action I (*passim*)
   and deed 21f.
   as abstract 25
   as complex 18
   as composite 25f., 46
   as intentional 89–107
   as logical construction 25
   as volition 2, 4
   as voluntary activity 1ff.
   as voluntary 71f., 85–89
   constitution of 16f.
   Collingwood on 21f., 25f., 46
   Davidson's conception of 11, 181.
   generation of 16
   identity of 26
   mental aspects of II (*passim*)
   on policy 140
   Prichard's conception of 1–26, 74
   psychokinetic 4, 46f. (note)
   reasons for identifying 16
   relation to thought 61–65, 74–84,
      119f.
   statements about 2f.
   three theories of 23–26, 103
action descriptions 5
   as teleological 6
action language 2
   secondary uses of 19ff., 85
adverbial modification 27–37, 90, 92–96
agency 8–12, 22
   Davidson on 10f.
   Prichard on 9
agents, theory of 1, 44ff.
Anscombe, G. E. M. 46, 66, 108, 109,
   143, 198, 200
Åqvist, Lennart 182, 184ff., 195, 198
Aristotle 6, 55, 74, 80, 82, 108, 142, 143,
   198, 132, 136
   on choice 114

on deliberation 112ff., 117, 123f., 135
on ends 117f., 135
on practical syllogism 112f., 119
Aune, Bruce 48, 49, 108, 143, 194, 198
Austin, J. L. 5, 47, 54, 71, 108, 198
axioms
   of deontic logic 184f.
   of hope 164
   of resignation 162

Barber, Patricia XI
Bayesian deliberation 137–142, 177f.,
   181
Beck, L. W. 107, 199
belief 45f.
   analysis of 62, and justification, 141f.
   relation to action 61–65, 74–84,
      119f.
Binkley, Robert 109, 143, 195, 198, 199
   his system discussed 158–167
Black, Max 47, 110, 199
Bratman, Michael XI, 109
Bronough, Richard 198
Burnet, John 114

Carnap, Rudolf 47, 88, 109, 198
Castañeda, Hector-Neri XI, 143, 193, 194,
   195, 196, 198, 200
   his theory of practical inference dis-
     cussed 167–181
   on normatives 182–185, 188, 190,
     192
   on paradox of knower 182, 184f.
causation 1ff.
   agent variety 5
   and explanation 40 (*see also* explanation)
   and laws 41
   and reasons 83
   and relations 37–44
   and singular statements 37–44
   concept of 8

PHILOSOPHICAL STUDIES SERIES
IN PHILOSOPHY

Editors:

WILFRID SELLARS, Univ. of Pittsburgh and KEITH LEHRER, Univ. of Arizona

Board of Consulting Editors:

Jonathan Bennett, Alan Gibbard, Robert Stalnaker, and Robert G. Turnbull

1. JAY F. ROSENBERG, *Linguistic Representation.* 1974, xii + 159 pp.

2. WILFRID SELLARS, *Essays in Philosophy and Its History.* 1974, xiii + 462 pp.

3. DICKINSON S. MILLER, *Philosophical Analysis and Human Welfare.* Selected Essays and Chapters from Six Decades. Edited with an Introduction by Lloyd D. Easton. 1975, x + 333 pp.

4. KEITH LEHRER (ed.), *Analysis and Metaphysics.* Essays in Honor of R. M. Chisholm. 1975, x + 317 pp.

5. CARL GINET, *Knowledge, Perception, and Memory.* 1975, viii + 212 pp.

6. PETER H. HARE and EDWARD H. MADDEN, *Causing, Perceiving and Believing.* An Examination of the Philosophy of C. J. Ducasse. 1975, vii + 211 pp.

7. HECTOR-NERI CASTAÑEDA, *Thinking and Doing.* The Philosophical Foundations of Institutions. 1975, xviii + 366 pp.

8. JOHN L. POLLOCK, *Subjunctive Reasoning.* 1976, xi + 255 pp.

DAT'